Kay Newbold

CONTENTS

PREFACE

This book was written by four avid quilters: Mary Hickey, Nancy Martin, Marsha McCloskey, and Sara Nephew. As authors, quilt designers, and teachers, they are each well known for their contributions to quilting in the areas of rotary cutting and quick piecing.

Luckily, these talented women are all friends who live in the Pacific Northwest and are members of the same large quilt guild, Quilter's Anonymous. They also belong to a smaller satellite group, the Monday Night Bowling League, named in the interest of remaining "anonymous." These friends have tested each other's patterns, made samples for quilt books, and even occasionally collaborated on a book together. Each of these authors produces her own uniquely beautiful quilts, and all four prefer to make quilts using speedy methods of cutting and construction.

Why are so many quilters trying quick quilting methods using the rotary cutter? Perhaps because rotary methods are fast and fun, in addition to being so accurate. Using these techniques, you can assemble a truly beautiful quilt top in a matter of days rather than months or even years. A busy mother or career woman now has time to try a new color scheme or quickly piece a gift. When the top goes together in hours, there's plenty of time to quilt it for a special occasion.

When done with care, rotary cutting is an extremely accurate cutting method that eliminates frustrating struggles to make the pieces match when assembling a quilt top. The logic and precision of rotary methods offer the quilter feelings of control and accomplishment hard to achieve in day-to-day life.

Rotary cutting is fun. In very little time and with little cutting effort, stacks and stacks of shapes in many colors appear almost magically, ready to be sewn into colorful quilt tops. Even the beginning quilter can achieve impressive results in record time.

In these rotary-cut quilts, you will find no tedious appliqué, no set-in or curved seams. The simplicity of straight seaming makes it possible to precisely piece sparkling quilt tops. Some quilts are pieced in exciting contemporary designs, while others evoke the warmth of cherished antique quilts. No matter what your style, there's a rotary-cut and quick-pieced quilt to match it. And once you master the techniques, you'll be designing your own quilts!

ACKNOWLEDGMENTS

Our sincere thanks to:

Pat Buck, Roxanne Carter, Shirley Gylleck, Teresa Haskins, Rose Herrera, Virginia Lauth, Hazel Montague, Alvina Nelson, Beverly Payne, Freda Smith, and Sue von Jentzen for their fine quilting stitches.

Amanda Miller for arranging for the fine hand quilting of Water Music, Secret Gardens, Woodland Cottages, Raven Dance, and Starry Path.

Martha Ahern, Roxanne Carter, Gretchen Greiker, Shirley Gundlach, Barbara Markham, Marion Morris, Bev Murrish, Shirley Nodell, Cleo Nolette, Judy Pollard, Carol Porter, Nancy Sweeney, Liz Thoman, and Sue von Jentzen for pattern testing.

Brenda Reed for loaning the Tulip Field Quilt made by the Busy Bee Quilters of Snohomish.

Judy Pollard for her usual generosity in designing, piecing, and quilting the Summer's End quilt.

Dr. Ray and Beth Robinson for the use of their home and belongings, shown in the photographs on pages 10 and 11.

Tony Angell for the use of his cedar ceremonial box in the photograph on page 7.

The Eddie Bauer Home Collection for the use of the green chairs in the photographs on page 10.

Philip Hickey for his enduring patience and kindness; Dan Martin for his constant encouragement and cheerful disposition; David McCloskey for reminders that there is a world outside of quilting; Dale Nephew for letting his wife do whatever she wants.

INTRODUCTION

Rotary cutting is a fast and easy way to cut the fabric pieces needed to make a quilt top. This wonderful tool looks somewhat like a pizza cutter with its round, razor-sharp blade attached to a handle. Using this modern tool, you can quickly and accurately cut through many layers of fabric at once. This contemporary tool can be credited with revolutionizing the quiltmaking process.

In this book you will be introduced to the cutting techniques that each of the authors originated, and you'll then use them to re-create the beautiful quilts pictured in each section of the book. The easy traditional designs, such as Rail Fence and Ninepatch quilts, are not included in this book. Instead, you will learn the authors' special techniques for making quilts with a variety of triangular shapes, a design area that often intimidates beginning quiltmakers. These techniques make it easy for a beginner to accurately cut and piece exciting quilts, using the triangular shapes required.

This book is organized for easy use. First, all the tools required for rotary-cut quilts are listed and described. Read through this section and assemble the necessary tools and supplies before beginning your first project.

General guidelines for selecting fabrics for your quilt follow. Additional thoughts on fabric and color selection are also included in each author's section of the book. Read carefully, as fabric type and color are an important consideration in planning a beautiful quilt.

Next, rotary-cutting tips and techniques and machine- and strip-piecing methods are reviewed. Finally, you will find a complete section on how to assemble a quilt, from sewing the pieces together to taking the final quilting stitch, then binding and labeling your finished masterpiece.

Following this complete introduction to quiltmaking basics, you will find four sections, each one dedicated to the special techniques of one of the featured authors. In each section, you will meet the author and learn about her background, her approach to the use of color, and the methods that are particularly appropriate for her individual quilts, including the special techniques she has developed for the use of the rotary-cutting rulers required for her quilts. The quilts reflect each author's favorite style of quiltmaking incorporating triangular shapes.

An easy warm-up project begins each quilt pattern section. This is a smaller quilt that can be done quickly as an introduction to the author's techniques and special look. Five or more patterns for larger quilts follow. Each was chosen for its beauty and relative ease of cutting and piecing. You'll find quilts with many different looks to appeal to a wide range of tastes, whether for you, for a favorite child, or for the man in your life.

For your convenience, you will find a resource list at the end of the book. If you are unable to find the special tools you need for a specific project, ordering addresses are given there.

Robust and masculine, *Raven Dance* and *Tumbling Blocks*
energize this handsome room. Painted cedar box by Tony Angell.

(Left) *Secret Gardens, Ohio Star Baby Quilt, Nancy's Nosegay,* and *Tulip Fields* beckon guests to enjoy tea on the porch on a sunny spring morning.

(Below) *The Fleet Is In* greets guests while *Tumbling Blocks* graces a welcoming chair.

The *Hill and Valley Quilt*, hung above a cheerful fire, forms the focal point for this friendly Christmas tea. The *Ohio Star Table Runner* adds warmth and interest to the table setting, and *Gardenia Bouquet* hangs on the quilt rack.

Woodland Cottages creates an amiable mood in this friendly family room, while the *Williamsburg Star Quilt* is just the right size to warm a lap on a frosty evening.

(Above) *Starry Path* and *Goose Tracks* provide calm beauty in a tranquil hideaway.

(Right) Romantic and rustic—*Summer's End* graces a twig bed in this feminine country retreat.

(Opposite) *Kelly's Green Garden*, a simple quilt in soft greens, forms a restful focal point in a charming bedroom. The *Ohio Star Baby Quilt* covers the table in the foreground.

Tulips provides inspiration for the gardener in a well-appointed potting shed. A quiet reading corner is adorned with *Flying Pinwheel*.

Quick & Easy Techniques

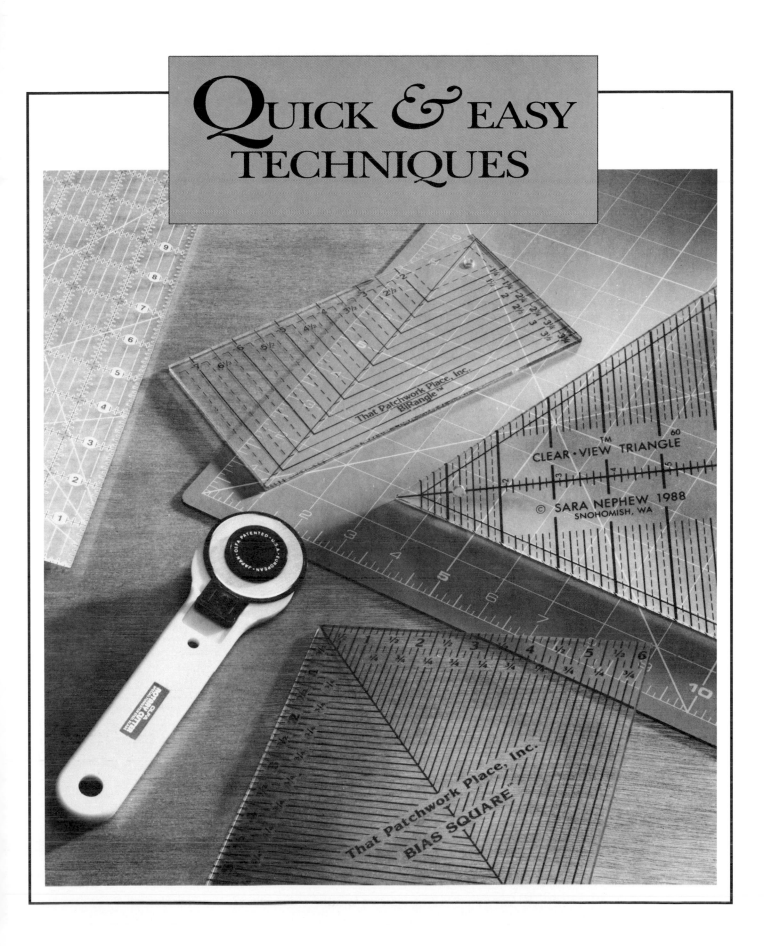

QUILTING TOOLS & SUPPLIES

Like the carpenter who uses specialized tools to complete a fine woodworking project, you as a quilt-maker will save time and energy by using the tools and equipment specifically designed for cutting and piecing your quilts.

The directions for the quilts in this book require rotary-cutting tools, so let's start by getting acquainted with them.

CUTTING RULERS

A good ruler is an invaluable tool and a necessity for rotary cutting the pieces for a quilt. The quilts featured in this book are made primarily with trian-gular-shaped pieces, and the directions for cutting them rely specifically on the use of the single-pur-pose, rotary-cutting rulers designed by the authors. These include the Bias Square®, designed by Nancy J. Martin; the BiRangle™, designed by Mary Hickey; and the Clearview™ Triangle, designed by Sara Nephew (Diagram 1).

While it is possible to cut these triangles using a general-purpose ruler, it is easier to use specialized rulers because they contain only the necessary cutting lines and strategic alignment guides to help keep the fabric grain line in the correct position. Since you don't have to visually screen out unnecessary lines, your eyes can quickly focus on only the lines you need. Using a specialized ruler also improves cutting accuracy and makes your quiltmaking experience more fun and free from the matching and stitching frustrations that can result from inaccurate cuts.

If these rulers are not available at your local quilt or fabric shop, they can be ordered from the sources listed on page 271. In addition, directions for adapting existing rulers or making cutting templates to use as substitutes appear in "Tip" boxes that follow.

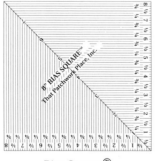

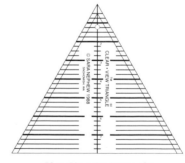

Bias Square®   BiRangle™   ClearView™ Triangle

Diagram 1

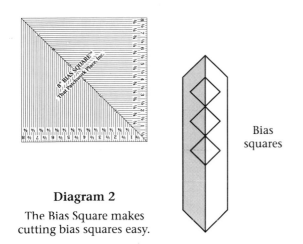

Diagram 2

The Bias Square makes
cutting bias squares easy.

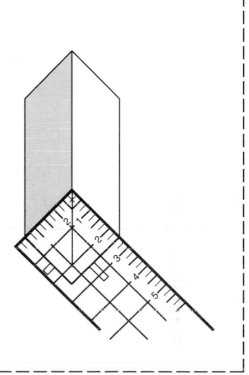

Bias
squares

The Bias Square is a clear acrylic ruler used to accurately cut squares composed of two half-square triangles (also called bias squares or Square One units in this book) from bias strip-pieced fabric units. The Bias Square is used for making the quilts on pages 65–100 and pages 190 and 202. This ruler is available in two sizes, 6" or 8" square, and is marked in ⅛" increments along two adjacent sides. It features a diagonal line, which is placed on the seam of a bias strip-pieced unit to cut the presewn, half-square triangle units required for the quilt you are making (Diagram 2).

Note: For detailed directions for using the Bias Square, see pages 59–64, 108–111, or 161–63.

The Bias Square is also useful when cutting small quilt pieces, such as squares, rectangles, and triangles. The larger, 8" size is ideal for quick-cutting blocks that require large squares and triangles as well as making diagonal cuts for quarter-square triangles. A 20cm-square metric version, designed by Marsha McCloskey, is also available for those who prefer to work in this format.

TIP

Converting a Rotary Ruler for Cutting Bias Squares

If the Bias Square is unavailable, you can adapt a general-purpose rotary ruler to work in a similar fashion.

1. Cut a square, see-through plastic template the size specified for the bias square in the quilt directions.
2. Draw a diagonal line on the template, bisecting the square.
3. Tape the template onto the corner of an acrylic ruler.
4. Follow the cutting directions given for the quilt you are making, substituting the template-adapted corner of the ruler for the Bias Square.

You will need to make a new template for each size bias square required for the quilt you are making. The most common sizes of bias squares required are 2", 2½", and 3".

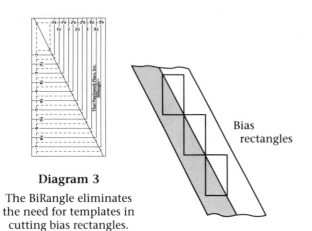

Diagram 3
The BiRangle eliminates
the need for templates in
cutting bias rectangles.

The BiRangle cutting ruler is used to quickly and accurately cut strip-pieced bias rectangles composed of two long, thin triangles joined on the diagonal. This ruler is a 4" x 7½" clear acrylic rectangle, marked in ¼" increments on two adjacent sides with a diagonal line that bisects it (Diagram 3). Placing the diagonal line on bias strips of fabric that are already stitched together makes it easy to quickly and accurately cut the bias rectangles required for the quilts on pages 164–208. Otherwise, templates are required for the triangles, and piecing them to make the rectangles is a time-consuming challenge.

Note: For detailed directions for using the BiRangle, see pages 155–60.

TIP

Converting a Rotary Ruler for Cutting Bias Rectangles

As a substitute for the BiRangle, make a clear plastic template to tape to your rotary ruler.

1. On a piece of paper, draw the pieced bias rectangle in the finished size. You will find these dimensions in the cutting chart provided for each project.
2. Draw a diagonal line from corner to corner.
3. Add ¼" seam allowances around the four sides of the rectangle. *Note that the diagonal line on the completed template intersects the opposite corners of what will be the size of the finished rectangle but not the corners at the outer edge of the template.* Cut out the bias rectangle template you have created.
4. Tape the plastic template to the corner of your rotary ruler and use it in place of the BiRangle, following the rotary-cutting directions given for the quilt you are making.

You will need to make a new template for each size bias rectangle required for the quilt you are making.

Finished size
bias rectangle

Bias rectangle with
¼" seam allowances added

Line intersects
inner corner but
not outer corner
of template.

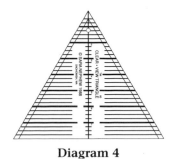

Diagram 4

Shapes with 30°, 60°, and 120°
angles are easy to cut with the
ClearView Triangle.

Sara Nephew designed the Clearview Triangle especially for creating quilts composed of equilateral triangles like those featured on pages 219–69. This acrylic triangle makes it easy to cut shapes with 30°, 60°, and 120° angles. The Clearview Triangle is marked in ¼", ½", and 1" increments with lines running parallel to the base. A perpendicular line from the tip to the base bisects the ruler and is used when cutting shapes related to the triangle. As an additional feature, ¼" seam lines are indicated (Diagram 4).

This triangular ruler is available in 6", 8", and 12" sizes, with the 8" ruler having additional lines in ⅛" increments.

Note: For detailed directions for using the Clearview Triangle, see page 213–18.

Tip

Making a Cutting Template for Equilateral Triangles

To make a template for cutting equilateral triangles and related shapes as a substitute for the Clearview Triangle:

1. Purchase two 6" 60° plastic triangles in the drafting section of a stationery or art supply store.
2. Place the two perpendicular sides together and tape securely, using 2"-wide transparent packaging tape. Tape on the front and the back.
3. Using a see-through ruler and a permanent marking pen, mark lines parallel to the base and 1" apart. Then add lines that are spaced ¼" apart between the 1" lines. For more permanent lines, scratch them into the template with a large needle.
4. Follow the rotary-cutting directions given for the quilt you are making, substituting the triangle template for the Clearview Triangle.

For larger triangle templates, purchase pairs of 8" and 10" plastic triangles.

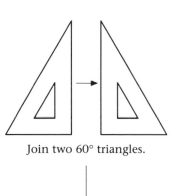

Join two 60° triangles.

Mark lines.

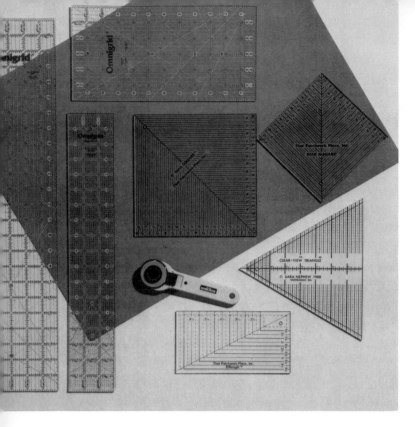

In addition to these specialized cutting rulers, there are a variety of general-purpose rulers for quilt-making.

When choosing a rotary ruler, consider the following:

- Rulers for cutting are made of clear, hard acrylic that is ⅛" thick. They come in all shapes and sizes with an assortment of markings. A basic ruler with ⅛" markings is a necessity. These ⅛" marks should appear on every inch line both horizontally and vertically.
- Rulers that are 24" long are useful for cutting large strips and shapes, and for working with fabric folded once, selvage to selvage. These rulers are generally 6" wide, which is helpful when cutting wide border strips.
- A 3" x 18" or 6" x 12" ruler is a nice size for most work as long as the fabric is folded twice—folded selvage to selvage and then folded again, with the first fold aligned with the selvages.
- Keep a 1" x 6" ruler by the sewing machine to constantly check your work for accuracy. This ruler is definitely a must when working with small pieces or making small quilts.
- Although 6" x 24" rulers can be used to cut large squares in conjunction with the lines on the rotary mat, it is very helpful to have a large square ruler, such as a 15" x 15" size, to more easily achieve the same goal.

ROTARY CUTTER AND MAT

Rotary cutters are available in two sizes. The larger one with the 2"-diameter blade enables you to cut easily through several layers of fabric. Be sure to keep several replacement blades on hand, as blades do become dull or nicked over time.

To hold the fabric in place and to protect the cutting blade and the table on which you will be cutting, you also need a mat designed specifically for rotary cutting. The surface should be slightly textured to hold the fabric, but not so bumpy that it interferes with accurate cutting.

An 18" x 24" mat is essential for cutting long strips. A smaller mat is ideal when working with scraps. Many cutting mats are available with a 1" printed grid and a bias or 45° line, which can be quite helpful when squaring up blocks (Diagram 5).

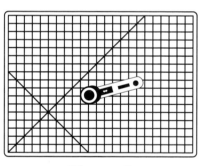

Diagram 5
Cutting mat with 1" grid and 45° bias lines

TIP

Remove the lint that builds up between the blade and the front sheath of your rotary cutter. Dismantle the cutter, paying careful attention to how the pieces go together. Carefully wipe the blade with a soft, clean cloth, adding a very small drop of sewing-machine oil to the blade where it lies under the front sheath. Try this first, *before* changing to a new blade when the cutting action is not what you expect.

SEWING MACHINE

Stitching quilts on a sewing machine is fast and enjoyable. Get to know your machine and become comfortable with its use. Keep it well oiled and maintained.

Machine piecing requires a straight-stitch machine in good working order. It should make an evenly locked straight stitch that looks the same on both sides of the seam. In addition, the machine should have a manually controlled backstitch so you can take "two stitches forward and two stitches back" with precision and ease.

Make sure the tension is adjusted so you can produce smooth, even seams. A puckered seam causes the fabric to curve, distorting the size and shape of the piecing and the resulting quilt.

A throat plate with a small, round hole for straight stitching (as opposed to an oblong hole for zigzagging) prevents poor feeding and eliminates the common problem of fabric being pushed down into the throat-plate hole by the needle.

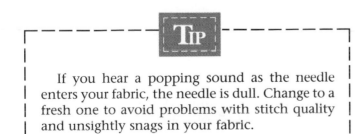

TIP

If you hear a popping sound as the needle enters your fabric, the needle is dull. Change to a fresh one to avoid problems with stitch quality and unsightly snags in your fabric.

OTHER NECESSARY TOOLS

Needles—For machine piecing, use a machine needle, size 70/10 or 80/12. For hand sewing, you will need Sharps, and for hand quilting, use Betweens, size 7, 8, 9, or 10, in the size you prefer.

Removable Tape—Use this to secure paper templates to cutting rulers (page 35).

Pins—Use long glass- or plastic-headed ones to pin pieces together for stitching. For machine quilting, you will need lots of rustproof 1" safety pins to pin-baste the quilt layers together.

Iron and Ironing Board—Locate these close to the sewing machine for frequent and careful pressing.

Scissors—You need paper scissors for cutting the occasional template required. Use high-quality shears for cutting fabric only. Thread snips or embroidery scissors are handy for clipping stray threads.

Markers—Use a sharp pencil to mark quilting lines on the quilt top. Use a mechanical pencil, EZ Washout marking pencil, or Berol silver pencil, and be sure to test your choice for easy removability. White pencils and solid or powdered chalk are available for marking dark fabrics.

Seam Ripper—This tool makes it easy to remove offending stitches in an unevenly stitched seam.

QUILTING MATERIALS

Fabric

Fiber Content

For best results, select lightweight, closely woven, 100% cotton fabrics. Small patchwork pieces are often difficult to cut and sew accurately when cut from fabrics with polyester content.

While 100% cotton is ideal, it is not always possible with quilts created from fabric collections of long standing. Some of the most interesting prints may have been purchased before following the 100% rule; they are often polyester/cotton blends of uncertain content. The colors and prints are unobtainable today, but they often serve a unique design purpose in the quilt. You may want to make an exception and use them in your quilts.

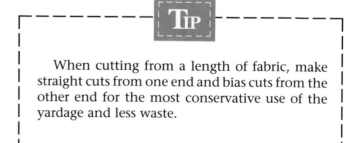

Fabric Preparation

Wash all fabrics first to preshrink, test for colorfastness, and remove excess dye. Wash light and dark colors separately with soap or detergent. Continue to wash fabric until the rinse water is completely clear. Add a square of white fabric to each wash cycle. When this white fabric remains white after washing, the fabric is colorfast.

There is a current trend among several noted quiltmakers to use unwashed fabrics in their quilts. Instead, they gently wash their completed quilts in Orvis soap when they require laundering. Some quilters avoid prewashing their fabrics because they prefer to work on "fresh fabric" or because they plan to have the item dry-cleaned. However, it's important to remember that colors in the fabrics may run if they get wet accidentally, and dark-colored dyes, such as black and deep reds and blues, are also apt to rub off onto other fabrics.

Recipients of your quilt in later years may not know how to best care for a quilt. If the fabrics in the quilt were prewashed, there is less likelihood that the quilt will be damaged through improper care. Do take the extra time required to make sure all of your fabrics are colorfast.

After washing, press fabric and fold lengthwise

into fourths, if you will be rotary cutting. Make straight cuts with the rotary cutter across each end to square up the piece. Fold fabric and store it with other fabrics in the same color family.

If you make it a habit to wash and prepare fabrics after they are purchased and *before* they are placed in your fabric library, your fabric will be ready to cut and sew when you are.

Thread and Batting

For machine piecing light-colored fabrics, select high-quality thread in a light, neutral color, such as beige or gray. Use a dark neutral, such as dark gray, for darker fabrics.

Thread for hand quilting is available in a wide range of colors. It is thicker than ordinary thread and coated so it does not tangle as readily.

Batting is the filler between the backing and the top of the quilt. A lightweight, cotton/polyester (80%/20%) combination batting works well. Battings of 100% cotton are also excellent, but some of them must be closely quilted to prevent shifting and separating during laundering. Less quilting is required with a 100% polyester bonded batting. However, some polyester may creep through the fabric and create tiny "beards" on the surface of the quilt. This problem is most obvious on dark fabrics and those made of poly/cotton blends.

Whether quilting by hand or by machine, most quilters prefer a low-loft or thin batting. Fluffy batting or fat batts are available and work well in tied quilts. Generally, these batts are too thick for fine hand quilting and too bulky to fit under the presser foot for machine quilting.

> ### TIP
>
> When cutting from a length of fabric, make straight cuts from one end and bias cuts from the other end for the most conservative use of the yardage and less waste.

FABRIC AND COLOR FOR QUILTS

FABRIC SELECTION

Quiltmakers share a passion for fabric. Color and visual texture are only part of the motivation for this love. Fabric is tactile, flexible, and forgiving, too.

Begin with a color idea and a fabric style. Shaded sketches that accompany each quilt project give an idea of how many colors or color groups are required. Your color idea may come from another quilt, a holiday, something from nature, or the colors in your home furnishings.

The fabric style can start with a single print as the key inspiration. This main fabric or idea print provides clues about other fabric designs and colors that will work with it. Is the main fabric flashy and wild, or subdued? Is it modern in design and color, or old-fashioned or scrappy looking? Is it a romantic floral, or a small, country-style floral? Does it have an oriental flavor, or is it French Country?

You may like the large prints that are popular in quilts today, including oversized floral, chintz decorator prints and contemporary batik and Japanese prints. Wild florals, jungle prints, and zany geometrics are also being used in quilts.

Contrast, in both color and visual texture, makes pieced designs visible. Visual texture is the way a print looks. Ask yourself if the print is spotty, smooth, plain, dappled, linear, rhythmical, or swirly? Are the figures far apart or close together? Generally accepted quilt wisdom tells us to mix large prints with small prints, and flowery, allover designs with linear, rhythmical prints. Too many similar prints can create a dull surface or one that is visually confusing. But, sometimes, visual complexity is just what is needed in a quilt. Using all small prints can be really boring; mixing in some large prints adds excitement. Large prints work hard for you, making a quilt surface look more complex than just the pieced design. Small, regular prints, however, quiet down larger, more flamboyant designs, making them more usable. In the end, you, the quiltmaker, must be the judge of what you want in your quilt.

COLOR RECIPE

Working with a color recipe will add variety to your quilt. Select a quilt or block and study its design. Assign a color family to a particular area of the block. An example is shown in Diagram 6.

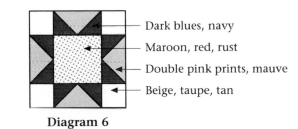

— Dark blues, navy
— Maroon, red, rust
— Double pink prints, mauve
— Beige, taupe, tan

Diagram 6
Using a color recipe, assign a color family to each area of the block.

Then, pull a run of colors from each color family in your fabric library, selecting a variety of prints and visual textures. Do not overmatch the colors, but select a range of colors instead. For instance, if you are pulling a color run of red fabrics, select maroons,

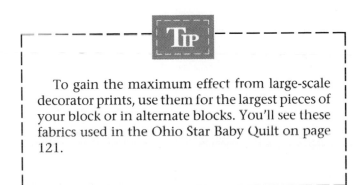

TIP

To gain the maximum effect from large-scale decorator prints, use them for the largest pieces of your block or in alternate blocks. You'll see these fabrics used in the Ohio Star Baby Quilt on page 121.

deep reds, rusty reds, true reds, and possibly even a warm brown print with red overtones. As you stitch each block, combine different fabrics from the various color families, adhering to your color recipe. Try to make blocks with both high and low contrast. The result is a scrappy-looking quilt, where each block is not identical but is unified by the repetition of colors in the color recipe.

It's fun to follow a color recipe when you make a quilt because each resulting block is different. Feel free to experiment with unusual prints and color arrangements. Be adventurous and go beyond what you consider "safe" fabric and color usage. Forget about centering large motifs; cabbage roses and other large prints often work better when they are cut randomly. Stripes and plaids can be cut randomly, too—even off-grain if you wish. Try using the wrong side of some prints to get just the right tone. If you make a mistake in piecing, consider leaving it in to create interest. Most of all, have fun as you try the many options that can make your quilt unique.

Each of the quilts in this book follows a color recipe. The featured quiltmaker selected a color for a specific unit in the quilt and used it every time that unit appeared. However, the fabrics were varied within that color family. This expands the possibilities for adding shading and visual character to the quilt while allowing the quiltmaker to use rotary-cutting and speed-piecing methods.

EVALUATING COLORS

Color choice is probably the most critical factor in determining the success of your quilt. One way to overcome the fear associated with color choice when you begin quilting is to copy the color scheme of an existing quilt that you admire. This is a good way to learn to combine colors and patterns. As you gain experience, you'll soon be following your own instincts and developing color palettes that are pleasing to you and to others.

You may find the following color strategies helpful in evaluating the fabrics for your quilts. No one strategy is the only answer, but taken together, these tips will help you avoid that dreaded quilter's condition known as the fabric-store nervous breakdown.

The Idea Fabric

Select one fabric that inspires you. Then, stand away from it to determine the color it "reads." Squint at it to get an overall impression. Resist the temptation to use a fabric because it has a few tiny dots of the perfect shade—or to reject it because it has a speck of the "wrong" color.

Next, look for fabrics in colors that relate to and contrast with your main fabric. Vary the size and textural appearance of the prints you select. Mix larger prints with the smaller ones and linear or geometric ones with flowery ones.

Overlap your fabric choices so you can observe their effect on each other. Remember that fabrics add color to and subtract color from each other when they are side by side in a quilt.

Natural Color Schemes

Natural objects are valuable sources of color inspiration. Study flowers, birds, animals, fish, seeds, leaves, trees, seashells, sunsets, and landscapes. Notice the proportions of the colors and color gradations within a single color family from light to dark and from muted to intense in natural objects.

One-Color Quilts (Monochromatic)

These quilts are made with light, medium, and dark values of a single color. To make an interesting monochromatic quilt, try a variety of lights, mediums, and darks of the color you've chosen. Use a small amount of a deep, dark shade of your color to add depth to your design and include a brilliant splash of your color to add life and visual interest. For a slightly different approach to a one-color quilt, try combining one strong color with a neutral, such as black or white.

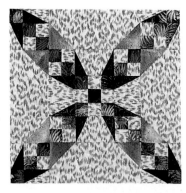

To add spark and interest, include a small amount of one brilliant color.

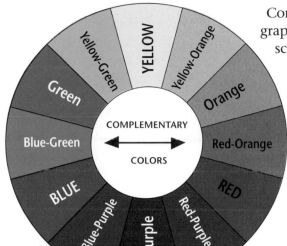

Two-Color Quilts (Complementary)

Consider making a two-color quilt for a strong graphic statement. Many traditional quilt color schemes, such as red and green, were based on two colors. The secret to a successful two-color quilt is to move both colors all over the surface of the quilt. A simple, traditional block design can look stunningly contemporary when interpreted in two strong colors. Use a color wheel to help you choose your colors, remembering that colors opposite each other are complements and therefore intensify each other.

When combining complementary colors in a quilt, warm colors dominate a design and appear to come forward. If you want cool colors to dominate, reduce the amount of warm colors in relation to the cool colors or use light and dark versions of the warm colors to reduce their impact.

Reds and greens complement each other in Marsha McCloskey's "Hill and Valley" quilt. She used a variety of reds in shades from rusty brown to pink and set them off with an equally diverse palette of greens.

TIP

If you have chosen a color and cannot seem to find a complement for it, try to see its afterimage. Stare at the fabric for about sixty seconds. Then, close your eyes to see what color appears in your eyes. Usually, you see a pastel form of the perfect complementary color.

A color with warm tones in it, such as barn red, usually looks best with a complement that has warm tones, such as moss green. The same holds true for cool tones.

Three-Color Quilts (Analogous)

Use colors that are next to each other on the color wheel to create lovely color schemes. Working with neighboring colors is a fun way to stretch self-imposed creative limits. Use a variety of light, medium, and dark tones of your colors and use a small amount of a brilliant color for added interest.

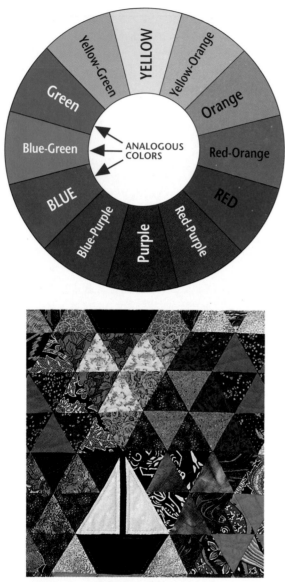

Sara Nephew's "Sailing" quilt sparkles in related shades of blue. Periwinkle, blue, and turquoise fall next to each other on the color wheel.

Multicolored Quilts

A single strong color used more than all the rest of the colors in a multicolored quilt often will give order and composition to an otherwise wild color scheme.

DEVELOPING A FABRIC LIBRARY

The success of a scrappy-looking quilt, which relies on color groups or color runs rather than repeating the same prints, depends on a well-stocked fabric library. Making scrappy quilts, which was easy for early quiltmakers who relied on their scrap bags for quilt fabrics, has affected the way quilters buy fabric.

Today, quiltmakers often buy new fabric to enrich their fabric libraries, rather than for a specific quilt. If your budget allows, it is a good idea to purchase 3–4 yards of any fabric that would make a good background. These are mainly lighter fabrics—white, beige, taupe, ecru, or pastels on a white background. Purchase ½–2 yards of medium- to dark-toned prints, depending on how much you like the fabric.

As quilting teachers, we have all seen the problems created by purchasing too little fabric. There is no flexibility to make the quilt bigger, to make a mistake, or to change your mind. So, the fabric requirements given in this book are generous, based on yardage 42" wide *after* prewashing. If your fabric is wider than 42", there will be a little left over at the end of your strips. If your fabric is narrower than 42", you may need to cut an extra strip. Use any extra yardage to help build up your fabric library.

It is rarely possible to make a complete quilt using only fabrics already in your fabric library, but it can also be difficult to make a quilt from only the fabrics available at any one time in the quilt shop. We all feel it is important to value yourself as a quilt artist, creating heirlooms for your family, friends, and cul-

---

TIP

If there is not enough variety of prints, design scales, and colors in your fabric collection, look for "fat quarters" at the quilt store. Fat quarters measure 18" x 22" and are one-half of a half yard of fabric (18" x 44"). A fat quarter has more fabric than a standardly cut quarter yard, which measures 9" x 44". Some of the quilt patterns in this book that require a variety of prints suggest buying fat quarters.

ture. Respect yourself and your work by giving yourself permission to purchase plenty of fine cottons to make your quilts. If this makes you feel guilty, think about the money some enthusiasts spend on computer software, or fishing gear, or football tickets. And remember, there are no calories in your fabric library, just beautiful quilts begging to be made!

SAMPLE BLOCKS

Once you have determined your color recipe and pulled color runs of fabric from your fabric library, it is time to test the recipe by making sample blocks. Since cutting directions on each pattern page are given for the entire quilt, you will need to study the sample block illustration found on each pattern page to determine which pieces to cut for just one block.

Make several sample blocks to determine the effectiveness of the color recipe for a scrappy quilt. Overuse of a color, color integration, contrast, and unity are difficult to see in a single block, so make several before you evaluate your work. Making sample blocks also enables you to test the accuracy of your rotary cutting.

ROTARY CUTTING A SCRAPPY QUILT FROM YARDAGE

A Template-Free™, rotary-cutting approach can be used for most quilts. With a little planning, you can rotary cut a scrappy-looking quilt that doesn't repeat too many fabric combinations.

For each quilt in this book, a "Materials" list specifies the total amount of fabric needed for a particular color group. Pull appropriate amounts of differing fabrics within that color group from your fabric library. If a total of three yards of dark blue fabrics is required, pull half-yard pieces of at least six different blue prints from your collection.

It sometimes helps to vary the amount of each print used within a color grouping. Some prints are too dominant and eye-catching to be used often. Since they interrupt the unity of the quilt, use them in smaller amounts. Use larger amounts of smaller, more restful prints, which help the design flow from one area of the quilt to another.

When a quilt requires bias squares (also called Square One units), that is the first cutting specification given. From half-yard pieces of fabric (or smaller squares when using Marsha's technique on page 108), cut bias strips of fabric. If the bias squares are to be constructed of light blue and dark blue fabrics, for example, cut light blue and dark blue bias strips from the six different blue prints.

Use the same procedure when cutting larger squares and triangles. If you need thirty-five assorted dark squares, 6⅞" x 6⅞", cut several from each fabric. If seven different dark fabrics are used, cut five from each dark fabric. Using the rotary cutter will save you time since you won't need to make templates. You merely cut a 6⅞"-wide strip from each piece of fabric. Then, stack the strips and make 6⅞"-wide cuts across each strip to make the squares.

As you use these units in your blocks, be sure to select different bias-square color combinations as well as triangles and squares of different colors. Vary the emphasis within each block. One block may blend with restful prints and low-contrast colors, while another offers high contrast with a variety of stripes and polka dots.

When you lay out the blocks for your quilt top, also vary the placement of strong prints and high- and low-contrast blocks. By scattering these elements evenly across your quilt top, you will keep the eye moving, causing the viewer to spend more time looking at the quilt.

As an alternative, try grouping all the low-contrast or soft colors in one area of the quilt, creating a flow into areas with stronger contrast or brighter colors. Each step of the quilt construction will give you the opportunity to make new design choices and add more individuality.

TIP

When cutting squares in half to yield triangles, make the diagonal cuts *before* moving the stack of squares. Work with a small mat, turning it to get the proper angle for cutting. Moving the squares may cause the fabric layers to shift, creating inaccurate cuts.

 ROTARY CUTTING

Quiltmakers have been using scissors and templates to cut quilt pieces for centuries, but when the rotary cutter was introduced to the quilt world in the early 1980s, cutting and piecing techniques changed radically and quickly. Strip piecing without templates, introduced by Barbara Johanna in the 1970s, became more and more popular because the strips were so much easier to cut with a rotary cutter than with scissors.

Thick acrylic rulers in various shapes and sizes and with a variety of helpful markings proliferated as quilters analyzed their needs and devised appropriate tools for the new techniques. Among the many rotary cutting rulers invented were the Bias Square by Nancy J. Martin, the BiRangle by Mary Hickey, and a complete line of Clearview Triangle rulers by Sara Nephew. With these rulers and a few others that are described on page 20, quilters can quickly cut all the shapes needed for thousands of quilt designs.

Not every quilt design is a good candidate for quick-and-easy rotary cutting and strip piecing. The quilts in this book were carefully chosen and the directions written to make the quiltmaking process as simple and pleasurable as possible for both beginning and more experienced quilters.

SAFETY FIRST

A rotary cutter has a *very sharp* blade. It is so sharp that you can cut yourself without even knowing it. If you are not extremely careful, you can also cut other people and objects that you had no intention of slicing. Before you begin rotary cutting for the first time, it is important to know some simple safety rules.

1. Keep the rotary cutter safety shield on when not in use.
2. Roll the cutter *away* from yourself. Plan the cutting so your fingers, hands, and arms are never at risk.
3. Keep the cutter out of the reach of children.
4. Dispose of used blades in a responsible manner. Wrap and tape cardboard around them before placing them in the garbage, or better yet, recycle them. Sharpening services are often advertised in the classified section of popular quilt magazines.

GETTING READY TO CUT

For comfort's sake, think about your posture and the table height as you cut. Stand to cut—you'll have more control than when sitting. Assume a comfortable stance with your head and body centered over the cutting line. Many quilters find they are more comfortable and can work longer if the cutting table is higher than a normal sewing table so they don't have to bend as they cut. Experiment to determine the work-surface height that is best for you.

When making all cuts, place the fabric to your right and the ruler to your left. Reverse the direction if you are left-handed. It also helps to cut at a table that you can walk around so you can easily position yourself for safe and efficient cutting without repositioning the fabric or the cutting mat.

THE IMPORTANCE OF FABRIC GRAIN LINE

Fabric is made of threads (technically, yarns) woven together at right angles. Threads that run the length of the fabric, parallel to the selvage, are called the lengthwise straight of grain. Those that run across the fabric width, from selvage to selvage, are the crosswise straight of grain. All other grains are considered bias. True bias runs at a 45° angle across the intersection of the two straight grains (Diagram 7).

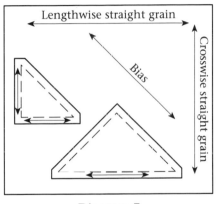

Diagram 7

Fabric Grain Line

For the small pieces in patchwork, both types of straight grain are considered equal. For long strips for borders and lattices, however, it is best to use the lengthwise grain as it is the more stable of the two. However, some quiltmakers prefer to cut and piece these strips across the fabric width because it requires less yardage.

Bias stretches and straight grain holds its shape, so whenever possible, cut fabric pieces with one or more edges aligned with the straight grain.

The straight grain of the fabric should fall on the outside edge of any pieced unit (Diagram 8).

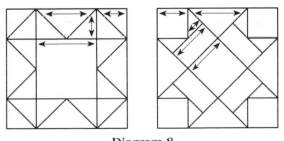

Diagram 8

Straight grain should be on the outside edges.

This applies to pieced units; design blocks; set pieces, which are used to join design blocks in larger quilts; and the edge pieces that are added to pieced borders (Diagram 9).

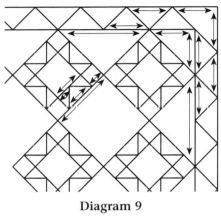

Diagram 9

Straight grain should fall on the outside edges on most pieces.

However, this rule does not necessarily apply to the 60° triangle methods shown in this book. (See page 218.)

Cutting directions for each fabric shape in this book were planned for the proper placement of grain lines in the pieced design.

TIP

In order to use a special print so the design is positioned in the direction you wish it to run, you may find that a bias cut edge falls on the outside edge of the block. On such a piece, sew a line of staystitching ⅛" from the cut bias edge to stabilize the fabric and keep it from stretching while you work with it. Take care not to stretch the piece as you stitch.

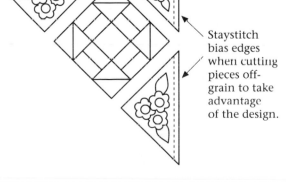

Staystitch bias edges when cutting pieces off-grain to take advantage of the design.

CUTTING STRAIGHT STRIPS

Rotary cutting squares, rectangles, and other fabric shapes begins with cutting strips of fabric. These strips are then crosscut to the proper dimensions and angles. Long strips of fabric are used for borders, and shorter ones are used for lattices or sashing, which are the strips often used to join quilt blocks together. Long, narrow strips are sometimes required in design blocks as well.

All strips are cut with the ¼"-wide seam allowances included. Some are cut from the crosswise grain and some are cut from the lengthwise grain.

To cut strips from the crosswise grain:
1. Fold and press the fabric with selvages matching, aligning the crosswise and lengthwise grains as much as possible. Place the folded fabric on the rotary-cutting mat, with the folded edge closest to your body. Align the Bias Square with the fold of the fabric and place a cutting ruler to the left, as shown in the photo for step 1 below.
2. Remove the Bias Square and make a rotary cut along the right side of the ruler to square up the edge of the fabric. Hold the ruler down with your left hand, placing the smallest finger off the edge of the ruler to serve as an anchor and prevent slipping. Stand comfortably, with your head and body centered over the cutting line.

As you cut, carefully reposition your hand on the ruler to make sure the ruler doesn't shift and the markings remain accurately placed. Use firm, even pressure as you cut. Begin rolling the cutter on the mat before you reach the folded fabric edge and continue across. For safety's sake, always roll the cutter away from you. Remember that the blade is very sharp, so be careful!

3. Fold fabric again so that you will be cutting four layers at a time. Cut strips of fabric, aligning the clean-cut edge of the fabric with the ruler markings at the desired width. Open the fabric strips periodically to make sure you are cutting straight strips. If the strips are not straight, use the Bias Square to realign the ruler on the folded fabric and make a fresh cut as in step 2 to square up the edge of the fabric before cutting additional strips. Don't worry. This adjustment is common!

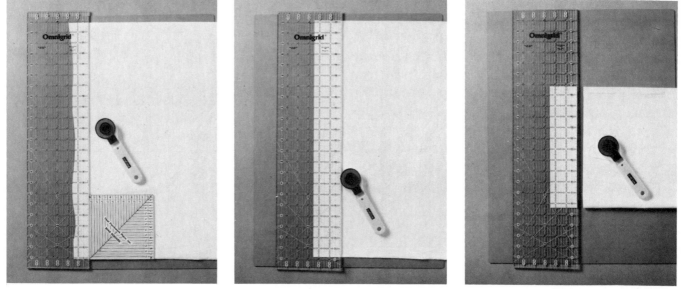

| Step 1 | Step 2 | Step 3 |

To cut strips from the lengthwise grain:

1. Fold the fabric in half crosswise, matching the selvages along each side, and press. Place the folded fabric on the rotary-cutting mat, with the folded edge closest to your body. Align the Bias Square with the fold of the fabric and place a cutting ruler to the left.

2. Remove the Bias Square and make a rotary cut along the right side of the ruler, cutting off the selvage about ¼" from the edge. Hold the ruler as described in step 2 for cutting strips from the crosswise grain.

3. Fold fabric in half again across the fabric width so that you will be cutting four layers at a time. Cut strips of fabric the desired width as shown in Diagram 10. Open fabric periodically to make sure you are cutting straight strips. If the strips are not straight, use the Bias Square to realign the ruler and make a fresh cut as in step 2 to square up the piece before cutting additional strips.

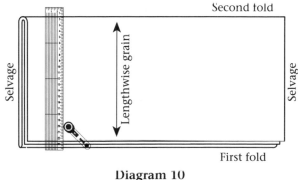

Diagram 10

Cutting straight strips

CUTTING SQUARES AND RECTANGLES

Strip Method

1. Determine the desired finished measurement of the square and add ½" for seam allowances (Diagram 11).

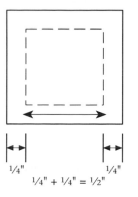

Diagram 11

Add ½" for seam allowances to finished measurement of square.

2. Cut strips of this determined measurement.

3. Align the top and bottom edge of the strip with adjacent edges of the Bias Square at the cut measurement for the square; cut into squares as shown in the photo below.

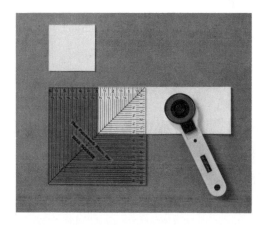

4. Cut rectangles in the same manner, first cutting strips the desired finished width of the rectangle plus ½" for seam allowances (Diagram 12).

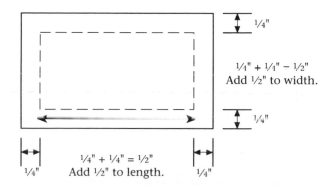

Diagram 12

Add ½" for seam allowances to finished measurement of rectangle.

Then, using the Bias Square, cut rectangles of the required length plus ½" for seam allowances.

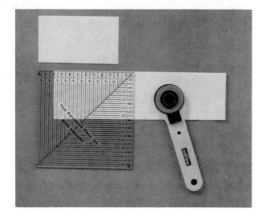

Stacked Scrap Method

The strip method of rotary cutting yields many squares of one fabric in a hurry. To cut just a few squares of many different fabrics for a scrappy look, you can also use the Bias Square ruler. One to six layers can be cut at one time, so several fabrics can be stacked before cutting.

1. Position the Bias Square on a corner of the fabric stack. Using a measurement slightly larger than the final cut size of the square, make two cuts along the edges of the ruler to separate the square from the rest of the fabric.

2. Carefully turn the separated squares around (or turn the mat) and position the Bias Square at the desired cutting measurement. Make the final two cuts to true up the fabric square.

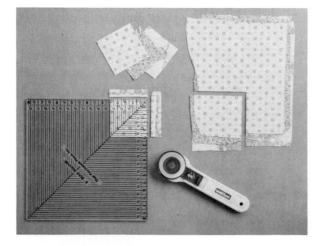

CUTTING TRIANGLES

There are three kinds of triangles used in the quilts in this book: The correct geometric terms for them are right isosceles triangles, right scalene triangles, and equilateral triangles (Diagram 13). Each kind can be cut out by itself or cut from strip-pieced units. You don't have to remember their names to cut and use them in your quilts.

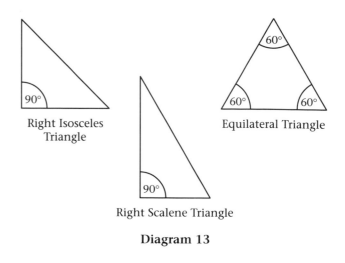

Right Isosceles Triangle

Right Scalene Triangle

Equilateral Triangle

Diagram 13

Half-Square and Quarter-Square Triangles

Right isosceles triangles, which have two equal sides, are the ones most commonly used in patchwork designs. They can be strip pieced and cut into bias squares (Square One units) or they can be strip pieced, cut, and then stitched together to make the Hourglass block (Square Two units). In some designs, you may need only a few of these triangles, which can also be cut and assembled as single units.

To keep the straight grain of the fabric on the outside edges of blocks and pieced units as described on page 29, you need to know how to cut two types of these triangles: half-square triangles and quarter-square triangles. The difference between them is in the placement of the straight of grain.

Half-square triangles result when a square is cut in half on the diagonal. When cut this way, the straight grain is on the short sides and the bias on the long side (Diagram 14). To allow for seam allowances, cut the square ⅞" larger than the finished measurement of the short side of the triangle (Diagram 15).

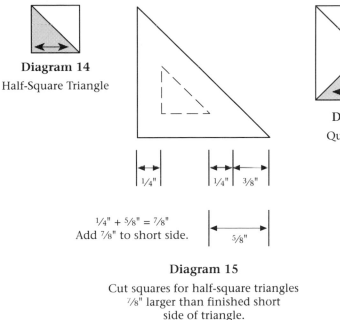

Diagram 14
Half-Square Triangle

$1/4" + 5/8" = 7/8"$
Add $7/8"$ to short side.

Diagram 15
Cut squares for half-square triangles
$7/8"$ larger than finished short
side of triangle.

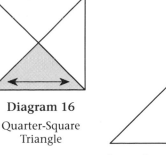

Diagram 16
Quarter-Square
Triangle

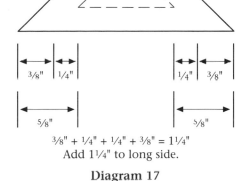

$3/8" + 1/4" + 1/4" + 3/8" = 1 1/4"$
Add $1 1/4"$ to long side.

Diagram 17
Cut squares for quarter-square
triangles $1 1/4"$ larger than the
finished long side of the triangle.

To cut half-square triangles:
1. Cut a square, using the finished measurement of the short side of the triangle plus $7/8"$.
2. Stack squares two to six layers deep and cut diagonally, corner to corner.

To cut quarter-square triangles:
1. Cut a square the finished measurement of the long side of the triangle, plus $1 1/4"$ for seam allowances.
2. Cut the square diagonally, corner to corner. Without moving the resulting triangles, line up the cutting ruler and make another diagonal cut in the opposite direction. Each square will yield four quarter-square triangles.

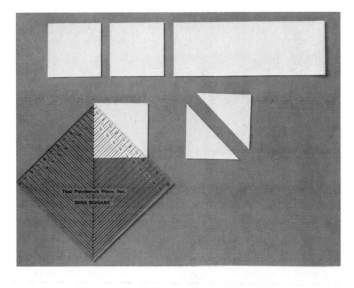

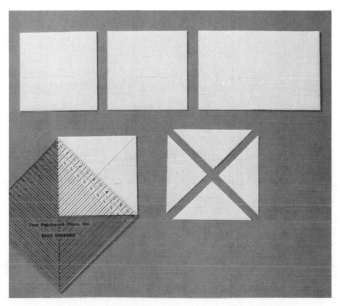

Quarter-square triangles result when a square is cut in quarters on the diagonal. When cut this way, the straight grain is on the long side, and the short sides are on the bias (Diagram 16). To allow for seams, cut the square $1 1/4"$ larger than the finished measurement of the long side of the triangle (Diagram 17).

It is important to remember the grain lines of these two kinds of triangles and the ⅞" and 1¼" rules for adding necessary seam allowances because these shapes are used in many patchwork designs.

Half-square and quarter-square triangles are also used as set pieces in diagonally set quilts. Study Diagram 52 on page 43 and note that the corner triangles within the borders are half-square triangles and the triangles along the sides are quarter-square triangles. Cut them this way to keep the straight grain along the outside edges of the quilt so the edges will not stretch out of shape when assembling and finishing the quilt.

Long Triangles

Right scalene triangles have two unequal sides. Whenever these long triangles are required for quilt designs in this book, they form bias rectangles. Long triangles can be cut individually and then assembled into rectangles, but it is far easier and much more accurate to make them using the BiRangle cutting ruler and Mary Hickey's ingenious strip-piecing method (Diagrams 18 and 19). The segments are cut into bias rectangles, each made up of two long, thin triangles. See pages 155–60 for detailed instructions on how to make bias rectangles.

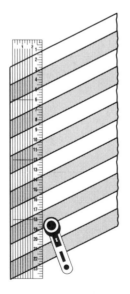

Diagram 18
The strip-pieced unit is cut into segments.

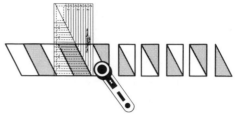

Diagram 19
Then segments are cut into bias rectangles, each made up of two long, thin triangles.

Equilateral Triangles

Equilateral triangles have three equal sides, and all three of its angles are 60° (Diagram 20).

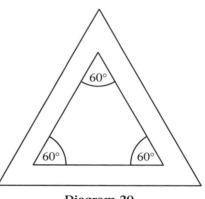

Diagram 20
Equilateral triangles have three equal sides.

Special cutting instructions for the equilateral triangles and their related shapes begin on page 213.

To cut single equilateral triangles:
1. Determine the height of the triangle (including seam allowances) by measuring from the point to the base; cut a strip of fabric in a width equal to this measurement. For the sake of illustration in the following steps, we will use a triangle with the height of 3" (including seam allowances) so the strip you cut would be 3" wide.

2. Position the tip of the Clearview Triangle ruler at one edge of the strip, and the 3" ruled line at the other edge of the strip.

3. Rotary cut along the two sides of the triangle ruler.

4. Slide the ruler along the same edge of the fabric strip to position it for the next cut, lining up the cut edge of the fabric strip with the 3" line on the ruler. (Do not flip the ruler over.) Check to be sure the strip edge is right along the ruled line.

5. Cut along both sides of the triangle ruler (Diagram 21). All resulting triangles are usable pieces.

Note: Strips may be stacked up to six thicknesses and cut all at once, if desired.

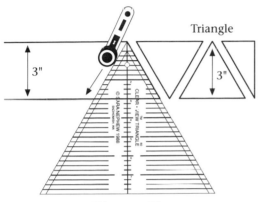

Diagram 21
Cutting equilateral triangles

USING PAPER TEMPLATES

Although the focus of this book is on rotary cutting fabric shapes without templates, sometimes shapes and cut dimensions of pattern pieces do not correspond with markings on standard cutting rulers. The simplest way to cut odd-sized or complicated shapes is to make an accurate paper template of the shape (including the ¼"-wide seam allowance) and tape it to the bottom of your cutting ruler with removable tape. The template marks the proper dimensions for cutting the shape, without measuring for each cut.

The quilt instructions in this book indicate when and where a paper template is needed and include template patterns of the required shapes. To make a paper template, carefully trace the needed shape from the book page onto a piece of typing paper. Accuracy is important. Use removable tape to secure the paper to the page in the book to keep it from shifting. Removable tape is easy to lift from the page without harming the book.

The type of paper template most often used for the quilts in this book is a "cutaway" triangle used to cut octagons—squares with the corner triangles cut away.

To cut an octagon:

1. Make a paper "cutaway" template of the triangle template given with the quilt pattern you are using, and tape it to the bottom of your ruler.

2. Cut a square the desired width of the octagon, including seam allowances.

3. Position the ruler as shown in Diagram 22 and trim off the four corners of the square with your rotary cutter.

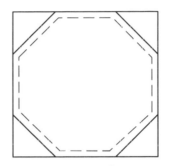

Cut a square first.

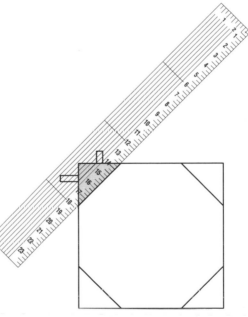

Trim the four corners, using a ruler
with a "cutaway" template.

Diagram 22

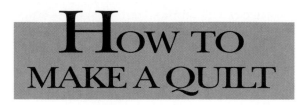

HOW TO MAKE A QUILT

STRIP PIECING

When you make a quilt using strip-piecing methods, you replace your scissors with a rotary cutter and exchange your templates for a clear acrylic ruler. For many shapes, you cut long strips of fabric with the rotary cutter and then cut squares and triangles and other shapes for the quilt from that strip. For some of the shapes, you sew several different-colored strips together to make a strip-pieced unit (Diagram 23). Then, you cut the required shapes from the strip-pieced unit. The shapes are very accurate because they are already sewn and pressed *before you cut.*

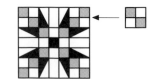

Diagram 23
Sew strips together to make a strip-pieced unit.

In the section on rotary cutting, beginning on page 28, you learned how to use the rotary cutter and special rulers as cutting guides to cut the strips and shapes you need for the quilts featured in this book. Now it's time to learn how to use the strips and shapes to create a quilt top.

Straight-Grain Squares

Many blocks have sections that are made of small squares. For example, the corner sections of the Water Music quilt blocks used in the quilt on page 176 are made of four squares (Diagram 24).

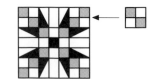

Diagram 24
Water Music Block

To construct this section, cut one light strip and one dark strip, each 2" wide. The 2"-wide strip includes a ¼"-wide seam allowance on each long edge of the strip. Sew the strips together on one long edge and press the seam toward one of the strips, usually the darker of the two colors. Then, cut the strip unit into 2"-wide pieces. Sew the pieces together to create a unit known as a Four Patch block (Diagram 25).

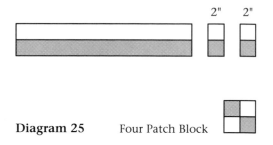

Diagram 25   Four Patch Block

Because the necessary ¼"-wide seam allowances are included in every strip measurement given in *Quick and Easy Quiltmaking,* you simply cut the strips to the size given in the quilt plan, and if you stitch accurate ¼"-wide seams, the finished pieces will be the correct size for your block. Since you cut long strips of each color, you have the components to make Four Patch units for many blocks.

Now consider applying this idea to the Nine-patch unit in the center of the same block (Diagram 26). Simply sew three strips of fabric together in each of the required color combinations, press, and cut across the pieced strips of fabric to create units

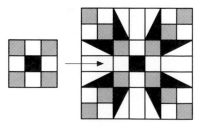

Diagram 26
Water Music Block

composed of three squares already pieced and pressed. Then join three of these units to create the Ninepatch unit easily and accurately (Diagram 27).

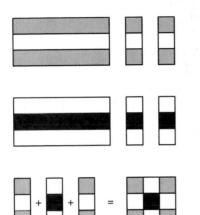

Diagram 27

Cut segments from strip-pieced units. Assemble Ninepatch block.

Other Strip-Pieced Units

Once you understand the principles of strip piecing units composed of simple squares, you can apply them to other units commonly found in patchwork designs.

Bias squares (or Square One units), made of two triangles sewn together on the diagonal, can be cut from bias strips sewn into units (Diagram 28). Complete directions for bias squares begin on page 59, 108, or 161, depending on which method you want to use.

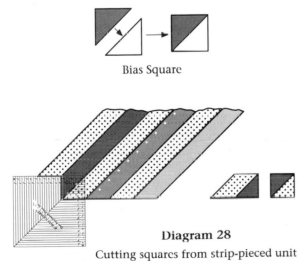

Bias Square

Diagram 28

Cutting squares from strip-pieced unit with Bias Square

Square Two units, also known as Hourglass, can be made by cutting bias squares as shown in Diagram 28, then cutting them in half and stitching them together (Diagram 29). Other related units can also be made, beginning with strip-pieced bias squares. Complete directions for these begin on page 112.

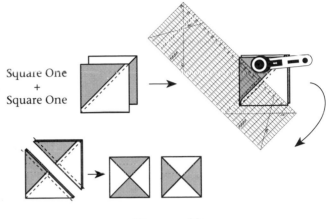

Square One
+
Square One

Diagram 29

Making Square Two

Strip piecing and cutting bias rectangles is much easier than cutting long, skinny triangles and piecing them together (Diagram 30). Directions for this innovative method begin on page 155.

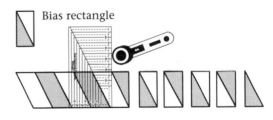

Bias rectangle

Diagram 30

Rotary cutting bias rectangles with the BiRangle

Units that contain equilateral triangles also can be cut from strips of fabric that have been sandwich pieced together (Diagram 31). This is a simple variation of strip piecing. Directions for this method are shown with the individual quilt plans in this book where sandwich piecing is most effective.

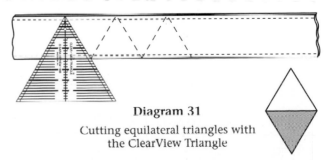

Diagram 31

Cutting equilateral triangles with the ClearView Triangle

Quilt Plans for Strip-Pieced Quilts

To determine what size to cut the fabric strips and pieces for a quilt, you use measurements that are similar to the ingredients listed in a recipe. These "recipes" are called quilt plans. The quilt plan will tell you how much fabric to buy and how to cut it and make it into a quilt. With these quilt plans, you can make a quilt faster and more accurately than your grandmother could have. As you sew the strips and assemble the blocks, here are some basic quiltmaking guidelines to keep in mind.

SEWING GUIDELINES

The Correct Seam Allowance

Patchwork pieces are sewn together to create a quilt top, using ¼"-wide seams. If your ¼" seam is off by as little as ¹⁄₁₆", then a block that is eight squares wide will be ½" off kilter on one side. If your quilt is eight blocks wide, then it will be 4" wider on one side than on the other. If you have ever tried to ease an extra 4" of collar into a neckband, you know this is a little like trying to squeeze a cow into a mayonnaise jar. And since you want your quiltmaking experience to be fun and a loving expression of the art practiced by our foremothers, *your seams must be exactly ¼" wide.*

Most sewing machines have markings on the throat plate to indicate a ¼"-wide seam allowance. Don't trust them! Many sewing machines are thought to have a presser foot that measures ¼" from the needle to its outer right-hand edge. Don't believe it, unless you've checked it and found it to be true!

Locate an accurate ¼"-wide stitching guideline on your machine by placing a template with an accurate ¼"-wide seam allowance under the presser foot and lowering the needle through the right edge of the seam line to anchor it in place. Mark the location of the outside edge of the template by placing several layers of masking tape alongside it on the throat plate of the machine (Diagram 32).

While the accurate template is in position, lower the presser foot to check its

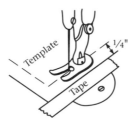

Diagram 32
Making a ¼" stitching guideline

width. If it is truly ¼" wide, you can use that as a guide. Zigzag sewing machines usually have a left-to-right needle adjustment. If your machine has this feature, try adjusting the needle position to achieve the correct seam-allowance width in relation to the outside edge of the presser foot.

A few minutes of experimenting and adjusting for an accurate ¼"-wide seam allowance before you begin eliminates frustration later when you are assembling your quilt blocks.

Stitching, "Reverse Stitching," and Backstitching

Set the stitch-length dial on your sewing machine for 12 stitches per inch (2.5 on the dial of some machines).

If you must remove a line of inaccurate stitching (a process lovingly called "reverse stitching"), use a seam ripper. Slip the long point of the ripper under one stitch and carefully slide the point farther under the stitch until the sharp curve of the ripper cuts the thread. When ripping stitches made along the straight grain, cut about every third or fourth stitch and pull the seam apart. However, on a bias seam, cut every stitch to avoid stretching the bias as you open the seam.

Since every seam in these quilts is crossed by another seam, you do not need to backstitch at the beginning of a seam. However, if you feel you must backstitch (for many of us, the habit is quite ingrained), go ahead and do so as long as it does not affect your stitching accuracy.

Piecing-Order Diagrams

To make a quilt block, you sew small shapes to each other to make progressively larger shapes until each block is complete. A piecing-order diagram shows you the easiest way to join the pieces to avoid difficult inset corners.

For example, when two right triangles are joined, they form a square. When two squares are joined, they form a rectangle (Diagram 33).

Diagram 33
Two right triangles form a square.
Two squares form a rectangle.

These shapes, in turn, are sewn together to create the block. In general, it's best to sew in an order that allows you to sew progressively longer straight lines. For example, the Shoofly block requires that you sew a rectangular unit between two of the square units composed of triangles. Next, you sew a small square between two rectangles. Then join the long sides of these two shapes (Diagram 34).

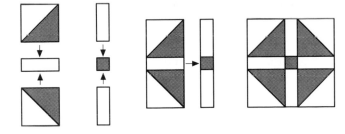

Diagram 34

Making the Shoofly block

If you had sewn a rectangle to the other side of the square unit first, you would have been faced with the frustrating task of sewing the small square into the corner created by the three shapes (Diagram 35).

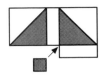

Diagram 35

Avoid sewing small squares into a corner.

The piecing-order diagrams are a quick way for you to see where the longest straight seams are.

Chain Piecing

Chain piecing is an efficient sewing system that saves time and thread. Place the pieces that are to be joined, right sides together. Arrange them in a stack with the side to be sewn on the right (Diagram 36).

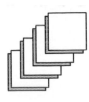

Diagram 36

Arrange pieces to be sewn
in a stack for chain piecing.

Be consistent when you chain piece. Start with the same edge on each pair and the same color on top to avoid confusion (and to eliminate the necessity of snipping apart incorrectly joined pieces).

To chain piece:

1. Stitch the first seam but do not lift the presser foot or cut the threads.

2. Feed the next pair of pieces under the presser foot, as close as possible to the first pair, and stitch. A thread "chain" will form between the pieces.

3. Continue feeding the remaining pairs into the machine in the same manner; remove the chain of pieces.

4. Take the whole chain of pieces to the ironing board and snip the pairs apart as you press them (Diagram 37). Chain piecing leaves very few hanging threads to clip, thus saving time and thread.

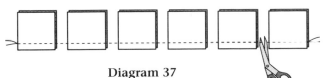

Diagram 37

Snip the thread between the pieces.

TIP

You can use a "chain leader" and a "chain follower" to make chain sewing even easier. Keep a supply of four or five squares of scrap fabric, each about 3" x 3", next to your sewing machine. Before you start your chain, fold one of the scrap squares in half and send it through your sewing machine to lead the other pieces under the presser foot. Add a "follower" at the end of the chain. It becomes the leader for the next chain.

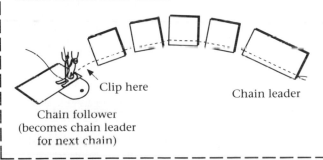

Clip here

Chain leader

Chain follower
(becomes chain leader
for next chain)

Aiming for the X

When pairs of triangles are sewn together, the stitching lines cross each other on the back, creating an X. As you sew triangle units to other units, sew with the triangle units on top and aim your stitching through the center of the X to maintain the crisp points on your triangles (Diagram 38).

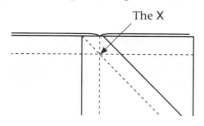

Diagram 38
Aim your stitching through the X
when sewing triangles together.

Matching Equilateral Triangles

When you sew with equilateral shapes, tiny triangles extend beyond the diagonal seams at the seam edges (Diagram 39). Do not trim these. They are helpful as guides for matching with other sections, like the notches on a garment pattern. If a dark triangle shows through on the front after the quilt top is complete, trim it away.

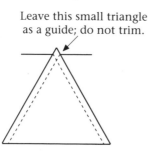

Leave this small triangle
as a guide; do not trim.

Diagram 39

Easing

If a fabric piece is no more than ⅛" shorter than the one it must match, pin the places where the two pieces should match and put them under your presser foot with the shorter one on top (Diagram 40). The feed dog will ease the two pieces together.

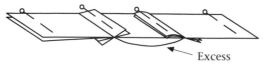

Excess

Diagram 40
Put the shorter piece on top; the feed dog will
help ease the longer piece on the bottom.

Pinning Short Seams

"Less is better" is the general rule for pinning patchwork pieces or units together for stitching. This saves time, too. It is not necessary to pin small shapes together unless there are points to match.

When two pieces of 100% cotton fabric are placed together, tiny fibers reach out and grab hold of each other, preventing the fabrics from slipping and sliding as you sew. (Even 42"-long strips will not slip.) A well-adjusted sewing machine will walk the fabric layers through, between the presser foot and feed dog, without causing puckering, shifting, or stretching. However, if you feel unsure and would prefer sewing with pins, go ahead and pin.

Pinning Long Seams

Pin the long seams of a block where there are seams and points to match. Begin by pinning the points of matching where seam lines or points meet. Once these important points are firmly in place, pin the remainder of the seam.

Using Positioning Pins

To establish the proper point of matching, carefully push a pin straight through two points that must match and pull it tight (Diagram 41). Pin the rest of the seam normally and remove the positioning pin before stitching.

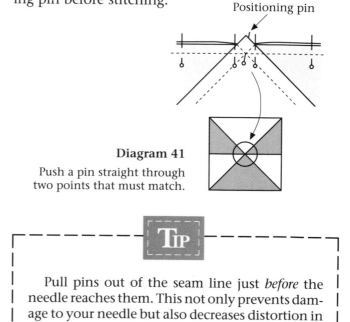

Positioning pin

Diagram 41
Push a pin straight through
two points that must match.

> **TIP**
>
> Pull pins out of the seam line just *before* the needle reaches them. This not only prevents damage to your needle but also decreases distortion in the fabrics as you stitch.

PRESSING GUIDELINES

Precise piecing is a combination of accurate sewing and gentle pressing. There is a difference between ironing and pressing. When ironing, you exert a downward pressure on the fabric with a hot iron. Quilters let the weight of the iron do the work and move the iron gently and quickly over the fabric. In other words, when pressing, don't press down.

Keep your iron and ironing board close to the sewing machine. Frequent light pressing enables you to see where the pieces should be matched. Some quilters use a dry iron, some prefer steam, some favor a shot of steam, and some like to use a damp press cloth on the blocks and large sections of the quilt. Experiment with your iron to find the method that best suits you. *The important point to remember is to press frequently but lightly.*

Directional Pressing

The traditional rule in quiltmaking is to press seams to one side, toward the darker color whenever possible (Diagram 42). Pressing this way adds strength to the quilt, evenly distributes the fabric bulk, and prevents the darker fabrics from showing through the right side of the completed quilt.

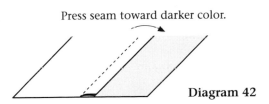

Press seam toward darker color.

Diagram 42

Pressing for Opposing Seams

Occasionally, the instructions in a quilt plan will tell you to press the seams in opposite directions or toward a particular shape or color to make it easier to match the points or corners. This creates opposing seams (Diagram 43).

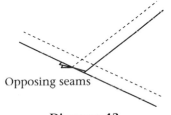

Opposing seams

Diagram 43

In some quilt plans, identical blocks are sewn directly to one another without lattices or set pieces between them (Diagram 44). Matching the points of these blocks can be difficult sometimes. Starry Path on page 202 is an example.

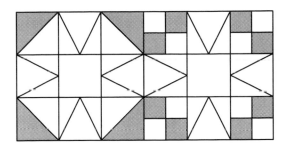

Diagram 44
Sewing blocks directly to each other

One way to overcome this difficulty is to ignore the rule about pressing toward the darker color. Instead, press seams of adjoining blocks in opposite directions. To make this easy, designate some of the blocks as Block A and some as Block B.

As you stitch the units of the A blocks, press all seams toward the center of the block. As you stitch the B blocks, press all seams toward the outer edges (Diagram 45). This pressing strategy creates opposing seams between the blocks.

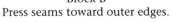
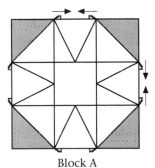
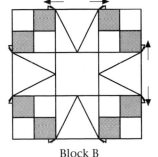

Block A
Press seams toward center.

Block B
Press seams toward outer edges.

Diagram 45

SETTING THE QUILT

The previous guidelines describe techniques for stitching and pressing the blocks of a quilt. The next consideration is the arrangement of the blocks into a quilt top. This arrangement is traditionally called the "set." There are several ways to "set" the blocks:

1. Blocks can be sewn directly to each other (Diagram 46).

Diagram 46
Blocks sewn directly to each other

2. Blocks can be separated by alternating them with plain or pieced blocks, checkerboard style (Diagram 47).

Diagram 47
Pieced blocks alternating with plain blocks

3. Blocks can also be separated by lattice strips with set squares where the lattices intersect (Diagram 48).

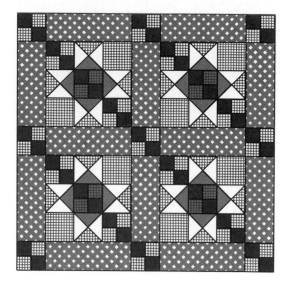

Diagram 48
Blocks separated by lattice strips and pieced set squares

All three of these sets can be arranged in straight rows and columns, or they can be arranged in diagonal rows. When the blocks are arranged in diagonal rows, their corners point toward the top of the quilt, so they are said to be set "on point." Diagonal sets require side and corner triangles to transform the blocks into square or rectangular quilts (Diagram 49).

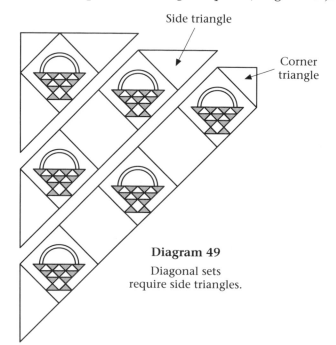

Side triangle

Corner triangle

Diagram 49
Diagonal sets
require side triangles.

Set pieces can be sewn in different ways to add to the overall quilt design. Pieced lattices and alternate blocks link the design blocks, obscuring their boundaries and creating fascinating secondary patterns (Diagram 50). Lattices and alternate blocks usually have some large pieces that offer a change of rhythm in the design of the quilt. The larger unpieced areas also provide space for some lovely quilting designs.

Diagram 50
Alternate Snowball blocks obscure the boundaries of pieced blocks to create secondary patterns.

As you examine the quilt plans in this book, notice that some of the quilts are constructed in bars. In a bar quilt, the quilt is sewn together in rows or block segments, rather than in complete blocks. The block pattern emerges *after* the quilt top is sewn together (Diagram 51).

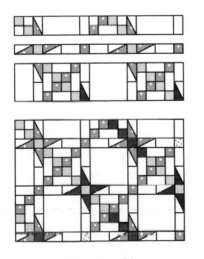

Diagram 51
Summer's End is a good example of bar construction.

All quilt projects in this book include the setting arrangement, but you can change or adapt them, if you wish. Whatever set you choose for your quilt, the following general-construction rules for sewing unit blocks still apply.

- 💜 Sew precise ¼"-wide seams from edge to edge.
- 💜 Look for the longest straight seams to stitch.
- 💜 If possible, keep straight grain on the outside edges of the quilt. (This does not necessarily apply when working with equilateral triangles.)
- 💜 Press for opposing seams.
- 💜 Pin the points of matching.

Preparing the Blocks

All the blocks in your quilt should be the same size. Remember trying to squeeze your feet into a pair of shoes that were a size too small? You *could* do it, but by the third dance you'd wish you hadn't. Trying to sew blocks of different sizes together is the same sort of torment. That is why it is so important to sew accurate ¼"-wide seams.

As you sew the blocks, measure them to make sure they are the size given in the pattern or at least that they are all the same size. Some quilters trim their sewn blocks to the proper size. Unfortunately, this often trims away a significant part of the seam allowance. It is a better idea to cut and sew as accurately as possible from the beginning.

Cutting the Set Pieces

The set pieces should be cut to fit your blocks. Measure your blocks and adjust the measurements given in the pattern to fit your blocks. Alternate squares and rectangles for lattices are cut on the straight grain. If you are sewing your blocks in a diagonal set, then cut the side triangles so that the straight grain will fall at the outside edges of the quilt top when the blocks and set pieces are joined together (Diagram 52). See page 29.

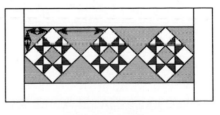

Diagram 52
Cut set triangles so straight grain falls on the outside edge of the quilt top.

Sometimes, the way you wish to position a printed pattern on your fabric within the quilt will mean that the outside edges are on the bias, going against the general rule. In that case, it's important to handle the fabric gently, and staystitch the bias edges as suggested on page 29.

Laying Out the Quilt Top

Arrange the completed blocks and set pieces on the floor or on a design wall. (Tack a large sheet of batting or flannel to a bare wall. Your quilt blocks will adhere to the surface so you can stand back and examine the quilt layout before stitching.)

Look for the longest seams to determine the construction rows. Diagonal sets are made up of diagonal rows of blocks and side and corner triangles that are of different lengths (Diagram 53). Laying the whole top out in this way helps you identify which pieces belong in each row for organized assembly.

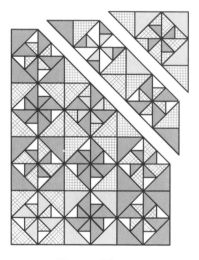

Diagonal Set
Diagram 53

Pressing and Pinning

Plan the pressing for the blocks and set pieces to create opposing seams (page 41). This will help you achieve crisp points and control excessive bulk where seam allowances intersect. In quilts with lattices or alternate blocks, this means pressing the seams that join them to the blocks, away from the pieced blocks.

When pieced blocks are sewn side by side, the pressing can be a little more complex, so think ahead to how the blocks will be joined. Plan a piecing and pressing order that, whenever possible, creates opposing seam allowances where the blocks meet, so matching points and seams is easy.

In blocks with symmetrical designs, the pressing can be identical in all the blocks (Diagram 54). Then, you simply rotate the blocks as needed to create opposing seams for matching purposes.

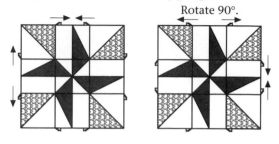

Diagram 54
Raven Dance is an example of a symmetrical design. Press blocks identically and rotate to create opposing seams.

You may find it necessary to do more pinning while setting a quilt top than when you are piecing the blocks. Pin to secure the points of matching and to ease the pieces together. Easing blocks to set pieces and vice versa is fairly normal. It helps to do the pinning on the ironing board. A shot of steam here and there seems to help the rows fit together and to make the sewing go more smoothly.

ADDING THE BORDER

While not every quilt needs a border, many quilts are transformed by the frame that a border provides. Quilt borders can grab your attention and draw your eye in, to focus on the center blocks. Borders emphasize and give significance to the designs that they surround.

Whether the border is made of a single strip of fabric or of several different strips pieced together to make a multistrip border, thoughtfully planned and sewn borders greatly enhance a quilt. The best way to decide whether or not your quilt will benefit from the addition of a border is to experiment.

Borders should echo the color, size, and shape of the pieces in the blocks. The borders for the quilt projects in this book were planned with this in mind. The color of the outside border will bring out the same color in the quilt. For example, if a quilt is rust, cream, and blue in about equal amounts, adding a blue border will intensify the blue in the blocks.

Borders can also be used to enlarge a quilt to the desired size without making additional blocks. Be careful, though, not to make the borders so wide that they outweigh the quilt design in visual importance.

The borders used in quilts in this book include:

♥ Plain strips with straight-cut and -sewn corners (Diagram 55)

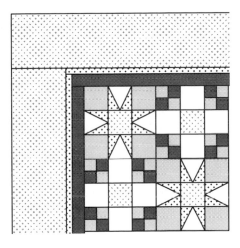

Diagram 55
Border with straight-cut and -sewn corners

♥ Pieced strips with straight-cut and -sewn corners (Diagram 56)

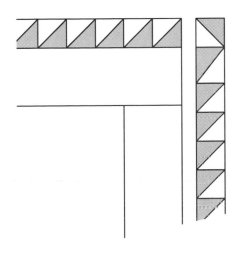

Diagram 56
Pieced border with straight-cut and -sewn corners

♥ Plain strips with mitered corners (Diagram 57)

Diagram 57
Border with mitered corners

Borders should be cut to fit the actual finished size at the center of the pieced quilt top, *not* the outer edges, which are often different on opposite sides. This ensures that the finished quilt will be "square," with 90° corners and with opposite edges that are of equal lengths.

At first, cut the border strips longer than you think you'll need. Trim them later to fit the measurements of the center of the quilt as directed below.

Straight-Cut and -Sewn Borders

These borders can be made of multiple strips or of single strips of plain fabric. If the border is cut from a striped fabric or border print, it can look fancy but still be easy to construct. (See Starry Path on page 202.)

Cut one strip of fabric for each side of the quilt and for the top and bottom. The ideal method is to cut the strips from the lengthwise grain of the fabric so you do not have to piece them. The lengthwise grain is more stable than the crosswise grain, so borders cut on the lengthwise grain stretch less. However, cutting continuous border strips from the length of the fabric requires more yardage, adding to the overall cost of the quilt. If expense is a consideration, you can purchase less fabric and cut the border strips across the fabric width, but if the quilt measures more than 40" on a side, it will be necessary to piece strips to the appropriate lengths, using straight or diagonal seams (Diagram 58).

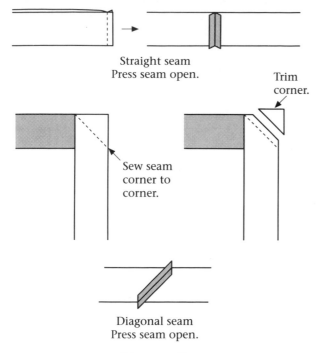

Straight seam
Press seam open.

Trim corner.

Sew seam corner to corner.

Diagonal seam
Press seam open.

Diagram 58

To add straight-cut and -sewn borders of single strips:
1. Measure the length of the quilt at the center (Diagram 59).

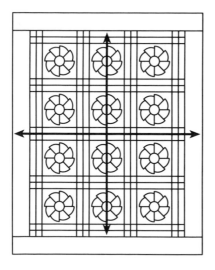

Diagram 59
Measuring for straight-cut and -sewn borders.

2. Trim two of the border strips to match that measurement.

3. Sew these strips to the long sides of the quilt,

easing as necessary. By encouraging the quilt to fit the measured strips, your finished quilt will be square with flat borders. This is an important step, so don't skip it.

Note: It's not unusual to ease one side of your quilt to fit a border and stretch the opposite side slightly to fit the same dimension.

4. To measure for the top and bottom borders, measure horizontally across the quilt, including the side borders and seam allowances as shown in Diagram 59.

5. Cut the borders to this length and sew them to the quilt, easing or stretching as necessary.

If you plan to have several strips of plain borders with straight-cut and -sewn corners, follow the same order as outlined above, attaching each additional border to the sides first and then to the top and bottom edges (Diagram 60).

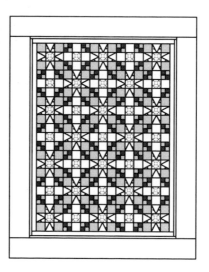

Diagram 60
When attaching several borders
with straight-cut and -sewn corners,
sew sides first, then the top and bottom.

Mitered Borders

Quilts with several borders often look better with mitered corners rather than straight-cut and -sewn ones. Mitered corners are not difficult and are particularly attractive when using a stripe, a border print, or another directional design.

If you are using multiple borders, sew them together, creating a "striped" fabric that can be treated as a unit. Sewing the borders together makes it easier to match the fabrics at the corners and simplifies sewing the strips to the quilt top (Diagram 61).

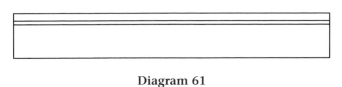

Diagram 61

Sew strips together for multiple borders with mitered corners before sewing to the quilt top.

1. Determine the finished outside dimensions of the quilt, *including the borders* as indicated by the arrows at the outside edges of Diagram 62. Add about 4" to this measurement for seam allowances and ease of matching.

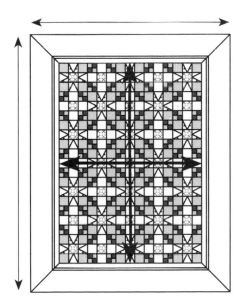

Diagram 62

Add 4" to the outside dimensions of the quilt top, including borders.

2. Measure the width and length of the quilt top through the center, seam line to seam line, not including seam allowances (as indicated by the arrows in the center of the quilt in Diagram 62).

3. Pin-mark each border strip, placing a pin at the center and one at each end to mark the length of the quilt side, which was measured at the center, as shown in Diagram 62 (Diagram 63).

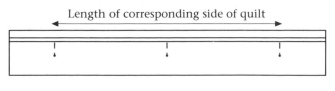

Length of corresponding side of quilt

Diagram 63

4. Pin a border strip to the corresponding edge of the quilt top, matching centers and corners. The border strip should extend exactly the same length beyond the quilt edge at both corners. Pin generously. If necessary, ease or stretch to fit. A little steam pressing can be helpful when adjusting borders to fit the outer edges of the quilt.

5. Begin stitching the border to the quilt top ¼" in from one corner and stop ¼" from the other end. In other words, leave the first and last ¼" of the seam unsewn (Diagram 64).

¼" from quilt corner ¼" from quilt corner

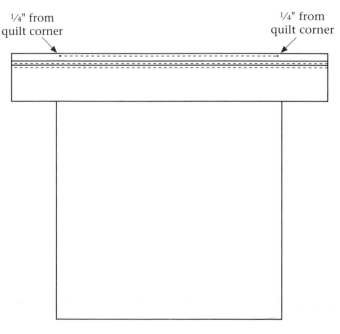

Diagram 64

Pin and stitch the remaining three border strips to the quilt top in the same manner.

6. Arrange one corner of the quilt, right side up, on the ironing board. Fold one border strip under at a 45° angle to the other strip. Work with each strip in the multiple border so they each miter perfectly at the corners (Diagram 65).

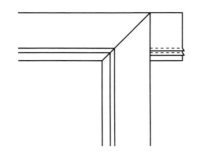

Diagram 65
Fold border strip under at a 45° angle.

7. Pin the fold, pointing all pins from the quilt center outward (Diagram 66). Press a crease in the fold. Use a Bias Square ruler to make sure that the corner is square and that the diagonal line from the inner to the outer corner is a true 45° angle.

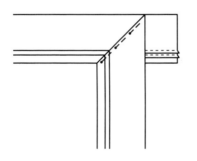

Diagram 66
Pin fold with pins pointing outward.

8. Center 1"-wide masking tape over the mitered corner, beginning at the outer edge of the border and removing pins as you work toward the quilt center (Diagram 67).

Diagram 67
Remove pins as you tape corner.

9. Turn the quilt over, fold diagonally (Diagram 68), and draw a light pencil line on the crease created by pressing in step 7.

10. Stitch on the pencil line and remove the tape.

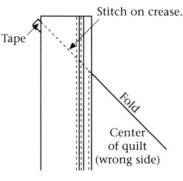

Diagram 68

Note: If your border strip is made of striped fabric or multiple strips of fabric, use a basting stitch on the sewing machine. After stitching, remove the masking tape on the right side and examine each mitered corner to make sure the seam lines within the border match. If not, remove stitches where needed, then tape and restitch the seam in the unstitched areas. Check again. When you are satisfied with the match, change to a regular stitch length and stitch permanently. Remove basting stitches.

11. Trim away excess border, leaving a ¼"-wide seam; press seam open.

12. Repeat steps 6–11 on the remaining corners.

FINISHING THE QUILT

Suggested quilting patternss are included with each quilt plan in this book. They are designed to help you see how the quilting relates to the piecing and to give you ideas for your quilt. Feel free to change or add to the designs. Remember that it is difficult to hand quilt through the layers of fabric in a seam allowance, so plan your design to avoid stitching across the seams, if possible.

MARKING THE QUILTING LINES

Mark the quilting design on the quilt top before layering it with and basting it to the batting and backing layers. Where you draw the lines will depend on the design you choose, the type of batting you select (page 22), and how much quilting you wish to do by hand or machine.

To mark the quilt top for quilting, first press the quilt top and spread it out on a large, flat surface. Then, trace the quilting designs onto it, using a sharp pencil, a mechanical pencil, a Berol silver pencil, or an EZ Washout marking pencil. Use powdered or solid chalk or a white marking pencil to mark quilting lines on dark fabrics.

TIP

Straight-line quilting patterns can be marked with ¼"-wide masking tape on the quilt top after the layers have been basted together. For grids or cross-hatched quilting patterns, 1"-wide masking tape is also very handy. Tape only small sections at a time and remove tape when finished to avoid leaving a sticky residue behind.

PREPARING THE BACKING

Cut or assemble a quilt backing that is at least 3" larger than your quilt top on all sides. For large quilts, it is usually necessary to sew two or three lengths of fabric together to make a backing of the required size. Press the backing seams open to make quilting easier (Diagram 69).

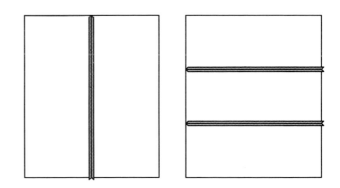

Diagram 69
For large quilt backings, sew fabric lengths together.

LAYERING AND BASTING THE QUILT LAYERS

1. Spread the backing, wrong side up, over a clean, flat table. Use masking tape or large binder clamps to anchor the backing to the table, being careful not to stretch it out of shape.

2. Spread and smooth the quilt batting over the backing, making sure it covers the entire backing.

3. With the right side up, center the pressed and marked quilt top on top of the batting. Make sure the borders and the straight vertical and horizontal seam lines of the quilt are parallel to the edges of the backing.

4. Pin-baste the layers together, using one of the following methods:

For machine quilting:

Use rustproof #1 safety pins, spaced about 2"–4" apart (no more than a hand's width). Begin pinning in the center and work toward the outer edges of the quilt, keeping pins away from the marked quilting lines (Diagram 70). Remember that smooth layering and careful pinning of your quilt top will prevent endless frustration as you quilt on the machine and will help ensure the success of your project.

Sew a row of basting stitches around the outside of the quilt about ¼" from the raw edges. This helps prevent the edges from fraying while you machine quilt and keeps the edges aligned while you stitch the binding to the quilt. You're ready to machine quilt without further basting.

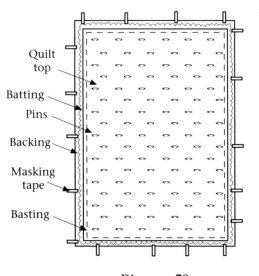

Diagram 70
Use safety pins to baste layers together
for machine quilting.

For hand quilting:

Carefully pin-baste the layers together, using large straight pins. Then, hand baste the three layers together, using a long needle and light-colored quilting thread. Thread the needle without cutting the thread from the spool, so you can baste at least one or two long rows without stopping to thread the needle again.

Baste a large **X** through the quilt, beginning at the center and stitching out to each corner. Take large stitches to make the work go faster.

Continue basting, creating a grid of parallel lines, spaced 6"–8" apart (Diagram 71).

Complete the basting with a row of stitches around the outside edges. After the basting is complete, remove the straight pins.

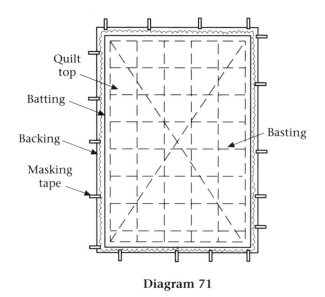

Diagram 71

QUILTING

The quilting stitch is simply a short running stitch taken through all three layers of the quilt. It may be done by hand or by machine (Diagram 72). While hand quilting is traditional, beautiful, and considered a relaxing and pleasant activity by many quiltmakers, it *is* time-consuming. Machine quilting is a practical alternative for smaller projects or baby quilts, which need to be laundered frequently.

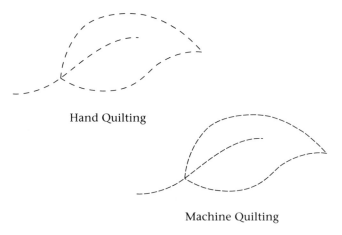

Hand Quilting

Machine Quilting

Diagram 72
Machine quilting is more dense than hand quilting.

Hand Quilting

You may hand quilt on a frame, in a hoop, on a table top, or in your lap. Be sure to use quilting thread; it is thicker and coated to prevent tangling while you stitch. Beginning quilters usually prefer to use a #7 or larger needle. As you become more familiar with hand quilting, you will find that it is easier to take smaller, more evenly spaced quilting stitches with a smaller (#8, #10, or #12) needle. Remember, the larger the number, the smaller the needle.

To hand quilt:

1. Thread the needle with an 18"–24" length of quilting thread and tie a small knot at one end.

2. About 1" from where you want the quilting to begin, insert the needle through the quilt top and batting only. Tug gently on the knot until it pops through the quilt top and is caught in the batting.

3. Take small, evenly spaced, straight stitches through all three quilt layers. Wear a thimble on the middle finger of your quilting hand to make it easier to guide and push the needle through the layers.

4. Rock the needle up and down through all layers, "loading" three or four stitches on the needle (Diagram 73). Place your other hand under the quilt and use your thumbnail to make sure the needle has penetrated all three layers with each and every stitch.

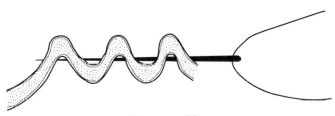

Diagram 73
Load three or four stitches on the needle.

5. Pull the needle through the layers and repeat.

6. To end a line of quilting (when you reach the end of your thread or the end of the marked line to be quilted), make a single knot close to the surface of the quilt top. Take a short backstitch, popping the knot into the top layer and running the needle through the batting only and then up

through the quilt top (Diagram 74). Clip the thread close to the surface of the quilt.

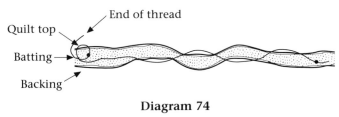

Diagram 74
Ending a line of quilting

7. When all quilting is completed, carefully remove all basting except the stitching that holds the layers together around the outside edges.

Machine Quilting

Machine quilting is a widely accepted alternative to hand quilting. As quilters discover that they can piece more quilt tops than they can quilt by hand, they realize that machine quilting is a very practical choice.

Choose a small quilt, such as one of the warm-up projects, for your first machine-quilting project. Plan a quilting design that involves long, continuous straight lines, gentle curves, and few direction changes. Allover grids, diagonal straight lines, or clamshells are good examples. Quilting "in the ditch" and outline quilting can also be done by machine (Diagram 75). To quilt in the ditch, take stitches in the seam line. Use outline quilting stitches to enhance existing shapes in the quilt.

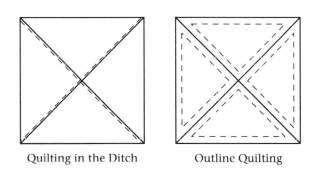

Quilting in the Ditch   Outline Quilting

Diagram 75

Keep the spacing between quilting lines consistent over the entire quilt. Avoid using complex, little designs and leaving large unquilted spaces. For most battings, a 2" or 3" square is the largest area that can be left unquilted. Read the instructions enclosed with the batting you have chosen.

Use a walking foot or even-feed foot (or the built-in, even-feed feature, when available) for your sewing machine to help the quilt layers feed through the machine without shifting or puckering. This type of foot is essential for straight-line and grid quilting and for large, simple curves. Read the machine instruction manual for special tension settings to sew through extra fabric thicknesses.

Curved designs require free fabric movement under the foot of the sewing machine. This is called free-motion quilting, and with a little practice, you can imitate beautiful hand quilting designs quickly. If you wish to do curved quilting designs with your machine, use a darning foot and lower the feed dog while using this foot (Diagram

Diagram 76

Darning foot

76). Because the feed dog is lowered for free-motion quilting, the stitch length is determined by the speed with which you run the machine and with which you feed the fabric under the foot. Practice running the machine fairly fast, since this makes it easier to sew smoother lines of quilting. With free-motion quilting, do not turn the fabric under the needle. Instead, guide the fabric as if it were under a stationary pencil (the needle).

Practice first on a piece of fabric until you get the feel of controlling the motion of the fabric with your hands. Stitch some free-form scribbles, zigzags, and curves (Diagram 77). Try a heart or a star. Then, practice on a sample block with batting and backing. Make sure your chair is adjusted to a comfortable height. At first, this type of quilting may feel a bit awkward, but with a little determination and practice, you will have the satisfaction of being able to complete a project with beautiful machine quilting in a few hours.

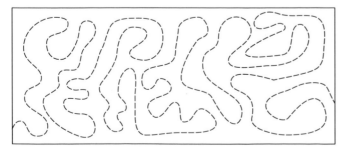

Diagram 77

Machine quilting can be cumbersome when the bulk of a large quilt makes moving it under the sewing-machine arm difficult. If you wish to machine quilt a large quilt, roll the quilt to fit under the sewing-machine arm and secure with bicycle pant-leg clips. As you work from the center of the quilt, gently unroll the quilt with the clips still in place.

Do not try to machine quilt the entire quilt in one sitting, even if it's a small quilt. Break the work up into short periods; stretch and relax your muscles regularly. Your shoulders, back, and arms will appreciate the rest.

When all the quilting is completed, remove the safety pins. Sometimes it will be necessary to remove safety pins as you work.

BINDING

After quilting, you're ready to finish the raw edges of the quilt with binding. First, trim the batting and backing even with the quilt top edges.

To bind the edges:

1. Cut 2½"-wide bias strips from the binding fabric. Use the 45°-angle marking on your large rotary-cutting ruler as a guide for cutting true bias strips.

2. Sew the bias strips together, end to end, to make a strip that is long enough to go all the way around the quilt, plus about 3" (Diagram 78). This measurement is provided for you in each quilt plan.

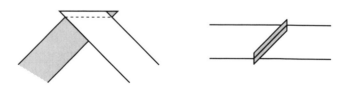

Diagram 78

Seam bias strips together for a
continuous length of bias binding.

3. Fold the strip in half lengthwise, *wrong sides together,* and press (Diagram 79).

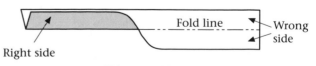

Diagram 79

Fold the strip in half lengthwise.

4. Turn under ¼" at one end of the bias strip and press (Diagram 80).

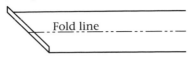

Diagram 80

Turn under ¹/₄" at one end.

5. Beginning just to the right of the center of one side of the quilt, stitch the binding to the quilt with raw edges even with the quilt-top edge; use a ¼"-wide seam (Diagram 81). End the stitching ¼" from the corner of the quilt and backstitch.

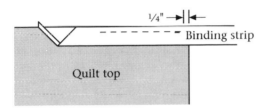

Diagram 81

End stitching ¹/₄" from corner.

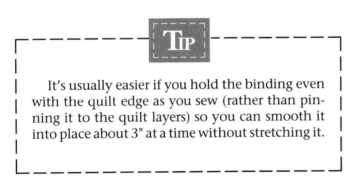

TIP

It's usually easier if you hold the binding even with the quilt edge as you sew (rather than pinning it to the quilt layers) so you can smooth it into place about 3" at a time without stretching it.

6. Remove the quilt from the sewing machine. Put a pin from the back of the quilt up through the end of your line of stitching, ¼" from the end of the quilt. Fold the binding back on itself, creating a 45° angle. The binding should form a straight line out from the next side of the quilt (Diagram 82).

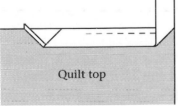

Diagram 82

Fold the binding back at a 45° angle.

7. Hold the fold down with your finger and fold the rest of the binding back over itself, even with the quilt-top edge (Diagram 83). Begin stitching the binding to the second edge of the quilt top ¼" from the corner—exactly where you stopped stitching the binding to the first edge of the quilt.

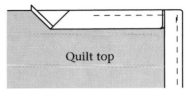

Diagram 83

Fold rest of binding down even with second edge of quilt top and start stitching ¹/₄" from corner.

8. Repeat the stitching and mitering process on the remaining edges and corners of the quilt. When you reach the point where you started stitching the binding to the quilt top, overlap the beginning stitches by about 1" and cut away any excess binding, trimming the end at a 45° angle (Diagram 84). Tuck the end of the binding into the fold.

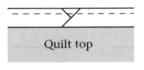

Diagram 84

Overlap the ends about 1" and trim end at 45° angle; tuck end into fold.

9. When all the binding is stitched, place your finger under each corner and push the fold toward the point. Fold the binding around to the back of the quilt and fold a miter on the back of the corner.

10. Whipstitch the binding to the back of the quilt by hand (Diagram 85).

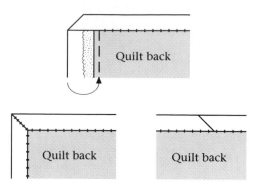

Diagram 85
Whipstitch binding to back of quilt.

LABELING

Labeling your quilt is an important finishing touch. Embroider or cross-stitch your name, city, and the date on the back of your quilt (Diagram 86). If you have too much information to stitch, letter a muslin label with a permanent pen or type the information on a muslin label. Stitch the label to the back of the quilt.

Diagram 86
Stitch a label to the back of your quilt.

L ET'S GET STARTED

Now it's time to get acquainted with each of the authors and to choose your first quilt project from those featured in the sections that follow. To make your quiltmaking an enjoyable experience, first review the following points:

♥ Read the complete cutting and piecing directions for the quilt you are going to make before you begin. Refer to the quiltmaking basics on pages 15–54 if you wish to refresh your memory on any of the required techniques.

♥ The yardage requirements for each quilt include fabric type and color suggestions to help you reproduce the quilt shown in the accompanying photo. Each fabric has a visual color key to help you identify the pieces as you cut and piece them into blocks. Feel free to substitute your favorite colors. If you do substitute colors, it's a good idea to make your own fabric key by mounting small squares of fabric on an index card and labeling each with the color it is replacing.

♥ Remember that the yardage requirements are based on fabric that is at least 42" wide after prewashing. If it's wider than 42", you may have a little left over at the end of each strip. If it is narrower, you may need to cut an extra strip.

♥ All measurements for the block pieces and borders include ¼"-wide seam allowances. Do not add seam allowances to the dimensions given in the cutting section. Measurements in the diagrams indicate the strip size before sewing even though the strips are illustrated as they appear after sewing.

♥ When individual triangles are required, you will be instructed to first cut a square and then to cut it in half on the diagonal, once for half-square triangles or twice for quarter-square triangles.

♥ Unless otherwise indicated, all border strips are cut across the crosswise grain of the fabric and seamed together as necessary to make strips of the required lengths for the sides and top and bottom edges of the quilt. If you wish to cut borders lengthwise to take advantage of a particular fabric design, such as a vertical stripe, you must purchase extra yardage.

MEET
Nancy J. Martin
&
HER BIAS SQUARE
QUILTS

My interest in quilting began with the bicentennial celebrations in 1976. At that time, I lived in Oakland, New Jersey, a small town located twenty-one miles from New York City and steeped in colonial history. The town sponsored several demonstrations of crafts and folk art that had been practiced in earlier times. The demonstration on quilting appealed most to me, especially since I already enjoyed sewing and stitchery projects.

I learned embroidery as a young child from my grandmother. I loved to feel the raised threads that created neat, geometric stitches, and I loved to create flowers and birds from strands of floss. I dabbled in various types of stitchery over the years—crewel, needlepoint, bargello, and counted cross-stitch—but none had the same appeal as quilting.

I was an avid home stitcher, self-taught but very capable and competent. At age seventeen, I realized I was three months away from starting college on a tight budget without a fashionable wardrobe. It was 1960, before the blue jeans-and-sweatshirt fashion rebellion.

Armed with practicality and perseverance, I purchased a Vogue pattern, borrowed a neighbor's sewing machine, and whipped up a red wool skirt with stitched-down pleats plus a coordinating plaid vest on my first try. It was "love at first stitch!" It wasn't long before I purchased a secondhand machine to take off to college with me. Doing alterations and mending for fellow students kept me in spending money through my college years.

As a young mother, I used the sewing machine as my creative outlet during those days at home with a new baby. The house sparkled with new curtains and bedspreads and homemade slipcovers. My son and I dazzled our friends in matching mother-son outfits. However, at age two, he rebelled at these "sissy" get-ups. I soon needed to find other creative outlets, so I returned to teaching elementary school.

It was about this time that I attended the craft demonstrations in Oakland and discovered quilting. A subsequent article on a Log Cabin quilt in *Decorating and Crafts* magazine was all that I needed to get me going. Never one to practice on a small project, I quickly put together a brown, queen-size Log Cabin quilt. Executed in the quilt-as-you-go style, my machine-sewn Log Cabin is truly the archetypical "first quilt." The exuberance of color and fabric is so naive and childlike (remember the limited fabric choices in 1976) that it more than compensates for the occasional pucker or mismatched seam.

As a seamstress for fifteen years, I had struggled mightily with all the fabric-matching rules, such as: "Never mix stripes and plaids," and "Don't combine prints." Patchwork afforded me the opportunity to break the rules and to purchase and combine all the wonderful prints available.

Quilting is very textural and sensory to me. I have an innate need to touch and feel all those fabrics. The varying prints represent texture to me. Quilting allows me to use color and pattern to develop and express my very own sense of style.

After I discovered quilting, it was difficult to maintain a full-time teaching position and still devote time to quiltmaking. I was also teaching an evening adult class in patchwork and quilting. I felt that I wanted to make a career change that would utilize my teaching background yet include quilting. My husband, Dan, and I always wanted to have our own business, and we searched for a solution that might combine all of our wants and needs.

The solution was That Patchwork Place, incorporated in New Jersey in 1976. It started as a mail-order company that produced kits with directions and quality fabric for patchwork items, such as purses, totes, vests, and clothing items, including men's neckties.

I have watched this business prosper and grow into a major publishing company that produces over twenty-four books on patchwork and quilting each year, thanks to the dedication of numerous authors and thirty-five employees. Even so, I seldom think of myself as Nancy J. Martin, President of That Patchwork Place.

In my eyes, I am first and foremost a quiltmaker. Each day is planned so that I have an opportunity to stitch. My studio is the heart of my home. I begin each day early in my studio. Some days I stitch at the machine, completing a quilt design for a new book. Other days are spent writing directions in longhand and sketching illustrations. I am quite happy to be "computer illiterate," for word processing doesn't have the tactile qualities that appeal to me.

It's not surprising that quiltmaking would appeal to me in so many ways. I've always been a mathematical person with an affinity for numbers. However, I now wish that I had been more attentive in my high school geometry class. A better knowledge of those triangles and angles could have helped me in my quiltmaking! I also enjoy jigsaw puzzles, and patchwork offers many of the same matching and assembling challenges.

Dan and I live in Woodinville, Washington, a suburb of Seattle. Our reproduction colonial home is located on the banks of Cottage Lake Creek, a salmon-spawning stream, beautiful in its natural splendor. The view from my studio window is of the stream and the perennial gardens I have cultivated.

Quilting is not my only creative outlet, for I love gardening, with its myriad textures and colors, and cooking, which offers opportunities to combine textures and tastes.

I'm an avid collector and enjoy arranging my various collections throughout the house: dolls, teddy bears, teapots, china, antique sewing notions, children's sewing machines, antique quilts, lace, and, of course, fabrics.

I also enjoy interior decorating and like to include some decorator fabrics in my quilts. These are 100% cotton fabrics normally used for draperies, slipcovers, and pillows. The large-scale decorator prints create movement and design interest when combined with other fabrics in a quilt.

My fabric library includes an assortment of chintzes and decorator fabrics in several color groupings. Although these fabrics are heavier than more traditional quilt fabrics, they are not difficult to hand quilt. Many of them, such as the chintzes, have a glazed finish, which adds a sheen, reflecting light from the quilt's surface.

As the photo of my studio illustrates, I am a firm believer in a well-stocked fabric library. (See page 57.) I use my fabric quickly and find that I need to constantly evaluate the fabric on hand, ensuring that I have a good variety of prints available in all color groups.

I have never made templates for my quilts, preferring instead to cut the correct shape from fabric, using an accurate ruler for measurement. The Olfa company provided me with one of their first rotary cutters in 1980, and I eagerly accepted this helpful tool. Not only did the rotary cutter save time, but it was much easier to use on the days that the cramping in my hand and wrist proved troublesome.

I was delighted with the accuracy of the Template-Free approach. Trudie Hughes (author of *Template-Free Quiltmaking* and *More Template-Free Quiltmaking*) helped me to refine my thinking in this area, and then Marsha McCloskey (author of *Feathered Star Quilts*) spurred me on with her bias-strip-piecing technique. Soon I devised the Bias Square, the ruler that is the key to making so many of my quilts with speed and accuracy.

Friends who sat next to me at workshops seemed amazed at the piecing shortcuts that I used in my quiltmaking. Their encouragement resulted in sharing my techniques for bias squares in the book *Back to Square One*.

Marsha McCloskey, a good friend and fellow quiltmaker, has worked with me, refining this process over the years. She takes the bias square or "Square One" process even further to create additional units, which she refers to as "Square Two" and even Square .5 and Square 1.5. Her recent book, *On to Square Two*, explores this concept.

One of the greatest pleasures to me as a quilting teacher and designer is to see these triangle techniques prove helpful to students and fellow quilters. It's always a joy to share what you believe in, and a reward to know that you are part of a quilt heritage and history that will survive over the years.

In the section that follows, you'll find instructions on how to make the bias squares that are used in the quilt projects I've included in this book. Reading through this section before attempting to make the quilts will save you a lot of time and make your quiltmaking a joyous experience.

MAKING BIAS SQUARES

Many traditional quilt patterns contain squares made from two contrasting half-square triangles. The short sides of the triangles are on the straight grain of the fabric while the long sides are on the bias (Diagram 1). These triangles are called bias squares or Square One units. It is easy to sew and cut bias squares in a variety of sizes, using bias strip piecing. This technique is especially useful for making small bias squares because pressing the seams is done in the strip piecing, not after joining the two triangles, a point when pressing after stitching can distort the shape (and sometimes burn fingers!).

Diagram 1

Half-square triangles have their short sides on the straight grain and their long sides on the bias.

1. To make fabric more manageable, cut two half-yard pieces of contrasting fabric and layer with the right side of both pieces facing up. That way, you can cut bias strips from both fabrics at the same time. Remember to cut the strips for the bias squares first, then cut the remaining quilt pieces.

2. Use the 45° marking on the Bias Square cutting ruler to locate the true bias and then use a longer ruler to make a bias cut (Diagram 2). Most of the resulting cut strips will have the same angle along the short ends. To utilize those that do not, see "Tip" on page 63.

BIAS-SQUARE BASICS

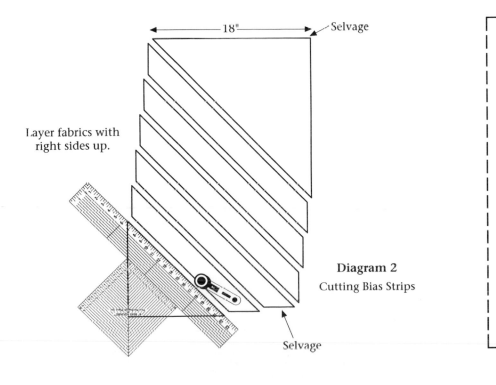

Layer fabrics with right sides up.

18"

Selvage

Diagram 2

Cutting Bias Strips

Selvage

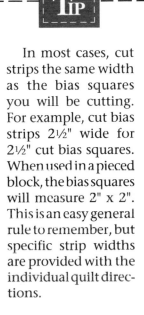

TIP

In most cases, cut strips the same width as the bias squares you will be cutting. For example, cut bias strips 2½" wide for 2½" cut bias squares. When used in a pieced block, the bias squares will measure 2" x 2". This is an easy general rule to remember, but specific strip widths are provided with the individual quilt directions.

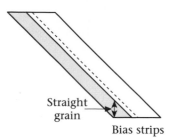

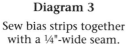

Straight grain

Bias strips

Diagram 3

Sew bias strips together
with a ¼"-wide seam.

3. With right sides together, sew the strips together ¼" from the long bias edge. Press seams toward the darker fabric (Diagram 3). (When cutting bias squares 1¼" square or smaller, you may want to press the seams open to evenly distribute the fabric bulk.)

4. Align the 45° mark on the Bias Square ruler with the seam line. Cut the first two sides of the square after measuring the distance from the cut edge to the opposite side of the square. Turn the fabric strip, then measure and cut the third and fourth sides in the same manner (Diagram 4).

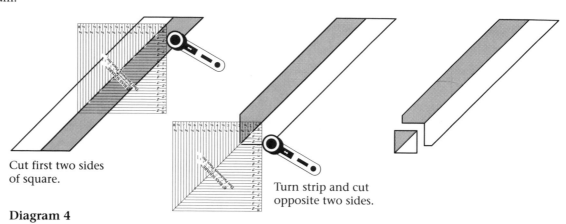

Cut first two sides
of square.

Turn strip and cut
opposite two sides.

Diagram 4

5. Align the 45° marking on the Bias Square ruler with the seam line before cutting the next bias square.

Note: All quilt directions in this book give the cut size for bias squares; the finished size after stitching will be ¼" smaller on each side.

EDGE TRIANGLES

When bias squares are cut from long bias strip-pieced fabrics, triangular pieces are left along each side. These pieces are called edge triangles, and in some of the featured quilts, they are used in constructing the blocks (Diagram 5).

To use these edge triangles, you must resize them first, following the directions on page 64 for resizing edge triangles. When the quilt does not require any leftover edge triangles, you can save them and resize them for other quilts, using the easy resizing technique or the template provided on page 270.

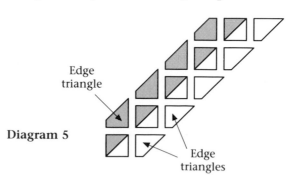

Edge
triangle

Diagram 5

Edge
triangles

CUTTING MULTIPLE BIAS SQUARES

To conserve time and fabric, the following cutting formats were devised for producing the required bias squares. Each format results in different colorations of bias squares and contains variations in the number of strips sewn together. All strips are cut from half-yard lengths of 44"-wide fabric.

A cutting format is illustrated with the cutting directions for each quilt. The size of the bias squares and the number of strips sewn together determine the cut width of the strips. The number of edge triangles needed for each quilt determines the number of strips sewn together. If the cutting format does not provide enough edge triangles for your design, you will find quick-cutting information for additional triangles with the directions.

Cutting Format #1: Bias Squares in Two Colors

1. Follow the basic technique on pages 59–60 to prepare strips for cutting bias squares, using the cutting width specified in the quilt directions.

2. Join two, three, four, five, or six bias strips of fabric together, alternating dark and light strips (Diagram 6).

1A yields edge triangles from both fabrics.

1B yields edge triangles from both fabrics.

1C yields edge triangles from one fabric.

1D yields edge triangles from both fabrics.

Diagram 6
Cutting Format #1
Join two, four, five, or six bias strips together.

3. Begin at the lower end of the strip-pieced unit and cut the first two sides of the bias squares, aligning the 45° marking of the Bias Square on the seam line (Diagram 7).

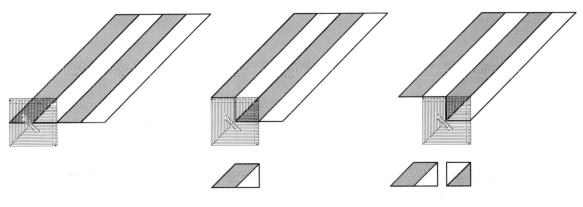

Diagram 7
Align 45° marking on seam line and cut first two sides.

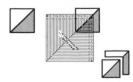

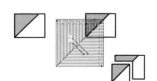

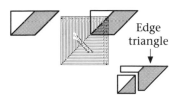

Edge
triangle
↓

Diagram 8

Turn cut segments and
cut opposite two sides.

4. Turn the cut segments and place the Bias Square ruler on the opposite two sides, accurately aligning the measurements on both sides of the cutting guide and the 45° marking. Cut the remaining two sides of the bias squares (Diagram 8).

5. Continue cutting bias squares in this manner, working up the strip-pieced unit, row by row, until you have cut bias squares from all usable fabric.

6. Resize any edge triangles needed for the quilt design, using the template on (page 270) or the resizing directions on page 64.

Cutting Format #2:
Bias Squares of a Consistent Background Color

If you are using a consistent background color in your bias squares, such as muslin with a variety of other prints, use the following technique:

1. Follow the basic technique on pages 59–60 to prepare strips for cutting bias squares, using the cutting width specified in the quilt directions.

2. Join three, four, five, or six bias strips of fabric together, alternating the chosen background fabric with the others (Diagram 9).

2A
yields edge
triangles
from dark
fabric.

2B
yields edge
triangles
from dark and
light fabrics.

2C
yields edge
triangles
from dark
fabric.

2D
yields edge
triangles
from dark and
light fabrics.

Diagram 9
Cutting Format #2
Join three, four, five, or six bias strips together.

3. Follow steps 3–6 of Cutting Format #1 to cut bias squares (Diagram 10).

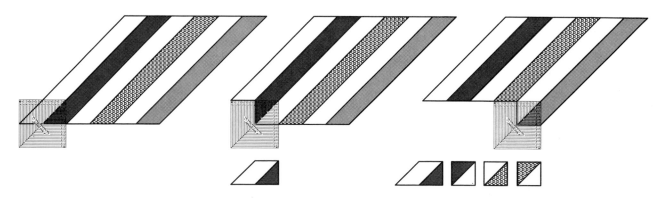

Diagram 10
Align 45° marking on seam line and cut first two sides.
Turn cut segments and cut opposite two sides.

Note: You can also make a dark variation, using black for a background color in place of the light color.

Cutting Format #3: Multicolor Bias Squares

1. Follow the basic technique on pages 59–60 to prepare strips for cutting bias squares, using the cutting width specified in the quilt directions.

2. Join six strips, each a different fabric (Diagram 11).

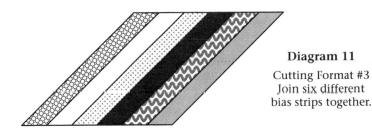

Diagram 11

Cutting Format #3
Join six different
bias strips together.

3. Follow steps 3–6 of Cutting Format #1 to cut bias squares. (Diagram 12).

Diagram 12

Align 45° marking on seam line
and cut first two sides.
Turn cut segments and cut
opposite two sides.

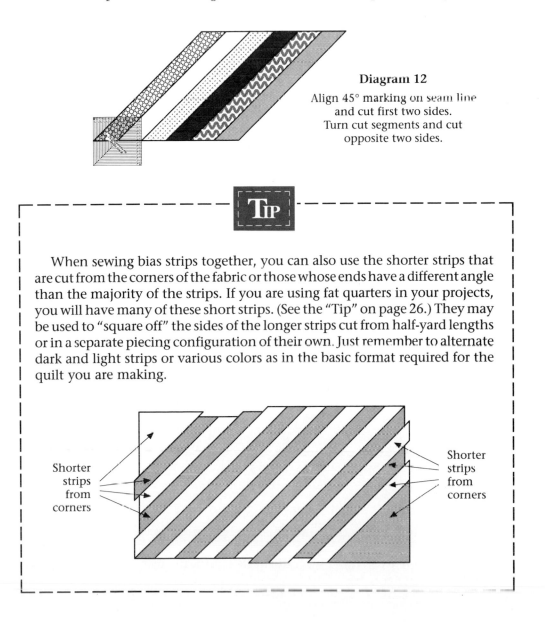

TIP

When sewing bias strips together, you can also use the shorter strips that are cut from the corners of the fabric or those whose ends have a different angle than the majority of the strips. If you are using fat quarters in your projects, you will have many of these short strips. (See the "Tip" on page 26.) They may be used to "square off" the sides of the longer strips cut from half-yard lengths or in a separate piecing configuration of their own. Just remember to alternate dark and light strips or various colors as in the basic format required for the quilt you are making.

Shorter
strips
from
corners

Shorter
strips
from
corners

RESIZING EDGE TRIANGLES

The edge triangles that result when bias squares are cut are not really waste (Diagram 13). They can be used for the half-square triangles that are needed for many of the blocks in this book (Diagram 13). In order to use these triangles, you must trim them to the correct size.

If the edge triangles need resizing for a particular quilt, that information is included in the directions. If you prefer to use templates for resizing, use the resizing template for edge triangles on page 270.

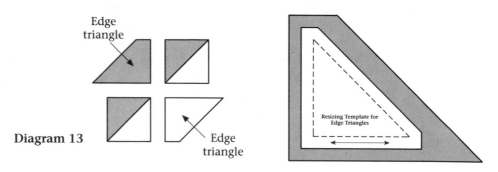

Using a template to resize edge triangles

If you prefer a Template-Free rotary-cutting method, follow the steps below. Although this works with any size edge triangle, the example shown is a 2" finished (2½" cut size) half-square triangle.

1. Use the Bias Square and rotary cutter to true up the 90° corner of the edge triangle (Diagram 14).

2. To trim the points of the triangle for easy matching, set the Bias Square at the 2½" mark on the triangle as shown in Diagram 15. Trim off the points that extend beyond the edge of the Bias Square. For other sizes of edge triangles, use the dimension that is the same size as the bias squares used in your design.

3. To cut the diagonal of the triangle, align one edge of the triangle with the 45°-angle line of the Bias Square where the first two ¼" marking lines meet in the corner. Trim the diagonal edge with the rotary cutter (Diagram 16).

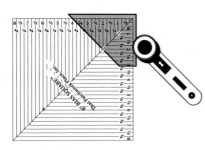

Diagram 14
True up the 90° corner.

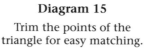
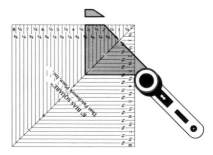

Diagram 15
Trim the points of the
triangle for easy matching.

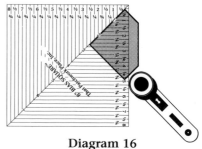

Diagram 16
Trim the diagonal.

Now that you are familiar with the basic technique used in the Bias Square quilts that follow, you are ready to begin a quilt project!

The Fleet Is In

Make this delightful quilt to practice making bias squares. For the background, select a deep blue print with swirly lines to resemble waves. Use a white print for the sails and a red for the ship to create a nautical color scheme. Choose a lighter blue for the smaller bias squares, which represent waves.

Dimensions: *26" x 48"*

3 blocks, each 12" square,
set straight across with
6" x 12" alternate blocks
and 2"-wide sashing strips;
1"-wide inner border and
3"-wide outer border

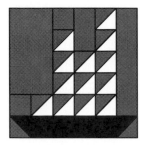

Tall Ships Block

Materials: *44"-wide fabric*

Yardages listed are generous and are based on 44"-wide fabric that has been preshrunk. Strips cut across the fabric width should measure at least 42", as shown in the strip dimensions in the cutting chart.

- 1 yd. deep blue print for background and alternate blocks
- ½ yd. white print for sails
- ¼ yd. light blue print for waves
- ¼ yd. red print for ships and binding
- ¼ yd. red plaid fabric for inner border
- ½ yd. blue fabric for outer border and binding
- 1½ yds. fabric of your choice for backing
- Batting and thread to finish

Cutting

> All rotary-cutting dimensions include ¼"-wide seam allowances. Cut the bias strips for the bias squares first and set aside any remaining fabric. Construct the bias squares and set aside. Then cut the pieces and strips shown in the cutting chart.

From the deep blue and the white prints:

Cut bias strips 2½" wide and piece 2 sets of strips, using Cutting Format #1C (Diagram 17). Cut 2½" x 2½" bias squares from the strip-pieced units. Each set of strips made using this format yields at least 28 bias squares, 2½" x 2 ½". You will need a total of 39 for this quilt, 13 for each Tall Ships block.

Diagram 17
Cutting Format #1C

From the deep blue and light blue prints:

Cut bias strips 1¾" wide and piece 1 set of strips, using Cutting Format #2A (Diagram 18). Cut 1½" x 1½" bias squares from the strip-pieced unit, which will yield at least 20 bias squares. You will need 18, 6 for each alternate block.

Diagram 18
Cutting Format #2A

From the deep blue and red prints:

Cut bias strips 2½" wide and piece 1 set of strips, using Cutting Format #1A (Diagram 19). Cut 2½" x 2½" bias squares from the strip-pieced unit, which will yield at least 7 bias squares. You will need 6, 2 for each Tall Ships block.

Diagram 19
Cutting Format #1A

COLOR KEY
■ Deep blue
□ White print
▨ Light blue
■ Red print
▦ Red plaid

CUTTING		
Fabric	No. of Pieces	Dimensions
Deep Blue		Alternate Blocks
	3	6½" x 10½"
	3	1½" x 6½"
		Sashing Strips
	2	2½" x 18½"
		Piece #1
	3	4½" x 8½"
		Piece #2
	6	2½" x 2½"
		Piece #3
	3	2½" x 4½"
		Piece #4
	3	2½" x 10½"
Red Print		Piece #5
	3	2½" x 8½"
Red Plaid		Inner Border
	3	1½" x 42"
Blue		Outer Border
	4	3¼" x 42"

Directions

Tall Ships Blocks

Assemble 3 Tall Ships blocks, using the deep-blue-and-white bias squares, deep blue/red print bias squares, and the cut fabric pieces.

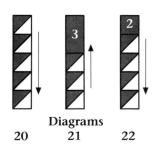

Diagrams
20   21   22

For each block, repeat steps 1–8:

1. Join 5 blue-and-white bias squares in a row. Press seams in the direction of arrow (Diagram 20).

2. Join 3 blue-and-white bias squares to deep blue Piece #3. Press seams in the direction of arrow (Diagram 21).

3. Join 4 blue-and-white bias squares to deep blue Piece #2. Press seams in direction of arrow (Diagram 22).

4. Join the rows from steps 1, 2, and 3 as shown in Diagram 23, carefully matching seams.

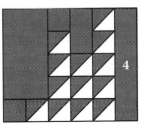

Diagram 23

Diagram 24

5. Join a blue-and-white bias square to deep blue Piece #2. Add to deep blue Piece #1 (Diagram 24).

6. Join pieces to form sail and sky (Diagram 25).

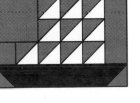

Diagram 25

7. Add a deep blue/red print bias square to each end of Piece #5 (Diagram 26).

8. Join to the sail and sky segment to complete the block (Diagram 27).

Diagram 26

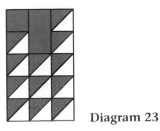

Diagram 27

Alternate Blocks

Assemble 3 alternate blocks, using the deep blue/light blue bias squares and the deep blue cut fabric pieces.

For each block, repeat steps 1–2:

1. Join six 1½" bias squares in a row as shown in Diagram 28.

2. Join the 6½" x 10½" rectangle, the row of bias squares, and the 1½" x 6½" rectangle as shown in Diagram 28 to complete the block.

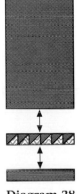

Diagram 28

Quilt Top Assembly

Join Tall Ships blocks, alternate blocks, and deep blue sashing strips to form quilt top as shown on page 66.

Borders

1. Measure the quilt for borders as shown on page 46. Trim the 1½"-wide red plaid border strips to correct length and stitch first to the sides of the quilt top. Press seams toward borders. Then add red plaid border strips, trimmed to the correct length, to the top and bottom. Press seams toward borders.

2. Add the 3¼"-wide blue outer borders as described in step 1, stitching the border strips to the sides of the quilt top first, and then to the top and bottom.

Quilt Finishing

1. Layer the quilt top with batting and backing; baste.

2. Quilt in the design of your choice, or follow the Quilting Suggestion.

3. Cut and piece 154" of 2½"-wide bias for binding from the remaining blue fabric, following the directions on pages 52–53. Bind the quilt edges.

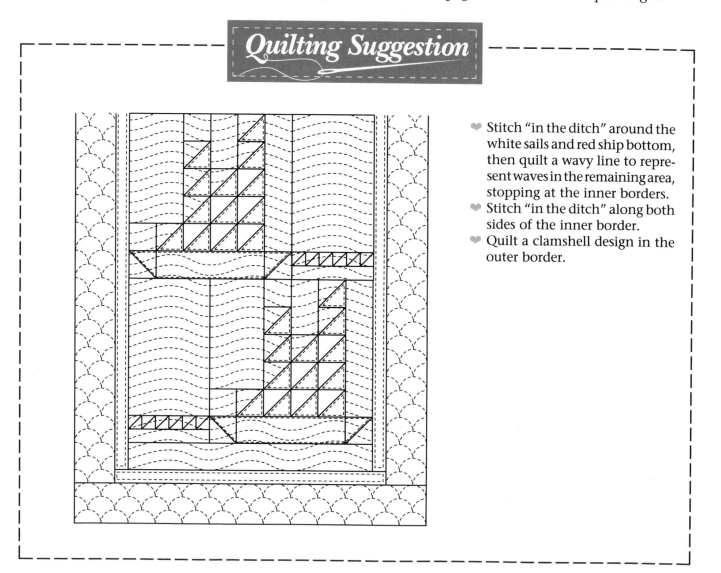

Quilting Suggestion

- Stitch "in the ditch" around the white sails and red ship bottom, then quilt a wavy line to represent waves in the remaining area, stopping at the inner borders.
- Stitch "in the ditch" along both sides of the inner border.
- Quilt a clamshell design in the outer border.

Kelly's Green Garden

Each block in Kelly's Green Garden is divided diagonally into lights and darks, much like traditional Log Cabin blocks are. These blocks can be arranged in any of the traditional Log Cabin settings, but my personal choice is the dramatic "Barn-Raising" setting used here. The soft peach center square in each block accents the shades of teal in soft and more dramatic tones.

Dimensions: *85" x 85"*

36 blocks, each 12½"
square, set straight across,
6 blocks x 6 blocks;
5"-wide outer border

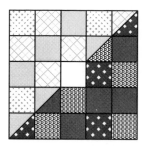

Kelly's Green Garden Block

Materials: *44"-wide fabric*

*Yardages listed are generous and are based on 44"-wide fabric that has
been preshrunk. Strips cut across the fabric width should measure at
least 42", as shown in the strip dimensions in the cutting chart.*

⬜ ⅜ yd. peach print for center squares

⬜ ▨ ⬜　3 yds. total of assorted light teal prints

⬛ ▪ ▨　3 yds. total of assorted dark teal prints

⬛　1⅜ yds. dark teal for borders (cut crosswise)

　5 yds. fabric of your choice for backing

　⅝ yd. green striped fabric for binding

　Batting and thread to finish

Cutting

> *All rotary-cutting dimensions include ¼"-wide seam allowances. Cut the bias strips for the bias squares first and set aside any remaining fabric. Construct the bias squares and set aside. Then cut all remaining pieces as directed in the cutting chart. No directions appear in the second column, when additional cuts are not needed.*

From the light and dark teal prints:

Cut bias strips 3" wide and piece 6 sets of strips, using Cutting Format #3 and alternating the dark and light prints (Diagram 29). Cut 3" x 3" bias squares from the strip-pieced units. Each set of strips made using this format yields at least 25 bias squares, 3" x 3". You will need a total of 144 bias squares, 4 for each block.

Diagram 29
Cutting Format #3

Fabric	FIRST CUT		ADDITIONAL CUTS	
	No. of Strips	Dimensions	No. of Squares	Dimensions
Light Teal	Blocks			
	26	3" x 42"	360	3" x 3"
Dark Teal	26	3" x 42"	360	3" x 3"
Peach Print	3	3" x 42"	36	3" x 3"
Dark Teal	Border			
	9	5¼" x 42"		

Directions

Kelly's Green Garden Blocks

Assemble 36 blocks, using the bias squares and the plain squares.

For each block, repeat steps 1–2:

1. Join bias squares and plain squares in rows as shown, pressing seams in the direction of the arrows (Diagram 30).

2. Join the rows together to complete the block (Diagram 31).

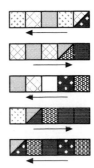

Diagram 30

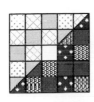

Diagram 31
Make 36.

Quilt Top Assembly

1. Join 6 blocks together to form a row, arranging the dark and light sides of the block as shown in Diagram 32.

Make 4 rows.

Diagram 32

Make 2 rows.

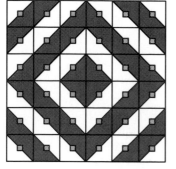

Diagram 33

2. Join the 6 rows together to form the quilt top, as shown in Diagram 33.

Borders

Measure the quilt for borders as shown on page 46. Trim the 5¼"-wide teal border strips to correct length and stitch first to the sides of the quilt top. Press seams toward borders. Then add border strips, trimmed to the correct length, to the top and bottom. Press seams toward borders.

Quilt Finishing

1. Layer the quilt top with batting and backing; baste.

2. Quilt in the design of your choice, or follow the Quilting Suggestion.

3. Cut and piece 346" of 2½"-wide bias for binding, following the directions on pages 52–53. Bind the quilt edges.

Quilting Suggestion

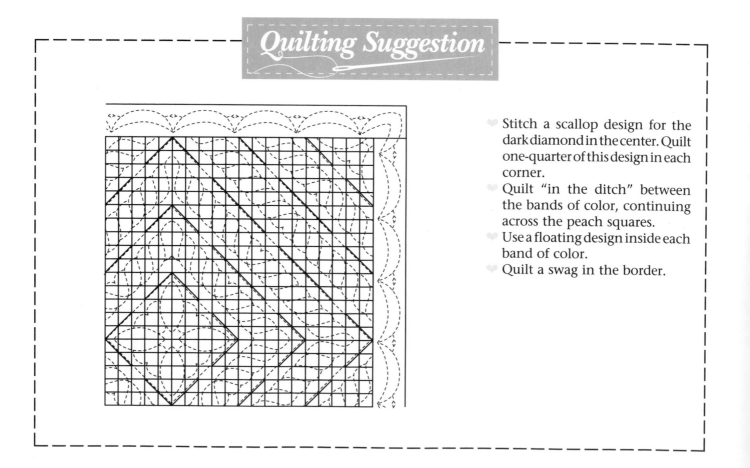

- Stitch a scallop design for the dark diamond in the center. Quilt one-quarter of this design in each corner.
- Quilt "in the ditch" between the bands of color, continuing across the peach squares.
- Use a floating design inside each band of color.
- Quilt a swag in the border.

Nancy's Nosegay

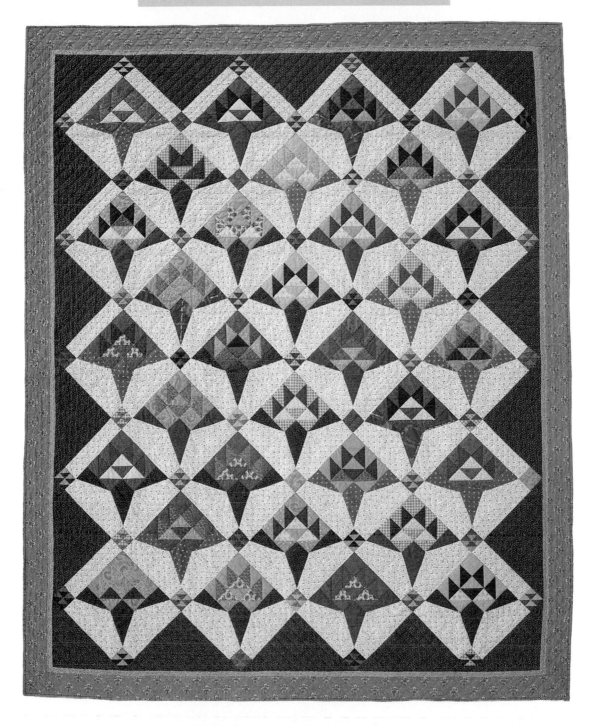

Lavender flower holders surround stylized flowers in shades of pink and yellow set against leafy green backgrounds in this quilt. The smaller pink and green bias squares are repeated in the sashing squares. The flower holders in this block are made of bias rectangles plus pieces cut using templates. The light print used in the background continues into the sashing strips. Lavender setting triangles and a multiple border surround the gaily colored nosegays.

Dimensions: *80¾" x 98½"*

Templates: *Page 270*

32 blocks, each 10" square, set diagonally with 2½"-wide sashing and pieced sashing squares; 1"-wide inner border and 4"-wide outer border

Nancy's Nosegay Block

***Materials:** 44"-wide fabric*

Yardages listed are generous and are based on 44"-wide fabric that has been preshrunk. Strips cut across the fabric width should measure at least 42", as shown in the strip dimensions in the cutting chart.

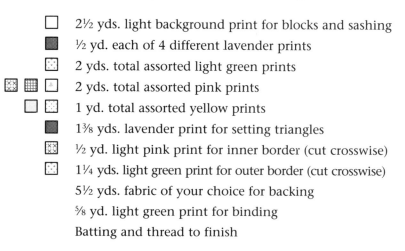

- 2½ yds. light background print for blocks and sashing
- ½ yd. each of 4 different lavender prints
- 2 yds. total assorted light green prints
- 2 yds. total assorted pink prints
- 1 yd. total assorted yellow prints
- 1⅜ yds. lavender print for setting triangles
- ½ yd. light pink print for inner border (cut crosswise)
- 1¼ yds. light green print for outer border (cut crosswise)
- 5½ yds. fabric of your choice for backing
- ⅝ yd. light green print for binding
- Batting and thread to finish

Cutting

All rotary-cutting dimensions include ¼"-wide seam allowances. Cut the bias strips for the bias squares first and set aside any remaining fabric. Construct the bias squares and set aside. Cut out the two template-cut shapes, following the instructions below. Then cut all remaining pieces as directed in the cutting chart. Some strips will not require additional cuts at this time so no directions appear in the second column.

From the assorted pink and light green prints:

Cut bias strips 3" wide and piece 6 sets of strips, using Cutting Format #3 and alternating the pink and green strips (Diagram 34). Cut 3" x 3" bias squares from the strip-pieced units. Each set of strips made using this format yields at least 25 bias squares, 3" x 3". You will need a total of 128 bias squares, 4 for each block. Edge triangles from bias squares are not used in this quilt. Save them for another quilt project.

From the remaining assorted pink and light green prints:

Cut bias strips 2" wide and piece 4 sets of strips, using Cutting Format #3 and alternating the pink and green strips (Diagram 35). Cut 1¾" x 1¾" bias squares from the strip-pieced units. Each set of strips made using this format will yield at least 50 bias squares, 1¾" x 1¾". You will need a total of 196 bias squares, 4 for each sashing square.

From the assorted yellow and light green prints:

Cut bias strips 3" wide and piece 4 sets of strips, using Cutting Format #3 and alternating the yellow and green strips (Diagram 36). Cut 3" x 3" bias squares from the strip-pieced units. Each set of strips made using this format yields at least 25 bias squares, 3" x 3". You will need a total of 96 bias squares, 3 for each Nosegay block.

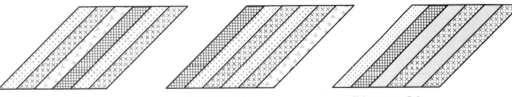

| Diagram 34 | Diagram 35 | Diagram 36 |
| Cutting Format #3 | Cutting Format #3 | Cutting Format #3 |

From the light background and 4 lavender prints:

Cut a ½-yard length from the light background print. From this piece and the lavender prints, cut 3¼"-wide strips for bias rectangles, following the directions on page 155. Piece 4 sets of strips, alternating lavender and light background fabrics. Cut 3" x 5½" bias rectangles from the strip-pieced units (Diagram 37). Each set of strips yields at least 20 bias rectangles, 3" x 5½". You will need a total of 64 bias rectangles, 2 for each block.

Diagram 37

Cut bias rectangles from strip-pieced units.

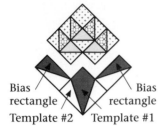

Bias
rectangle
Template #2

Bias
rectangle
Template #1

Diagram 38

Note: Divide the bias rectangles into sets of 2, which are mirror images of each other. You should have 32 sets. Refer to these sets when cutting Template #1 (below) from the 4 lavender prints. Within each block, Template #1 must be cut from the same print as the one in the set of bias rectangles (Diagram 38).

From the 4 different lavender prints, cut:
    32 from Template #1 (page 270).

From the light background print, cut:
    32 from Template #2 (page 270). Reverse the template and cut 32 more from Template #2. (Edge triangles from bias rectangles may be resized using Template #2.)

Fabric	FIRST CUT		ADDITIONAL CUTS		
	No. of Strips	Dimensions	No. of Pieces	Dimensions	No. of Triangles
	Nosegay Block				
Light Green Prints	3	3" x 42"	32	3" x 3"	
Light Background	Sashing Strips				
	20	3" x 42"	80	3" x 10½"	
	Setting Triangles				
Lavender Print	2	18¼" x 42"	4	18¼" x 18¼"	16* ⊠
	1	8" x 42"	2	8" x 8"	4 ◩
	*You will use only 14.				
Light Pink Print	Inner Border				
	9	1½" x 42"			
Light Green Print	Outer Border				
	10	4¼" x 42"			
◩ = Cut squares once diagonally to yield half-square triangles.					
⊠ = Cut squares twice diagonally to yield quarter-square triangles.					

Directions

COLOR KEY

☐ Light background

■ Lavenders

▨ Light greens

▨▨▨ Pinks

▨▨ Yellows

■ Lavender print

Nancy's Nosegay Blocks

Assemble 32 Nancy's Nosegay blocks, using the 3" bias squares, bias rectangles, and the 3" light green print squares.

For each block, repeat steps 1–4:
1. Stitch the light background Template #2 and the reversed Template #2 to the lavender Template #1, matching seam intersections as shown in Diagram 39 to make Unit 1.

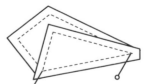

Diagram 39   Unit 1   Pin seam intersections to match.

2. Join 2 different bias squares as shown in Diagram 40, then join to a bias rectangle. Make a mirror image of this unit for each block.

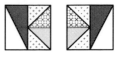

Diagram 40
Unit 2

3. Join the bias squares and light green print squares to create Unit 3 (Diagram 41).

Diagram 50
Unit 3

4. Join Units 1, 2, and 3 to complete the Nosegay block (Diagram 42).

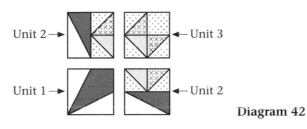

Unit 2 → ← Unit 3

Unit 1 → ← Unit 2

Diagram 42

Quilt Top Assembly

1. Using the 1¾" bias squares, make 49 sashing squares as shown in Diagram 43.

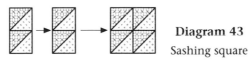

Diagram 43
Sashing square

2. Join Nancy's Nosegay blocks, sashing strips and squares, and side and corner setting triangles into diagonal rows to form quilt top as shown in Diagram 44.

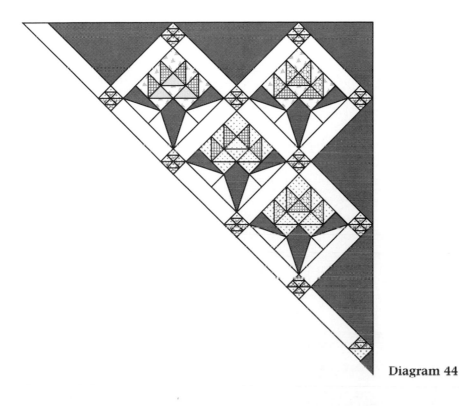

Diagram 44

Borders

1. Measure the quilt for borders as shown on page 46. Trim the 1½"-wide light pink border strips to correct length and stitch first to the sides of the quilt top. Press seams toward borders. Then add border strips, trimmed to the correct length, to the top and bottom. Press seams toward borders.

2. Add the 4¼"-wide light green outer borders as described in step 1, stitching the border strips to the sides first and then to the top and bottom.

Quilt Finishing

1. Layer the quilt top with batting and backing; baste.

2. Quilt in the design of your choice, or follow the Quilting Suggestion.

3. Cut and piece 370" of 2½"-wide bias for binding, following the directions on pages 52–53. Bind the quilt edges.

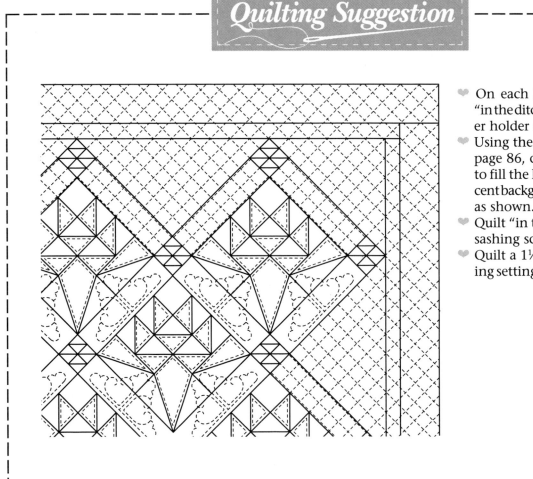

Quilting Suggestion

- ♥ On each Nosegay block, quilt "in the ditch," outlining the flower holder and bias squares.
- ♥ Using the quilting template on page 86, quilt the heart design to fill the lattice strips and adjacent background area of the block as shown.
- ♥ Quilt "in the ditch" around the sashing squares and strips.
- ♥ Quilt a 1¼" grid in the remaining setting triangles and border.

Sister's Chain

This eye-catching quilt is composed of two traditional quilt blocks. Colorful Sister's Choice blocks in a combination of assorted pink and contrasting navy prints are set off by Chain blocks with their large expanse of pink tone-on-tone print. The alternating blocks form a chain pattern across the quilt top, so the quilt is aptly named Sister's Chain.

Dimensions: 86" x 86"

49 blocks, each 10" square;
25 Sister's Choice blocks
alternate with 24 Chain
blocks, set straight across,
7 blocks x 7 blocks;
2"-wide inner border and
6"-wide outer border

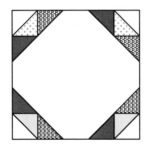

Sister's Choice Block

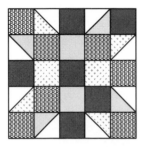

Chain Block

Materials: *44"-wide fabric*

*Yardages listed are generous and are based on 44"-wide fabric that has
been preshrunk. Strips cut across the fabric width should measure at
least 42", as shown in the strip dimensions in the cutting chart.*

☐   3 yds. pink tone-on-tone print for background and bias
     squares

☐ ⊡   1½ yds. assorted pink prints

■ ▨   2½ yds. assorted navy prints

☐   ⅝ yd. pink for inner border (cut crosswise)

■   1¾ yds. navy for outer border (cut crosswise)

     5 yds. fabric of your choice for backing

     ⅝ yd. blue print for binding

     Batting and thread to finish

Cutting

> All rotary-cutting dimensions include ¼"-wide seam allowances. Cut the bias strips for the bias squares first and set aside any remaining fabric. Construct the bias squares and set aside. Then cut all remaining pieces as directed in the cutting chart. Some strips will not require additional cuts at this time so no directions appear in the second column.

From the pink tone-on-tone and assorted pink prints:

Cut bias strips 2½" wide and piece 11 sets of strips, using Cutting Format #2C, alternating the pink tone-on-tone strips and the assorted pink print strips (Diagram 45). Cut 2½" x 2½" bias squares from the strip-pieced units. Each set of strips made using this format yields at least 28 bias squares, 2½" x 2½". You will need a total of 296 bias squares, 8 for each of the Sister's Choice blocks and 4 for each of the Chain blocks.

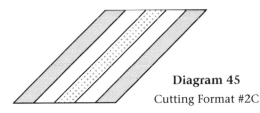

Diagram 45
Cutting Format #2C

Fabric	FIRST CUT		ADDITIONAL CUTS		
	No. of Strips	Dimensions	No. of Squares	Dimensions	No. of Triangles
Navy Prints	Sister's Choice Blocks				
	21	2½" x 42"	325	2½" x 2½"	
Pink Prints	7	2½" x 42	100	2½" x 2½"	
Navy Prints	Chain Blocks				
	7	2⅞" x 42"	96	2⅞" x 2⅞"	192 ◹
Pink Tone-on-Tone	6	10½" x 42"	24	10½" x 10½"*	
	*Trim the corners, using Sister's Chain cutaway template on page 270.				
Pink	Inner Border				
	8	2½" x 42"			
Navy	Outer Border				
	9	6¼" x 42"			
◹ = Cut squares once diagonally to yield half-square triangles.					

Directions

Sister's Choice Blocks

Assemble 25 Sister's Choice blocks, using the bias squares and the 2½" squares cut from navy and pink prints. Press all seam allowances toward the dark fabrics.

For each block, repeat steps 1–4:

1. Make 2 rows as shown in Diagram 46.

2. Make 2 rows as shown in Diagram 47.

3. Make 1 row as shown in Diagram 48.

4. Join the rows from steps 1, 2, and 3 to form a finished block (Diagram 49).

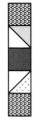

Diagram 46

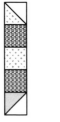

Diagram 47

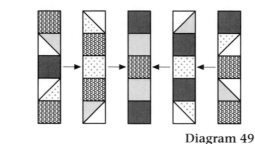

Diagram 48

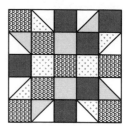

Diagram 49

Chain Blocks

Assemble 24 Chain blocks, using the bias squares and cut fabric pieces.

For each block, repeat steps 1–3:

1. Piece 96 triangle units, using the bias squares and the navy half-square triangles. Attach triangles to bias square (Diagram 50). Press seams in direction of arrows.

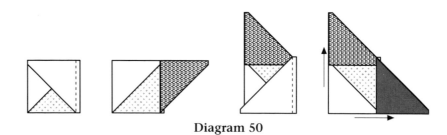

Diagram 50

2. Join 2 triangle units to opposite sides of the pink tone-on-tone background square (Diagram 51).

3. Add triangle units to the remaining sides to complete the Chain block (Diagram 52).

COLOR KEY

☐ Pink tone-on-tone

☐ Assorted pink prints

■ Assorted navy prints

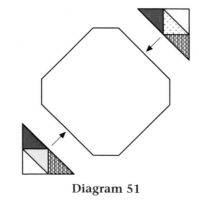

Diagram 51

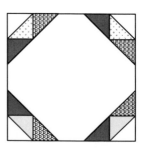

Diagram 52

Quilt Top Assembly

1. Join 4 Sister's Choice and 3 Chain blocks into Row A. Make 4 of these rows (Diagram 53).

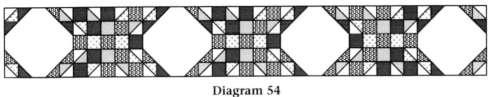

Diagram 53
Row A

2. Join 3 Sister's Choice and 4 Chain blocks into Row B. Make 3 of these rows (Diagram 54).

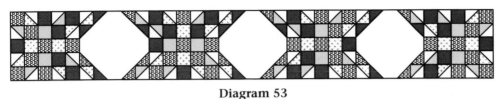

Diagram 54
Row B

3. Join Rows A and B to form quilt top, alternating them. Begin and end with Row A.

Borders

1. Measure the quilt for borders as shown on page 46. Trim the 2½"-wide pink border strips to correct length and stitch to the sides of the quilt top. Press seams toward borders. Then add border strips, trimmed to the correct length, to the top and bottom. Press seams toward borders.

2. Add the 6¼"-wide navy outer borders as described in step 1, stitching the side borders to the quilt top first and then the top and bottom borders.

Quilt Finishing

1. Layer the quilt top with batting and backing; baste.

2. Quilt in the design of your choice, or follow the Quilting Suggestion.

3. Cut and piece 350" of 2½"-wide bias for binding, following the directions on pages 52–53. Bind the quilt edges.

Quilting Suggestion

- ♥ Stitch a diagonal grid across the quilt top that crosses through the middle of each bias square and continues out into the borders.
- ♥ Stitch ¼" away from the seam line on the inside of each Chain block.
- ♥ Quilt a heart design, such as the one on this page, in the center of each Chain block.
- ♥ Use the heart design in the unquilted border area, spacing it evenly in the open areas between the grid.

Heart quilting design

Sparkling Stars

*A swirly blue print in the background sets off the brightly pieced star blocks
in this colorful quilt. The use of bias squares makes the star construction
easier than it might at first appear. Select brightly colored jewel-tone fabrics,
which will sparkle against the muted blue background.*

Dimensions: *82" x 82"*

A bar quilt (page 43), which is sewn together in segments to form 9 stars, 3 star units x 3 star units; 5"-wide outer border

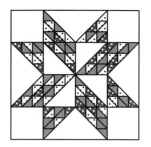

Sparkling Stars Block

Unit 1

Unit 2

Unit 3

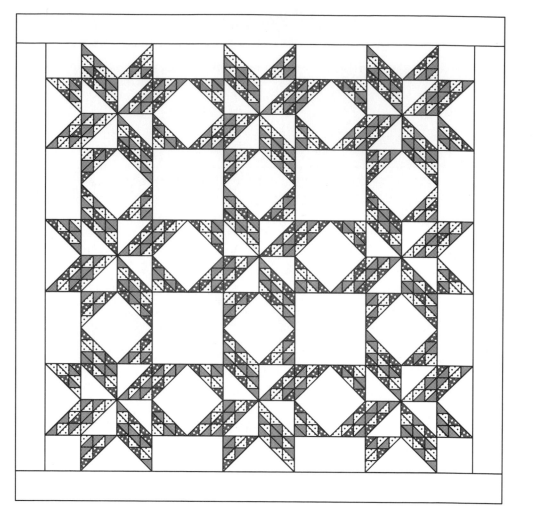

Materials: *44"-wide fabric*

Yardages listed are generous and are based on 44"-wide fabric that has been preshrunk. Strips cut across the fabric width should measure at least 42", as shown in the strip dimensions in the cutting chart.

☐   5 yds. blue swirly print for background and borders

    4 yds. assorted bright prints (purple, pink, green, teal, navy, blue) for stars

4¾ yds. fabric of your choice for backing

⅝ yd. blue swirly print for binding

Batting and thread to finish

Cutting

All rotary-cutting dimensions include ¼"-wide seam allowances. Cut the bias strips for the bias squares first and set aside any remaining fabric. Construct the bias squares and set aside. Then cut all remaining pieces as directed in the cutting chart. Some strips will not require additional cuts at this time so no directions appear in the second column.

From the assorted bright prints:

Cut bias strips 2½" wide and piece 10 sets of strips, using Cutting Format #3 (Diagram 55). Cut 2½" x 2½" bias squares from the strip-pieced units. Each set of strips made using this format yields at least 35 bias squares, 2½" x 2½". You will need a total of 324 bias squares. You will also need 324 separate triangles. Using the resizing template on page 270 or the resizing technique on page 64, resize the edge triangles that remain after cutting the bias squares. You will have approximately 140. For the additional triangles required, cut 92 squares, 2⅞" x 2⅞". Cut once diagonally for 184 triangles.

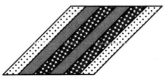

Diagram 55
Cutting Format #3

Fabric	FIRST CUT No. of Strips	FIRST CUT Dimensions	ADDITIONAL CUTS No. of Pieces	ADDITIONAL CUTS Dimensions	ADDITIONAL CUTS No. of Triangles
Blue Swirly Print		Outer Border			
	Note: Cut Outer Border strips first along the lengthwise grain of the fabric; then cut the remaining pieces from the remaining fabric.				
	2	5¼" x 72½"			
	2	5¼" x 82"			
		Unit 4			
	2	6½" x 21"	4	6½" x 6½"	
		Unit 5			
	3	6½" x 21"	8	6½" x 12½"	
		Unit 6			
	4	12½" x 21"	4	12½" x 12½"	
		Piece A			
	3	13¼" x 42"	3	13¼" x 13¼"	12 ⊠
		Piece B			
	3	6⅞" x 42"	18	6⅞" x 6⅞"	36 ◺
		Piece C			
	3	9" x 42"	12	9" x 9"	

◺ = Cut squares once diagonally to yield half-square triangles.

⊠ = Cut squares twice diagonally to yield quarter-square triangles.

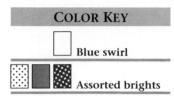

COLOR KEY

Blue swirl

Assorted brights

Directions

Basic Triangle Units

Units 1, 2, and 3 are made by combining pieced triangle units with other cut fabric pieces. You will need a total of 108 basic triangle units (Diagram 56) for the entire quilt top.

To piece each basic triangle unit, repeat steps 1–3:

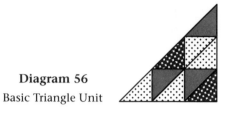

Diagram 56

Basic Triangle Unit

1. Attach 2 half-square triangles to a bias square. Press seams in direction of arrows (Diagram 57).

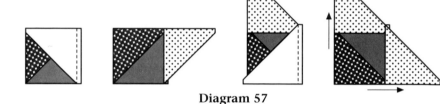

Diagram 57

2. Piece a row consisting of 2 bias squares and 1 half-square triangle. Press seams in direction of arrow (Diagram 58).

Diagram 58

3. Join the 2 units as shown in Diagram 59, matching opposing seams and using a positioning pin to secure them. Stitch through the **X** at seam intersections.

Note: When joining these pieced triangle units to other cut fabrics, match raw edges carefully and stitch with the pieced unit on top. Stitch through the **X** at seam intersections as shown in Diagram 60.

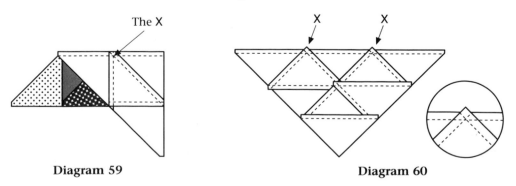

The X

X   X

Diagram 59   **Diagram 60**

Assembling Units 1, 2, and 3

1. Using 2 basic triangle units and 1 piece A for each unit, assemble 12 of Unit 1 (Diagram 61).

2. Using 4 basic triangle units and 4 piece B for each unit, assemble 9 of Unit 2 (Diagram 62).

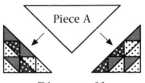

Diagram 61
Unit 1
Make 12.

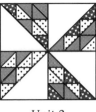

Make 4 for each unit.

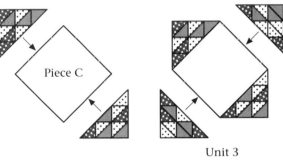

Unit 2
Make 9.

Diagram 62

3. Using 4 basic triangle units and 1 piece C for each unit, assemble 12 of Unit 3 (Diagram 63).

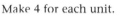

Diagram 63

Join 2 basic triangle units to opposite sides of Piece C. Press seams toward square. Stitch remaining triangle units to Piece C. Press seams away from center square.

Unit 3
Make 12.

Quilt Top Assembly

1. Assemble the quilt top in rows to form 9 stars. Make 2 of Row A by joining Units 1, 4, and 5 (Diagram 64).

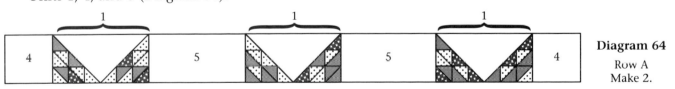

Diagram 64
Row A
Make 2.

2. Make 3 of Row B by joining Units 1, 2, and 3 (Diagram 65).

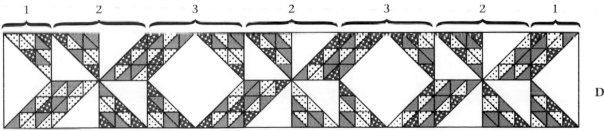

Diagram 65
Row B
Make 3.

3. Make 2 of Row C by joining Units 3, 5, and 6 (Diagram 66).

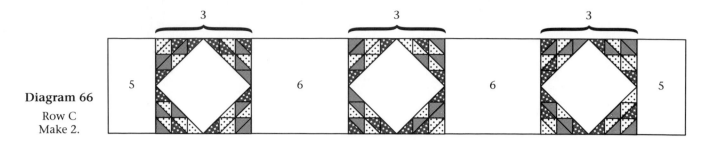

Diagram 66
Row C
Make 2.

4. Join Rows A, B, and C to form quilt top, alternating them as shown in the quilt plan on page 88.

Borders

Stitch a 5¼" x 72½" border strip to each side of the quilt top. Then, stitch the 5¼" x 82" border strips to the top and bottom edges of the quilt top.

Quilt Finishing

1. Layer the quilt top with batting and backing; baste.

2. Quilt in the design of your choice, or follow the Quilting Suggestion.

3. Cut and piece 334" of 2½"-wide bias for binding, following the directions on pages 52–53. Bind the quilt edges.

Quilting Suggestion

- Quilt "in the ditch" along the triangle shapes that form each star.
- Following some of the swirly lines in the blue background fabric, randomly quilt in the larger unpieced areas and in the border.

Colorful Baskets

Inspired by a Basket quilt made by Naomi Kajiyama, published in Quilts Japan, this multicolored quilt requires several sizes of bias squares. The basket colors begin with soft pastels in the upper-left corner and change to bright yellow, then to darker tones in the lower-right corner. The colors of the bias squares used in the sashing squares, set pieces, inner border, Sawtooth border, and outer border gradually change to reflect the colors of the adjacent baskets. Several soft beige fabrics unify the sashing, set pieces, and border.

First stitch the Basket blocks and then use the leftover bias squares in the Sawtooth border, matching the color to those in the adjacent blocks. This quilt is a challenging color study, but the results are well worth the time spent. Make a few blocks a day and enjoy the learning process.

Dimensions: *86" x 102"*

32 blocks, each 10" square, set diagonally with 2½"-wide sashing and pieced sashing squares; 1⅞"-wide (top and bottom) and 2⅝"-wide (sides) inner pieced borders, 2"-wide middle pieced border, and 3"-wide outer pieced border

Basket Block

Side Set Piece

Corner Set Piece

Materials: *44"-wide fabric*

Yardages listed are generous and are based on 44"-wide fabric that has been preshrunk. Strips cut across the fabric width should measure at least 42", as shown in the strip dimensions in the cutting chart.

5 yds. total of assorted light-background prints for Basket blocks and middle border

5 yds. total of assorted dark-background prints for baskets and middle border

3¼ yds. total of assorted beige prints for sashing, side set pieces, and inner and outer borders

7½ yds. fabric of your choice for backing

¾ yd. total assorted prints for binding

Batting and thread to finish

Cutting

All rotary-cutting dimensions include ¼"-wide seam allowances. Cut the bias strips for the bias squares first and set aside any remaining fabric. Construct the bias squares and set aside. Then cut all remaining pieces as directed in the cutting chart. Some strips will not require additional cuts at this time so no directions appear in the second column.

From the assorted light- and dark-background prints:

Cut bias strips 2½"-wide and piece 5 sets of strips, using Cutting Format #3 (Diagram 67). Cut 2½" x 2½" bias squares from the strip-pieced units. Each set of strips made using this format yields at least 35 bias squares, 2½" x 2½". You will need a total of 160 bias squares, 5 matching ones for each Basket block.

Using the resizing template on page 270 or the resizing technique on page 64, resize the dark edge triangles left over from cutting the bias squares. You will need a total of 192 triangles, 6 to match each basket. If additional triangles are needed, cut 2⅞" dark fabric squares and cut once diagonally. Light edge triangles are not required in this quilt. Save extra bias squares for the pieced border.

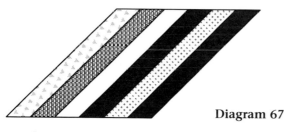

Diagram 67

Cutting Format #3

Cut bias strips 2¼"-wide and piece 1 set of strips, using Cutting Format #3 (Diagram 68). Cut 2¼" x 2¼" bias squares from the strip-pieced unit. One set of strips made using this format yields at least 40 bias squares, 2¼" x 2¼". You will need 28 of these for the side set pieces. Edge triangles from this strip-pieced unit are not required in this quilt.

Cut bias strips 2"-wide and piece 3 sets of strips, using Cutting Format #3 (Diagram 68). Cut 1¾" x 1¾" bias squares from the strip-pieced units. Each set of strips made using this format yields at least 55 bias squares, 1¾" x 1¾". You will need 142 bias squares for the sashing squares and triangles. Edge triangles from these strip-pieced units are not required in this quilt.

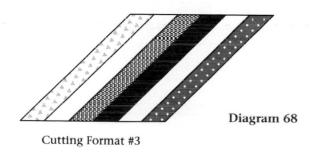

Diagram 68

Cutting Format #3

Fabric	FIRST CUT		ADDITIONAL CUTS		
	No. of Strips	Dimensions	No. of Pieces	Dimensions	No. of Triangles
Assorted Light Background Prints	Background Pieces				
	*	*	16	8⅞" x 8⅞"	32 ◻
	*	*	64	2½" x 6½"	
	*	*	16	4⅞" x 4⅞"	32 ◻
	*	*	32	2½" x 2½"	

*There are no first cuts here because the background pieces must match within each Basket block. They must be cut as sets.

Fabric	FIRST CUT		ADDITIONAL CUTS		
Beige Prints	Side Sashing Triangles				
	1	1¾" x 42"	10	1¾" x 1¾"	20 ◻
	Sashing Strips				
	20	3" x 42"	80	3" x 10½"	
	Side and Corner Set Pieces				
	1	4½" x 42"	2	4½" x 4½"	4 ◻
	4	2¼" x 42"	68	2¼" x 2¼"	
	1	8⅜" x 42"	4	8⅜" x 8⅜"	16* ⊠

*You will only need 14 of these for side set pieces.

Use the remainder of the beige prints to cut and piece the inner and outer pieced border as directed for borders on page 99.

Fabric	FIRST CUT		ADDITIONAL CUTS		
Dark Background Prints	Basket Blocks				
	7	2⅝" x 42"	96	2⅝" x 2⅝"	192* ◻

*Use 12 for each side set piece and 6 for each corner piece.

Fabric	FIRST CUT		ADDITIONAL CUTS		
	Top and Bottom Sashing Triangles				
	1	3" x 42"	4	3" x 3"	16 ⊠
	Side Sashing Triangles				
	1	1¾" x 42"	10	1¾" x 1¾"	20 ◻

◻ = Cut squares once diagonally to yield half-square triangles.

⊠ = Cut squares twice diagonally to yield quarter-square triangles.

Directions

Basket Blocks

Piece 32 baskets as described in the following steps. The light-background fabric in the bias squares may either match or contrast with the background fabric of the block. Stitch some blocks with both colorations.

For each basket, repeat steps 1–9:

1. Sew the 2½" bias squares and 2½" plain squares into rows as shown in Diagram 69. Press seams in direction of arrows.

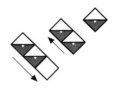

Diagram 69

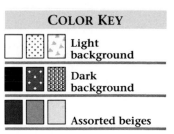

Light background

Dark background

Assorted beiges

2. Add a matching resized dark edge triangle to the top of each row (Diagram 70). Sew the rows together to form the basket shape (Diagram 71).

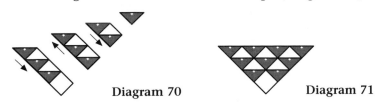

Diagram 70   Diagram 71

3. Stitch the remaining 2 dark basket triangles to the background rectangles (Diagram 72). Press seams toward the triangles.

4. Sew the rectangle units to the basket section (Diagram 73). Press seams toward the rectangle units.

Diagram 72

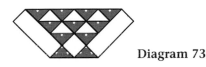

Diagram 73

5. For each basket handle, cut a bias strip, 1¼" x 14". Choose a fabric for the handle to match the darkest color in the basket base to which it will be joined. You will need a total of 32 strips in assorted colors.

6. To appliqué each basket handle to a 8⅞" background triangle, turn under ⅜" at each long edge of bias strip so raw edges meet in the center of the strip. Baste (Diagram 74).

Diagram 74

7. Appliqué handle to background triangle, as shown in Diagram 75, placing the outer edge of each side of the handle approximately 2⅞" from the triangle point. Remove basting.

2⅞"   2⅞"   Diagram 75

8. Complete each Basket block by stitching it to its handle/background triangle. Press seam toward handle. To each basket, add a 4⅞" light-background triangle at the lower corner. Press seam toward lower corner (Diagram 76).

Sashing

1. Piece 31 sashing square units, using four 1¾" bias squares for each unit. Be sure to position the dark triangles as shown in Diagram 77.

Diagram 77
Sashing Square Unit
Make 31.

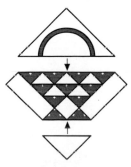

Diagram 76

Diagram 78

Sashing Triangle
Top and Bottom
Make 8.

Diagram 79

Sashing Triangle
Sides
Make 10.

2. Piece 8 sashing triangles for the top and bottom edges of the quilt. Use one 1¾" bias square and two quarter-square triangles cut from dark-background prints to complete each sashing triangle (Diagram 78).

3. Piece 10 sashing triangles for the sides. Use one 1¾" bias square and two half-square triangles cut from the light- and dark-background prints to complete each sashing triangle (Diagram 79).

4. Piece 14 side set pieces and 4 corner set pieces, using 2¼" bias squares and cut fabric triangles (Diagram 80).

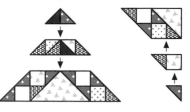

Side Set Piece
Make 14.
Join in rows.

Diagram 80

Corner Set Piece
Make 4.
Join in rows.

Quilt Top Assembly

Assemble Basket blocks, sashing squares, sashing strips, sashing triangles, and side set pieces into diagonal rows as shown in Diagram 81. Piece rows together to form the quilt top. Add corner set pieces.

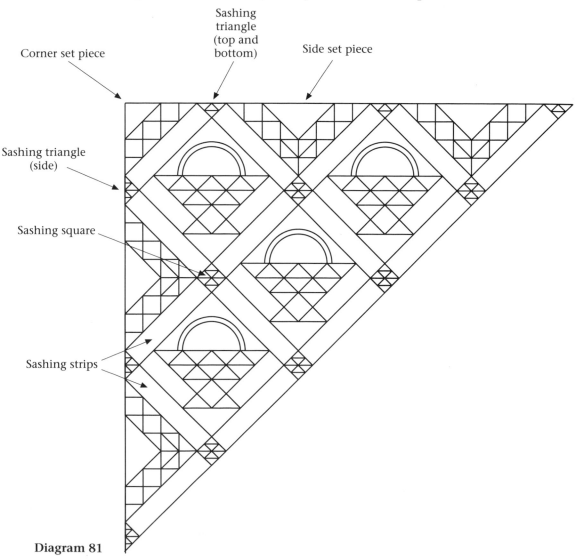

Corner set piece

Sashing triangle (top and bottom)

Side set piece

Sashing triangle (side)

Sashing square

Sashing strips

Diagram 81

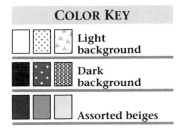

COLOR KEY

Light background

Dark background

Assorted beiges

Borders

Note: The inner borders for this quilt are made by piecing strips of assorted beige prints together to the appropriate length. Plan the color placement so when the borders are attached, the values change from light in the upper-left corner to dark in the lower-right corner. The finished top and bottom inner pieced borders are slightly narrower than the side inner pieced borders in order to create a quilt top with the correct dimensions so the Sawtooth (middle) border will fit.

1. To make the inner pieced borders for the top and bottom edges, cut 2⅜"-wide strips (cutting across the fabric width) from the remaining assorted beige prints. Piece the strips together in the required value progression, using diagonal seams (Diagram 82). You will need two completed border strips that each measure 2⅜" x 76½". Stitch the borders to the top and bottom edges of the quilt top.

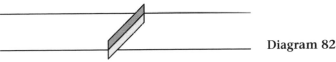

Diagram 82

Piece border strips with diagonal seams.

For the inner borders for the sides, cut strips 3⅛" wide and piece 2 borders in the correct value progression. Each side border strip should measure 3⅛" x 92½". Stitch the side borders to the quilt top, which should now measure 76½" x 92½" (Diagram 83).

2. To make the pieced Sawtooth (middle) border, you will need a total of 168 bias squares. Use any leftover 2½" x 2½" bias squares from the Basket blocks. If you need to make additional bias squares, cut bias strips 2½" wide from the assorted light- and dark-background fabrics and piece enough additional sets of strips, using Cutting Format #2D (page 62), to make the required number. Each set of strips made using this format yields at least 28 bias squares, 2½" x 2½".

Note: As you stitch the bias squares together for the pieced border, vary the color of the bias squares to match the colors used in the adjacent side set pieces and Basket blocks.

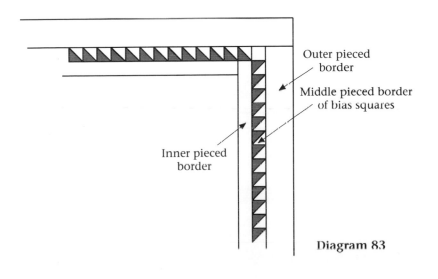

Outer pieced border

Middle pieced border of bias squares

Inner pieced border

Diagram 83

3. Stitch 38 bias squares together for the top and the bottom borders.

4. Stitch 46 bias squares together for each side border. Add a 2½" x 2½" square to each end of each side border before joining to quilt top (Diagram 83).

5. From the remainder of the assorted beige prints, cut and piece 3¼"-wide outer border strips as you did for the inner borders so the values change from light in the upper-left to dark in the lower-right corner. See step 1, above.

6. First, add side outer border strips, each pieced and cut to measure 3¼" x 96½". Then add top and bottom outer border strips, each cut and pieced to measure 3¼" x 86".

Quilt Finishing

1. Layer the quilt top with batting and backing; baste.

2. Quilt in the design of your choice, or follow the Quilting Suggestion.

3. Cut and piece 370" of 2½"-wide bias for binding from assorted remaining fabrics, varying the color of the strips used in the binding to match the color of the adjoining bias squares in the pieced border and following the directions on pages 52–53. Bind the quilt edges.

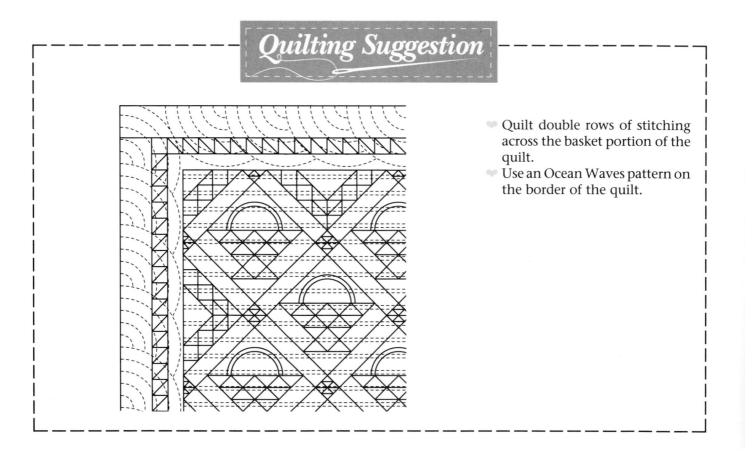

Quilting Suggestion

- Quilt double rows of stitching across the basket portion of the quilt.
- Use an Ocean Waves pattern on the border of the quilt.

MEET
Marsha McCloskey
&
HER SQUARE TWO
QUILTS

My first quilt was a pattern made entirely of triangles sewn in units of four, called Hourglass or Broken Dishes. I chose the design because my neighbor, Grace, loaned me a cardboard triangle for a template. She also let me pick fabrics from her scrap box. I dutifully traced around the template to cut the pieces and then sewed them together on my sewing machine. I also quilted by sewing machine and sewed the binding by machine as well. Having no background in quiltmaking, it never occurred to me that anyone might sew such a thing by hand.

I made the Hourglass quilt in 1969 for my daughter, Amanda, who was then one year old. She is now twenty-four. When I want to figure how many years I've been making quilts, I subtract one year from Amanda's age. In 1992, I have been quilting for twenty-three years.

I started quiltmaking with few books or experienced teachers to help me. I was so enthusiastic about the process that I simply stumbled through and made a lot of mistakes as I learned. In the early 1970s, I met Judy Martin in Eugene, Oregon, where my husband was attending graduate school. Judy and I were selling patchwork quilts and gift items at the weekly Saturday Market craft fair and became friends. She introduced me to quilt history and to graph paper and the Singer Featherweight sewing machine.

When my husband and I moved to Berkeley, California, in 1975 for his post-graduate work, I took classes from Glendora Hutson, who taught me how to draft my own patterns, make templates, and piece with precision. Both Glendora and Judy favored traditional quilt designs, and I came to share their love and knowledge of old quilts and quilt history.

For many years, when my children were young and my husband was in graduate school, I did production sewing to bring in extra income. I made quilts and wall hangings, toys, pillows, aprons, and potholders and sold them at street fairs and in gift shops. I worked at it for six to eight hours every day. Before I stopped in 1981, I had made over two thousand potholders! I'm not sure I should brag about that as an accomplishment, but I did learn a great deal in the process, including how to select fabric and color and which piecing techniques work best. I also learned that I didn't want to continue sewing for a living!

When my husband's job necessitated our move to Seattle, I met Sharon Yenter, the owner of a quilt shop called In The Beginning, where I started to teach quilt classes. It was 1977, and the quilt revival that had started in 1971 and hit its stride in 1976 with the national bicentennial was in full swing. Many women wanted to learn to make quilts. I knew just enough about it that I could teach others. I loved the connection with other women who were as interested as I was in quiltmaking. I have been teaching regularly ever since.

In 1980, Sharon asked me to do a Pattern-of-the-Month for the store—a one-page giveaway for her customers. It was a challenge to draft and fit pattern instructions and templates on one side of an 8½" x 11" sheet of paper. Obviously, the designs had to be fairly simple. These patterns were the basis for my first quilt pattern book, *Small Quilts*, published by That Patchwork Place in 1982.

Since that first book, I have written several others, including *Lessons in Machine Piecing* (1990) and *On to Square Two* (1992).

Through the success of these publications, I have been invited to teach and speak all over the United States and in Canada, Australia, and Europe. When I am in a place far from home, I marvel at the events that brought me there. Because I make quilts, I have held a koala in Australia, have taken a dog-sled ride

in Fairbanks, Alaska, and have walked down the Champs-Elysées in Paris. Because I make quilts, I am connected to other women all over the world in a very special way. Although they do not all speak English, they do speak the "language of quilting."

Of all my quilt designing and writing projects, the most important to me was *Feathered Star Quilts* (1987). Not only was it a major research project, but it required that I perfect my pattern-drafting skills. It also brought to light the importance of the bias strip-piecing technique for making the half-square triangle units that are the "feathers" in Feathered Star designs.

Bias strip piecing was first shown to me in 1981 by a quilter from Anacortes, Washington. The basic idea was to sew strips (which had been cut on the bias) together and, with a template, cut squares along the seam line. These squares had straight grain along the outside edge, where it belonged, and were absolutely accurate. This was a great improvement over cutting triangles, sewing them together, and pressing (which often distorted the square). It was the perfect technique for making the feather units for Feathered Star designs, which require precision piecing.

Nancy Martin liked the concept and its accurate results but didn't like working with templates, so she converted the method to a rotary-cutting technique by inventing a cutting ruler called the Bias Square. She wrote a book with my input, called *Back to Square One* (1988), in which we offered only patterns for quilts with half-square triangle units that could be made with bias strip piecing and rotary cutting. Later, we co-authored *Ocean Waves* (1989), in which we further refined the method and presented additional patterns in which to use it.

After completing *Ocean Waves*, I thought we had really exhausted the subject of bias strip piecing. But this technique doesn't stop with half-square triangle units. There are even more shapes and designs to be made with half-square and quarter-square triangles, using bias strip piecing. These are discussed in detail under "Bias Strip Piecing" on pages 106–107.

Quiltmaking is a lot of work and a lot of fun. I can't think of anything I'd rather do. Every quilter develops her own methods and a personal quiltmaking philosophy that suits her temperament and style. I am a perfectionist, a little obsessive, randomly creative, and more than a little bit lazy. I love to make traditional-looking quilts, but I am also anxious to adapt and experiment with design styles just a bit to discover something new. I want my quilts to be as technically perfect as I can make them and, to that end, I have developed a definite format for working that carries over to my teaching.

If you are following a preplanned quilt design, you would not need to use such a format. But, if you want to make a unique quilt, you may be interested in the procedure I use for designing my quilts.

Each quilt begins with a pencil sketch on graph paper. I play with the shapes and shadings until I develop a design that I feel is worth trying out in fabric. Then, I get a little more serious about the drawing and make a line drawing, to scale, of at least a portion of the quilt. I use graph paper with eight squares to the inch, with each square representing 1" in the finished quilt. From the drawing, I can tell the size of each piece and the dimensions of the finished project (Diagram 1). Since I started using a Macintosh® computer, I have learned to make my line drawings in a program called SuperPaint.

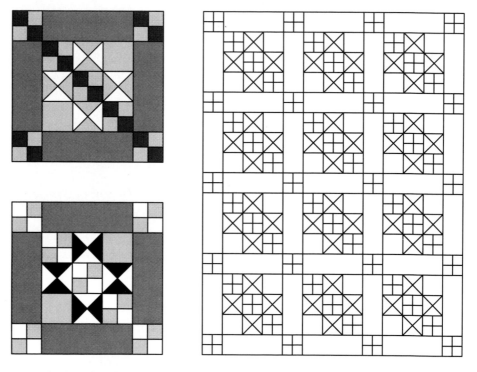

Diagram 1

Shaded Sketches   Scale Line Drawing

Next, I make several copies of the line drawing on a photocopy machine so I can experiment with different shadings. Working with a lead pencil (not colored pencils), I try to define the light, medium, and dark areas in the design. From a shaded drawing, I can tell how many colors will be needed to make the design, for instance, one dark, one medium, one lighter medium, and one light (four colors); or perhaps a dark, a darker dark, a medium, and two different lights (five colors). Choosing the actual fabrics and colors, using a "color recipe" like this, is discussed in further detail on pages 23–24.

The next step is to make a cutting guide or a "road map" for the design. This is a full-size drafting of the block and any set pieces needed to complete the design. Again, I generally work in pencil on large graph paper (17" x 22" sheets) with eight squares to the inch. I identify the shapes that need to be cut by coloring each one with colored pencils and adding a ¼"-wide seam allowance around each one to find its cut dimensions.

Then, I measure each shape and evaluate the design for rotary cutting, making notes on the drafting of anything I need to remember while I am cutting—dimensions, grain lines, quantities, and colors. I also draw little cutting sketches I call "quick-cut icons" to give me visual cues as to what to cut.

The sketch, the shaded line drawing, and the drafting get me started. The real fun in making a quilt begins when I start cutting and sewing and see the work grow and change before my eyes. A quilt-in-progress needs constant reevaluation. Sets and colors and size can be changed in hundreds of ways. That is what makes each quilt and quilter unique. However, don't let the endless possibilities and decisions paralyze you. At some point, it's important to stop "playing with the pieces" and sew the top together.

❤

Read the instructions that follow to learn how to make the pieced units required for my Square Two quilts.

TIP

Remember the carpenters' adage, "Measure twice and cut once." Take the time to develop good quilt-making skills and work habits. Working quickly is only a time-saver if the work is done correctly. Mistakes take more time to fix than to make, so concentrate on the process, be precise and accurate, and have a great time.

BIAS STRIP PIECING

Many quilters have experimented with bias strip piecing to make precisely pieced triangle units, and each has developed a slightly different approach to the technique. Nancy Martin's method for making bias squares, or "Square Ones," begins on page 59, and Mary Hickey's version is shown on page 161. In this section, I will present the method I use. All three approaches produce the same accurate results. Use the one that works best for you.

DEFINITIONS

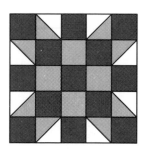

Diagram 3
Sister's Choice

The four design-and-construction units which can be made with the bias strip-piecing technique and cut with the Bias Square ruler include the following:

Square One: A pieced square made of two half-square triangles (Diagram 2). Also known as a "bias square" after the Bias Square ruler used to cut it. There are literally hundreds of patchwork designs that include the Square One unit (Diagram 3). All of the quilts in Nancy Martin's section, beginning on page 65, are "Square One" quilts.

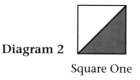

Diagram 2
Square One

Square .5 ("point five"): When a Square One unit is cut in half diagonally, two mirror-image units result (Diagram 4).

Diagram 5
Goose Tracks

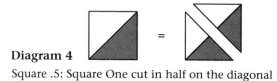

Diagram 4
Square .5: Square One cut in half on the diagonal

These pieced triangular units each consist of two quarter-square triangles. This is the most accurate way I have found to piece the smallest triangles in designs like Goose Tracks (Diagram 5).

Square Two: A pieced square made of four quarter-square triangles (Diagram 6).

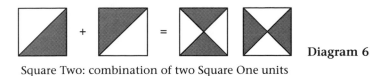

Diagram 6

Square Two: combination of two Square One units

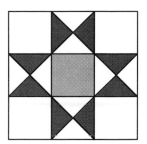

Diagram 7

Variable or Ohio Star

Two of these units result when two Square One units are placed right sides together, then cut on the diagonal and resewn. (See page 112 for detailed instructions.) The popular Ohio Star block is a good example of a design that requires Square Two units (Diagram 7).

Square 1.5 ("one point five"): A pieced square made of one half-square triangle and two quarter-square triangles (Diagram 8).

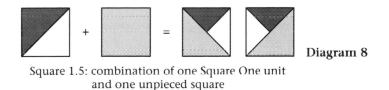

Diagram 8

Square 1.5: combination of one Square One unit and one unpieced square

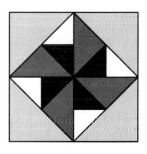

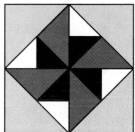

Diagram 9

Flying Pinwheel

Two mirror-image units result when a Square One unit is placed with right sides together with an unpieced square, then cut on the diagonal and resewn. (See page 114 for detailed instructions.) The Flying Pinwheel is a good example of a design using the Square 1.5 unit (Diagram 9).

Making Square One

Square One

To avoid struggling with a lot of yardage when cutting bias strips, I begin by cutting the fabric that will be cut into bias strips into manageable pieces. I cut strips from pieces of fabric, ranging in size from 9" to 15" square. I prefer working with squares because they fit nicely on my cutting mat and the strip lengths are predictable. With the Square One yield chart on page 111, it is possible to tell at a glance how many Square One units can be cut from a set of squares of a specific size.

To make Square One units using my method, follow these steps:

1. Cut two squares of contrasting fabrics and place right sides together so both layers will be cut at the same time.

2. Make the first cut diagonally, corner to corner (Diagram 10).

3. Measure the desired width of the bias strip from the first diagonal cut, and cut again. Continue until the whole square has been cut into bias strips. The width to cut the bias strips depends on the desired cut size of the Square One unit. The lengths of the strips will differ.

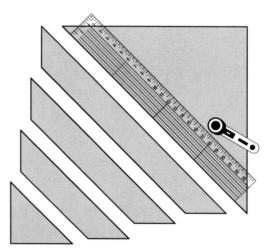

Diagram 10
Cutting Bias Strips

Sewing   Pressing

Diagram 11

4. Pick up pairs of contrasting strips; they will have right sides together and be ready to stitch. Sew them together on the long bias edge, using a ¼"-wide seam allowance. Press the seams toward the darker fabric (Diagram 11).

5. Sew the bias strip pairs together and press. There will be strip pairs of varying lengths. The most efficient configuration I have found for sewing them together is shown in Diagram 12. Sew the longest strip pairs together, then the next longest, continuing until they are all joined. Keep the Vs along the bottom edge even. The corner triangles left after cutting the strips can also be sewn together.

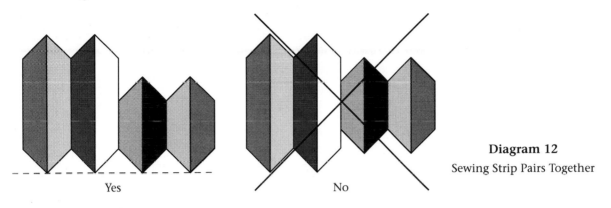

Yes   No

Diagram 12
Sewing Strip Pairs Together

6. Using a Bias Square and rotary cutter, begin cutting squares from the strip-pieced unit at the lowest points as shown in Diagram 13. Place the diagonal line on the ruler in the first seam line. Cut squares slightly larger (a few threads, but no more than ⅛") than the desired cut size of the Square One unit. Two cuts are required to separate the square from the sewn strips. Let your rotary cutter go a few threads beyond the seam line at the upper point of the square to cleanly separate each square from the strip-pieced unit.

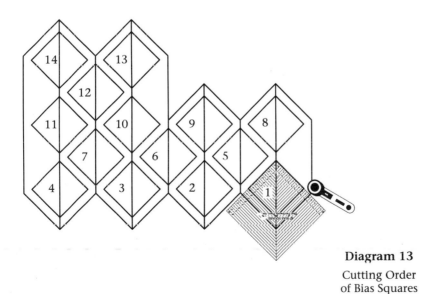

Diagram 13
Cutting Order
of Bias Squares

If you have joined two or more sets of strips, cut squares from alternate seam lines, working across the strips from the right to the left side (Diagram 14a). After cutting the first set of squares, go back and cut from the skipped seam lines (Diagram 14b). Numbers in Diagram 13 on page 109 show the order in which to cut the Square One units. (Left handers can begin cutting at the left side if it is a more comfortable way to work.)

7. The squares cut in step 6 now must be cut to the exact size desired. Turn each square so the two sides that were just cut are pointing toward you. Align the diagonal line of the Bias Square ruler with the seam line of the square and align the exact dimension on the ruler with the cut sides of the square. Make the final two cuts (Diagram 14c).

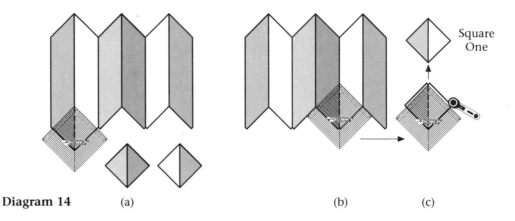

Diagram 14   (a)   (b)   (c)

RANDOM-SCRAP LOOK

Cutting bias strips from large beginning squares works especially well when making scrap or multifabric quilts. To get a random-scrap look to your quilt, cut 8" or 9" squares from each print you want to use. The idea is to use smaller beginning squares and to cut a lot of them for variety. The more fabrics you use, the scrappier your quilt will look.

Cut all the squares into identical bias strips. For the greatest variety of combinations, mix and match the strips before sewing them together (Diagram 15).

Save leftover bias strips and Square One units for future scrap quilts.

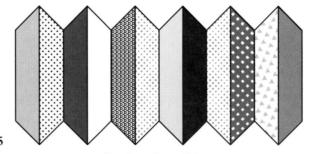

Diagram 15

Random-Scrap Setup

TIP

To determine how many Square One units can be cut from a certain amount of yardage when designing your own blocks and quilts, start by cutting one light and one dark 15" square of fabric. I use the 15" measurement as a base because that is the size of my largest square cutting ruler.

Following the steps on pages 108–110, cut and sew bias strips and cut out Square One units. Then, count the number of Square One units you were able to cut. Now you know the exact number of Square One units that you will get from that particular size of fabric square and strip width. Obviously, the larger the beginning fabric squares, the more Square One units you will get.

The Square One yield chart below shows:
- What size to cut the large fabric squares
- How wide to cut the bias strips
- What size to cut the Square One units and how many you will be able to cut from that amount of fabric

The "+" after the yield number indicates that, if you use the edge triangles, leftover corner triangles, and/or sew more strips together, a few more Square One units could be made.

SQUARE ONE YIELD CHART

Beginning Square Size	Strip Width	Square One Cut Size	Yield
10"	2½"	2½"	13+
12"	2½"	2½"	19+
15"	2½"	2½"	29+
11"	2¾"	2⅞"	13+
14"	2¾"	2⅞"	19+
9"	3½"	3⅞"	5+
14"	3½"	3⅞"	13+
15"	3½"	3⅞"	13+
12"	4¼"	4⅞"	5+

Making Square Two

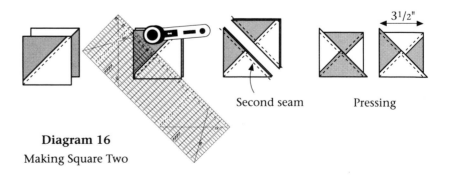

Square Two

This unit is used in the Ohio Star Table Runner on page 116, the Ohio Star Baby Quilt on page 121, Hill and Valley on page 145, and Star Stairway on page 139.

Bias strip piecing Square Two units is a perfect technique for miniatures and units in finished sizes up to about 4". For units much larger than that, I find it saves time and fabric to cut triangles and piece in the traditional manner.

The correct cutting dimensions for Square Two units are given for each quilt in this section.

For a Square Two unit with a finished size of 3", follow these steps:

1. Cut bias strips 3½" wide. Sew the strips together, using ¼"-wide seam allowances. Press the seam allowances toward the darker strip. Sew strip pairs together.

2. Cut two Square One units, each 3⅞" x 3⅞", using the Bias Square.

3. Place the Square One units right sides together, aligning opposing seams (Diagram 16). Cut the aligned pair once diagonally. Sew each of the two resulting triangle pairs together, using scant* ¼"-wide seam allowances to complete two Square Two units. For a scant seam allowance, you can just "eyeball" it, or adjust the stitching guide on your machine. Press seam allowances to one side. Trim the triangle points, if desired.

   *Square One units are easy to make accurately because they are cut after the first seam is sewn. However, the size of Square Two and Square 1.5 units may vary, depending on the width of the second seam. I find that the seam allowance used in step 3 needs to be a scant ¼" wide, in order for the pieced unit to be the right size.

Second seam   Pressing

3½"

Diagram 16
Making Square Two

4. Check your work for accuracy. Measure the completed units from cut edge to cut edge to make sure they are square and the proper size. In this example, the completed Square Two unit should measure 3½," which will give you a finished unit with a 3" dimension.

SQUARE TWO COLOR VARIATIONS

Square Two can be pieced with two, three, or four fabrics. A two-fabric Square Two unit is made from two identical Square One units, each containing the same two fabrics—a light and a dark. For this setup, sew bias strips of the two fabrics together in an alternating pattern as shown in Diagram 17.

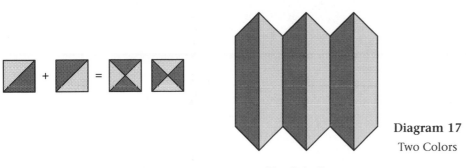

Diagram 17
Two Colors

Bias Strip Setup

To add a third fabric (a medium tone), one Square One unit must contain one light and one dark fabric, and the other unit must contain one medium and one dark. Sew the bias strips of the three fabrics together in succession, or make two different sets of strips, one dark/light and one dark/medium (Diagram 18).

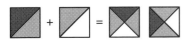

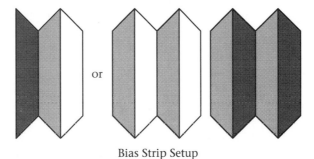

or

Diagram 18
Three Colors

Bias Strip Setup

If you want four different fabrics in the completed Square Two unit, each Square One must be made of different fabrics. This requires cutting strips from four different fabrics (Diagram 19). (You can use more than four fabrics to create a random-scrap look, if desired. See "Random-Scrap Look" on page 110.)

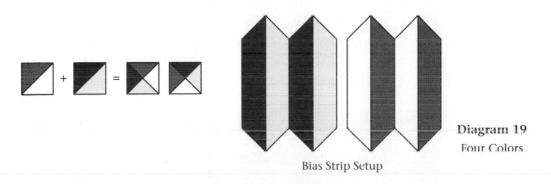

Diagram 19
Four Colors

Bias Strip Setup

Square 1.5

This unit is used in the Flying Pinwheel Quilt on page 134.

Square 1.5 contains three triangles. The two smaller triangles are half of a Square One unit. The larger triangle is half of an unpieced square. The correct cutting dimensions for Square 1.5 units are given in the quilt plan.

For a pieced Square 1.5 unit with a finished measurement of 3", follow these steps:

1. Cut bias strips 3½" wide from two different fabrics. Sew strips together, using ¼"-wide seam allowances. Press seam allowances toward the darker fabric. Sew strip pairs together. Press.

2. To make two Square 1.5 units (two mirror-image units), use the Bias Square to cut one Square One unit, 3⅞" x 3⅞", from the bias strips.

3. Cut one 3⅞" square from a third fabric.

4. Place the Square One unit and the 3⅞" square right sides together and cut once diagonally (Diagram 20). Sew resulting triangle pairs together, using ¼"-wide seams to complete two Square 1.5 units. Press seam allowances to one side. Trim triangle points, if desired.

5. Check your work for accuracy. The completed Square 1.5 unit should measure 3½" x 3½," which will give you a finished dimension of 3" x 3".

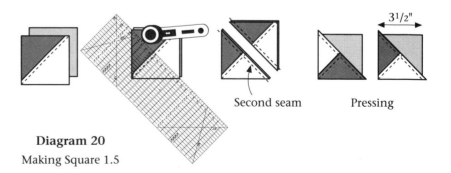

Second seam   Pressing

Diagram 20
Making Square 1.5

SQUARE 1.5 COLOR VARIATIONS

The colors in Square 1.5 can be varied in much the same way as Square Two. When working with Square 1.5 units, remember that the two pieced units from each set are always mirror images. Consider how these will work in the overall block and quilt design (Diagram 21).

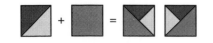  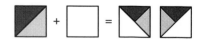

Diagram 21
Square 1.5 Color Variations

MAKING SQUARE .5

Square .5

This unit is used in the Goose Tracks Quilt on page 128 and the Hill and Valley Quilt on page 145.

Two mirror-image Square .5 units result when a Square One unit is cut in half diagonally. That means that Square .5 is a triangular unit consisting of two quarter-square triangles.

For a Square .5 unit with a finished short side of 2", follow these steps:

1. Cut bias strips from two different fabrics 2¾" wide. Sew strips together with ¼"-wide seam allowances. Press seam allowances toward the darker fabric. Sew strip pairs together. Press.

2. To make two Square .5 units (mirror-image units), use the Bias Square to cut one Square One unit, 2⅞" x 2⅞", from the bias strips.

3. Cut the Square One unit in half diagonally (Diagram 22).

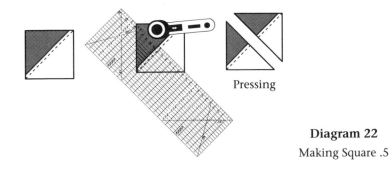

Pressing

Diagram 22
Making Square .5

4. Trim triangle points for easy matching, using the Bias Square placed at the 2½" mark (Diagram 23).

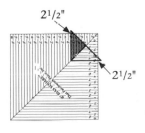

2¹/₂"

2¹/₂"

Diagram 23
Trimming Points on Square .5

Warm-Up Project

Ohio Star Table Runner

Making this Ohio Star table runner or wall hanging is an easy way to learn how to make Square Two units using the bias-strip-piecing technique. Many of my students complete the top in five to six hours.

In a simple pieced design like this one, large, chintzlike florals work beautifully to create a rich, complex look. Stripes in the star points provide a refreshing change in visual textures.

Dimensions: *21" x 46"*

3 blocks, each 9" square,
set diagonally; 3"-wide
border

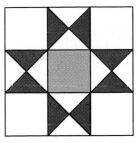

Ohio Star Block

Materials: *44"-wide fabric*

Yardages listed are generous and are based on 44"-wide fabric that has been preshrunk. Strips cut across the fabric width should measure at least 42", as shown in the strip dimensions in the cutting chart.

- ½ yd. large-scale red floral print for set pieces and star centers
- ⅞ yd. large-scale light floral print for borders and block backgrounds
- ½ yd. red stripe for star points and bias binding
- 1½ yds. fabric of your choice for backing
- Batting and thread to finish

Cutting

COLOR KEY

Red floral print

Light floral print

Red stripe

All rotary-cutting dimensions include ¼"-wide seam allowances. Using a rotary cutter, rotary ruler, and cutting mat, cut the strips and squares as described in the first column of the chart. Then from those squares, cut the pieces listed in the second column. Some strips and squares do not require additional cuts at this time so no directions appear in the second column. Cutting diagrams for each fabric are included as part of the "warm-up" phase of this quilt, so you can see how I cut the required pieces from the yardage. (Space limitations prohibit the inclusion of cutting diagrams for the other quilts in this section.)

| Fabric | FIRST CUT | | NEXT CUT |
	No. of Pieces	Dimensions	No. of Pieces
Red Floral		Set Piece I	
	1	13⅞" x 13⅞"	4 ⊠
		Set Piece II	
	2	7¼" x 7¼"	4 ◺
		Star Centers	
	3	3½" x 3½"	
Light Floral		Borders	
	3	4½" x 42"	
		Star Points	
	1	14" x 14"	
		Star Corners	
	12	3½" x 3½"	
Red Stripe*		Star Points	
	1	14" x 14"	

*Set aside the remaining stripe for bias binding. See step 3, page 120.

◺ = Cut once diagonally to yield half-square triangles.

⊠ = Cut twice diagonally to yield quarter-square triangles.

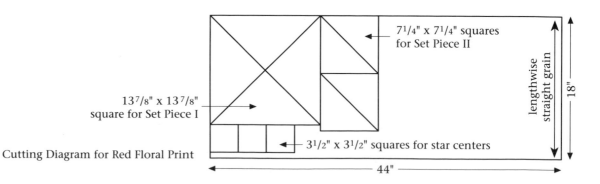

13⁷/₈" x 13⁷/₈"
square for Set Piece I

7¹/₄" x 7¹/₄" squares
for Set Piece II

lengthwise straight grain

18"

3¹/₂" x 3¹/₂" squares for star centers

Cutting Diagram for Red Floral Print

44"

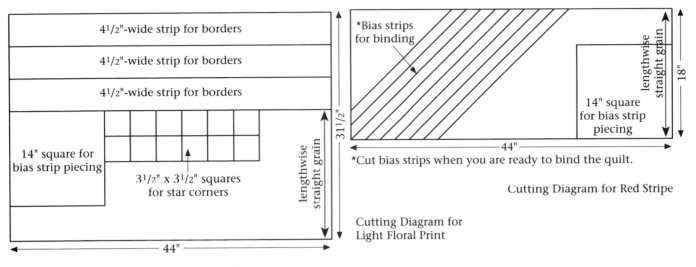

4½"-wide strip for borders

4½"-wide strip for borders

4½"-wide strip for borders

14" square for
bias strip piecing

3½" x 3½" squares
for star corners

lengthwise
straight grain

31½"

44"

Cutting Diagram for
Light Floral Print

*Bias strips
for binding

14" square
for bias strip
piecing

lengthwise
straight grain

18"

44"

*Cut bias strips when you are ready to bind the quilt.

Cutting Diagram for Red Stripe

Directions

Square Two Units

To make the Square Two units that are the star points, use bias strip piecing.

1. Place the 14" squares of the light floral print and red stripe right sides together; cut diagonally, corner to corner, to establish the true bias (45° angle). Cut bias strips 3½" wide (Diagram 24).

2. Sew bias strip pairs together in sets, using ¼"-wide seam allowances. Press the seams toward the dark strips. Sew the sets together.

3. Using Bias Square, cut 12 Square One units, each 3⅞" x 3⅞" (Diagram 25).

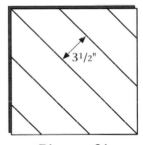

3½"

Diagram 24
14" squares

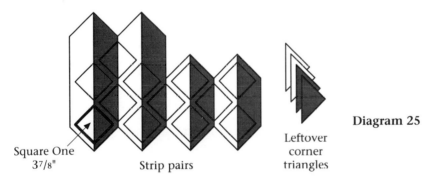

Square One
3⅞"

Strip pairs

Leftover
corner
triangles

Diagram 25

4. To complete the 12 Square Two units, match pairs of Square One units, aligning opposing seams. Cut pairs diagonally and sew resulting triangle pairs, using ¼"-wide seam allowances to make star-point units (Diagram 26). Press seams to one side. Check sewn units to make sure they measure 3½" x 3½" (cut edge to cut edge).

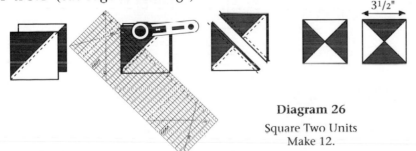

3½"

Diagram 26
Square Two Units
Make 12.

Ohio Star Blocks

Piece 3 Ohio Star blocks, joining the 3½" light floral and red floral print squares with the Square Two star point units in rows as shown in Diagram 27. Then join the rows. Press for opposing seams (page 41).

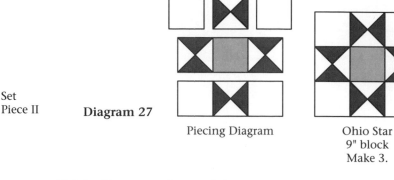

Diagram 27

Piecing Diagram

Ohio Star
9" block
Make 3.

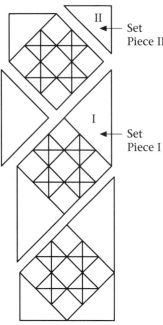

II → Set
Piece II

I → Set
Piece I

Diagram 28
Sewing Blocks Together
with Set Pieces

Table Runner Assembly

Join the Ohio Star blocks with Set Pieces I and II in diagonal rows, pressing for opposing seams (Diagram 28). Sew the rows together.

Borders

Measure the table runner for borders as shown on page 46. Trim the 4½"-wide light floral border strips to correct length and stitch first to the sides of the table runner. Press seams toward the borders. Then add border strips, trimmed to the correct length, to the top and bottom. Press seams toward the borders.

Table Runner Finishing

1. Layer the table runner with batting and backing; baste.

2. Quilt in the design of your choice, or follow the Quilting Suggestion.

3. From the remaining red stripe, cut and piece 144" of 2½"-wide bias for binding, following the directions on pages 52–53. Bind the quilt edges.

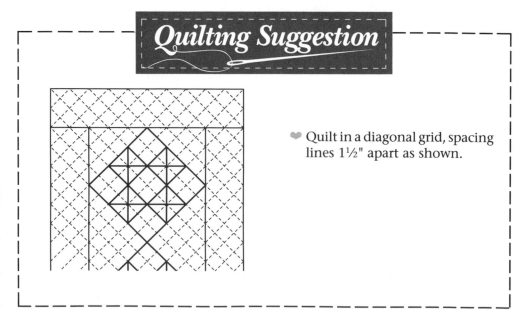

Quilting Suggestion

♥ Quilt in a diagonal grid, spacing lines 1½" apart as shown.

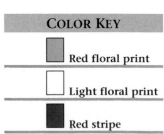

COLOR KEY

Red floral print

Light floral print

Red stripe

Ohio Star Baby Quilt

I like to make baby quilts large enough to last until a child is five or six years old. This quilt could provide many years of comfort to a small child or it could be used as a wall hanging.

Although most of the green and blue prints used in this quilt are large-scale florals, the stripe and smaller floral prints add visual texture, too. Soft, romantic pastels coordinate with the cabbage rose print in the set pieces. The pink stars were pieced from a darker print to stand out from the rest of the quilt. If you choose a softer fabric for the star points, the stars will not be as prominent.

Dimensions: *43½" x 59½"*

6 blocks, each 9" square,
set diagonally;
2"-wide inner border;
4"-wide pieced border made
of 38 Square Two units;
3¼"-wide outer border

Ohio Star Block

Materials: *44"-wide fabric*

Yardages listed are generous and are based on 44"-wide fabric that has been preshrunk. Strips cut across the fabric width should measure at least 42", as shown in the strip dimensions in the cutting chart.

- 2 yds. large-scale, medium-toned floral print for set pieces in central portion of quilt, outer border, and binding
- 1¼ yds. large-scale, light-toned floral print for inner unpieced border and block backgrounds
- 1 fat quarter (18" x 22") of unbleached muslin for block piecing
- 1 fat quarter pink print for block piecing
- 9 fat quarters in assorted prints for Square Two pieced border
- 1½ yds. fabric of your choice for backing
- Batting and thread to finish

Cutting

All rotary-cutting dimensions include ¼"-wide seam allowances. Using a rotary cutter, rotary ruler, and cutting mat, cut the strips and squares as described in the first column of the chart. Then from those squares, cut the pieces listed in the second column. Some strips and squares do not require additional cuts at this time so no directions appear in the second column.

	FIRST CUT		NEXT CUT
Fabric	**No. of Pieces**	**Dimensions**	**No. of Pieces**
Medium Floral*	Outer Border		
	4	3½" x 72"	
	Set Piece I		
	2	13⅞" x 13⅞"	8** ⊠
	Set Piece II		
	2	7¼" x 7¼"	4 ⟋
	Set Piece III		
	2	9½" x 9½"	

*Set aside the remaining fabric for bias binding. See step 3, page 126.

**You will use 6 of these.

	FIRST CUT		NEXT CUT
Light Floral	Inner Border		
	4	2½" x 42"	
	Star Corners		
	24	3½" x 3½"	
	Square Two Pieced Border		
	1	12" x 12"	
Muslin	Star Points		
	2	14" x 14"	
Pink Print	Star Points		
	2	14" x 14"	
	Star Centers		
	6	3½" x 3½"	
Assorted Prints	Square Two Pieced Border		
	9	12" x 12"	

⟋ = Cut once diagonally to yield half-square triangles.

⊠ = Cut twice diagonally to yield quarter-square triangles.

Directions

Square Two Units

To make the Square Two units that are the star points, use bias strip piecing.

Diagram 29

14" squares

1. Place the 14" squares of the unbleached muslin and the pink print right sides together; cut diagonally, corner to corner, to establish the true bias (45° angle). Cut bias strips 3½" wide (Diagram 29).

2. Sew bias-strip pairs together in sets, using ¼"-wide seam allowances. Press the seams toward the pink strips. Sew sets together.

3. Using the Bias Square ruler, cut 24 Square One units, each 3⅞" x 3⅞" (Diagram 30).

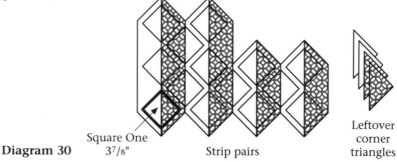

Leftover corner triangles

Square One 3⅞"

Diagram 30

Strip pairs

4. To complete the 24 Square Two units, match pairs of Square One units, aligning opposing seams. Cut pairs diagonally and sew resulting triangle pairs, using ¼"-wide seam allowances to make star-point units (Diagram 31). Press seams to one side. Check sewn units to make sure they measure 3½" x 3½" (cut edge to cut edge).

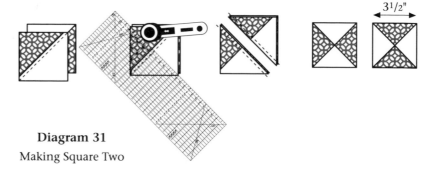

3½"

Diagram 31

Making Square Two

Ohio Star Blocks

Piece 6 Ohio Star blocks, joining the 3½" squares with the Square Two star-point units in rows as shown in Diagram 32. Then join the rows. Press for opposing seams.

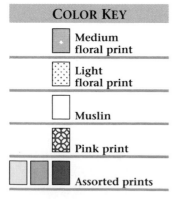

COLOR KEY
Medium floral print
Light floral print
Muslin
Pink print
Assorted prints

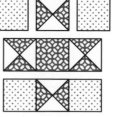

Diagram 32

Piecing Diagram

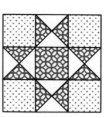

Ohio Star
9" block
Make 6.

Quilt Top Assembly

Join Ohio Star blocks with Set Pieces I, II, and III in diagonal rows, pressing for opposing seams from row to row (Diagram 33). Sew rows together.

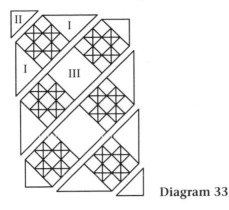

Diagram 33

Inner Border

Measure the quilt for borders as shown on page 46. Trim the 2½"-wide light floral border strips to correct length and stitch first to the sides of the quilt top. Press seams toward the borders. Then add border strips, trimmed to the correct length, to the top and bottom. Press seams toward the borders.

Square Two Pieced Border

To make the Square Two units for the pieced border, use bias strip piecing.

1. Place the 12" squares of assorted prints and light floral in 5 sets, right sides together (Diagram 34). One set will be composed of a light floral and a print. All others will be composed of two prints. Cut each set diagonally, corner to corner, to establish the true bias (45° angle). Cut bias strips, 4¼" wide, from each fabric set.

2. Sew bias-strip pairs together in sets, using ¼"-wide seam allowances and mixing the strips to get as many fabric combinations as possible. Also sew the corner triangles together. Press seams to one side. Sew strip sets together.

3. Using the Bias Square ruler, cut 38 Square One units, each 4⅞" x 4⅞", from the strip and triangle sets (Diagrams 35).

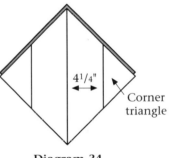

4¼"

Corner triangle

Diagram 34
12" squares
Make 5 sets.

Strip pairs

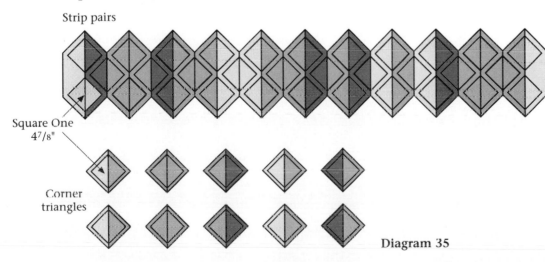

Square One
4⅞"

Corner triangles

Diagram 35

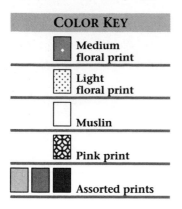

COLOR KEY

Medium
floral print

Light
floral print

Muslin

Pink print

Assorted prints

4. To complete the 38 Square Two units, match pairs of Square One units, aligning opposing seams. Cut pairs diagonally and sew resulting triangle pairs, using ¼"-wide seam allowances to make star-point units (Diagram 36). Press seams to one side. Check sewn units to make sure they measure 4½" x 4½" (cut edge to cut edge).

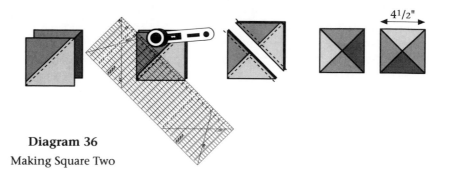

Diagram 36
Making Square Two

5. Sew the Square Two units together to make 2 border strips, each containing 10 units for the side borders, and 2 strips, each containing 9 units for the top and bottom borders. Sew the side borders in place, press seams toward the borders, then add the top and bottom borders.

Outer Border

Measure the quilt for borders as shown on page 46. Trim the 3½"-wide medium floral border strips to correct length and stitch first to the sides of the quilt top. Press seams toward the borders. Then add border strips, trimmed to the correct length, to the top and bottom. Press seams toward the borders.

Quilt Finishing

1. Layer the quilt top with batting and backing; baste.

2. Quilt in the design of your choice, or follow the Quilting Suggestion.

3. From the remaining medium floral print, cut and piece 216" of 2½"-wide bias for binding, following the directions on pages 52–53. Bind the quilt edges.

Quilting Suggestion

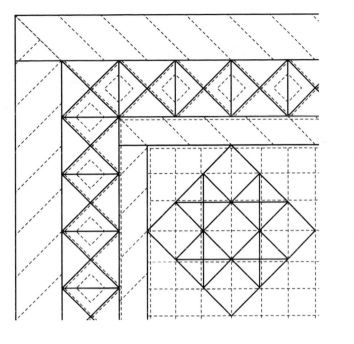

💜 Mark and quilt a grid of vertical and horizontal lines over the central portion of the quilt as shown.

💜 Outline the center section and each border with "in the ditch" quilting.

💜 Quilt the inner border with diagonal lines spaced 2" apart.

💜 Quilt the middle pieced border, outlining the pieces in the ditch, then add stitched diagonal squares ¼" in from seam lines as shown.

💜 Quilt the outer border with diagonal lines spaced 2" apart.

Goose Tracks

From 1870 to 1910, print styles in cotton fabrics were small and finely etched, often in only one color on a white ground. Two very popular quilt colors used in these prints were dark navy blue and pink.

The dark blue was made with indigo, a very reliable dye, and hundreds of small prints in blue on white were available. The pink has been called a "double pink" or "bubble-gum pink" and was also available in hundreds of variations.

For this bed-sized Goose Tracks Quilt, I chose a variety of prints in modern fabrics in pink and navy to approximate the look and colors of scrap quilts from that earlier time.

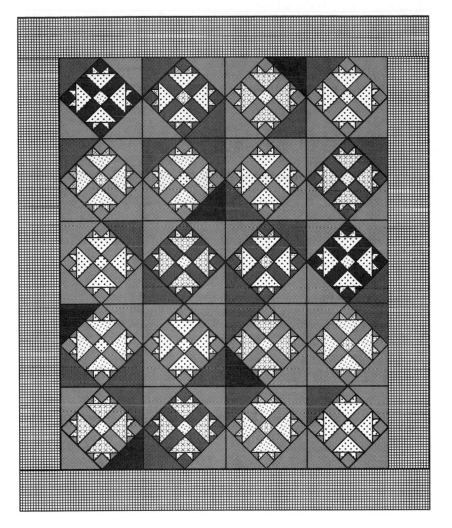

Dimensions: *70½" x 85½"*

20 blocks, each 10" square
and surrounded by 4 large
corner triangles;
7¼"-wide plain border

Goose Tracks Block

Materials: *44"-wide fabric*

Yardages listed are generous and are based on 44"-wide fabric that has been preshrunk. Strips cut across the fabric width should measure at least 42", as shown in the strip dimensions in the cutting chart.

 4 yds. assorted navy blue prints (8 different half-yard
   pieces) for block piecing and large corner triangles

2 yds. assorted pink prints (8 different fat quarters,
   18" x 22") for block piecing

2¼ yds. navy blue print for border

¾ yd. navy blue print for binding

5 yds. fabric of your choice for backing

Batting and thread to finish

Cutting

All rotary-cutting dimensions include ¼"-wide seam allowances. Using a rotary cutter, rotary ruler, and cutting mat, cut the strips and squares as described in the first column of the chart. Then from those squares, cut the pieces listed in the second column. Some strips and squares do not require additional cuts at this time so no directions appear in the second column.

	FIRST CUT		NEXT CUT
Fabric	No. of Pieces	Dimensions	No. of Pieces
Navy Prints	Goose Tracks Blocks		
	8*	11" x 11"	
	80	2½" x 2½"	
	80	2½" x 4½"	
	40	7⅛" x 7⅛"	80 ◻
	*Cut 1 square from each print.		
Pink Prints	8*	11" x 11"	
	40	4⅞" x 4⅞"	80 ◻
	20	2½" x 2½"	
	*Cut 1 square from each print.		
Navy Print	Border		
	4	7½" x 81"	

◻ = Cut once diagonally to yield half-square triangles.

⊠ = Cut twice diagonally to yield quarter-square triangles.

Directions

Square .5 Units

To make the Square .5 units that are the smallest triangles in the Goose Tracks block, use bias strip piecing.

Diagram 37
11" squares
Make 8 sets.

1. Place the 11" squares of the navy blue and pink prints right sides together (8 sets); cut diagonally, corner to corner, to establish the true bias (45° angle). Cut bias strips 2¾" wide (Diagram 37).

2. Sew bias strip pairs together in sets, using ¼"-wide seam allowances. Press the seams toward the navy blue strips. Sew sets together.

3. Using the Bias Square ruler, cut 80 Square One units, each 2⅞" x 2⅞" (Diagram 38).

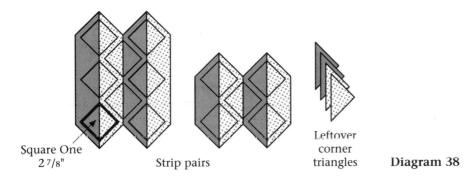

Square One 2⅞"　　　　Strip pairs　　　　Leftover corner triangles　　**Diagram 38**

4. To make the 160 Square .5 triangle units, cut the 80 Square One units in half diagonally (Diagram 39).

Diagram 39
Making Square .5

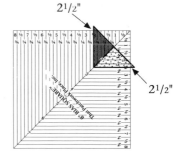

2½"

2½"

Diagram 40
Trimming Points on Square .5

Trim points for easy matching at the 2½" mark on the Bias Square ruler (Diagram 40).

Goose Tracks Block

Piece 20 Goose Tracks blocks.

For each block, repeat steps 1–4:

1. Sew 2 mirror-image Square .5 units to each 2½" navy square to make 4 A units (Diagram 41). Press to evenly distribute the bulk of the seam allowances.

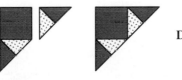

Diagram 41
A Unit
Make 4.

2. Sew a pink triangle to each A Unit to make 4 of Corner B Unit (Diagram 42). Press the seam toward the pink triangle.

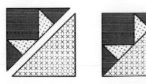

Diagram 42
Corner B Unit
Make 4.

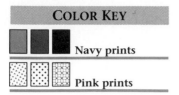

COLOR KEY

Navy prints

Pink prints

3. Assemble the block in rows, adding the navy rectangles and pink squares as shown in the piecing diagram (Diagram 43). Press for opposing seams from row to row. Sew the rows together to complete the block.

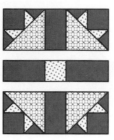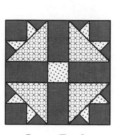

Diagram 43

Piecing Diagram

Goose Tracks
10" block
Make 20.

4. Add a large navy triangle to each side of the completed Goose Tracks block to complete the larger block (Diagram 44). Press seams toward the navy triangles.

Diagram 44

Piecing Diagram

Quilt Top Assembly

Sew the completed blocks together in 5 rows of 4 blocks each, pressing for opposing seams from row to row. Sew rows together.

Borders

Measure the quilt for borders as shown on page 46. Trim the 7½"-wide navy border strips to correct length and stitch first to the sides of the quilt top. Press seams toward the borders. Then add border strips, trimmed to the correct length, to the top and bottom. Press seams toward the borders.

Quilt Finishing

1. Layer the quilt top with batting and backing; baste.

2. Quilt in the design of your choice, or follow the Quilting Suggestion.

3. From the navy print for binding, cut and piece 305" of 2½"-wide bias for binding, following the directions on pages 52–53. Bind the quilt edges.

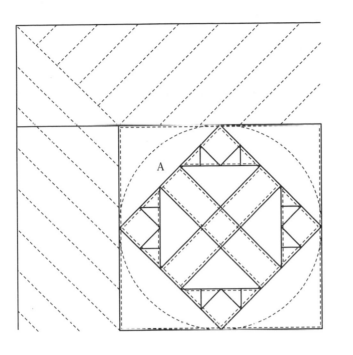

Outline each pieced block with "in the ditch" quilting.

In each large blue triangle, mark and quilt a curve based on a circle drawn from the center of the Goose Tracks block. Make a stiffened Quilting Template A* to guide the marking.

Quilt the border with diagonal lines spaced 2" apart.

* Trace the shape on paper, glue it to lightweight cardboard, and trace around it.

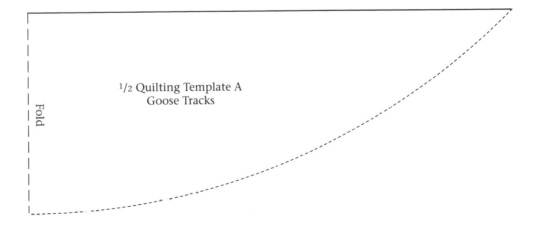

¹/2 Quilting Template A
Goose Tracks

Fold

Flying Pinwheel

In contrast to my usual fabric choices, which are most often darker colors, I chose soft pastel prints for this appealing bed-sized quilt. It is perfect for a sunny room with lots of lace and white eyelet curtains.

Soft stripes and plaids set off the large and small florals that predominate in the quilt. The quilting design was planned with straight lines and easy curves—a natural for machine quilting.

Dimensions: *60" x 82½"*

24 blocks, each 11¼"
square, set straight with
4 across and 6 down;
2"-wide inner border and
5½"-wide outer border

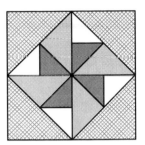

Pinwheel Block

Materials: *44"-wide fabric*

Yardages listed are generous and are based on 44"-wide fabric that has been preshrunk. Strips cut across the fabric width should measure at least 42", as shown in the strip dimensions in the cutting chart.

☐ ▨ ▩ 2 yds. assorted (or 8 fat quarters, 18" x 22") large-scale floral prints in medium-toned pastel colors for block piecing

▨ 2 yds. assorted (or 8 fat quarters) light pastel stripes and plaids for block piecing

▨ ¾ yd. light print for inner border

▥ 2⅛ yds. pastel stripe for outer border and binding

3¾ yds. fabric of your choice for backing

Batting and thread to finish

Cutting

All rotary-cutting dimensions include ¼"-wide seam allowances. Using a rotary cutter, rotary ruler, and cutting mat, cut the strips and squares as described in the first column of the chart. Then from the squares, cut the pieces listed in the second column. Some strips and squares do not require additional cuts at this time so no directions appear in the second column.

| Fabric | FIRST CUT | | NEXT CUT |
	No. of Pieces	Dimensions	No. of Pieces
Florals, Stripes, and Plaids	Pinwheel Blocks		
	16*	12" x 12"	
	Square 1.5 Units		
	48	4⅞" x 4⅞"	
	Block Corners		
	48	6½" x 6½"	96 ◻
	*Cut 1 square from each print.		
Light Print	Inner Border		
	8	2½" x 42"	
Pastel Stripe*	Outer Border		
	4	6" x 76½"	
	*Set aside the remaining fabric for bias binding. See step 3, page 138.		

◻ = Cut once diagonally to yield half-square triangles.

Directions

Square 1.5 Units

To make the Square 1.5 units that form the pinwheel at the center of each block, use bias strip piecing.

1. Place the 12" squares of assorted floral, plaid, and striped prints right sides together, medium to light, making a total of 8 sets. Cut diagonally, corner to corner, to establish the true bias (45° angle). Cut bias strips 4¼" wide (Diagram 45).

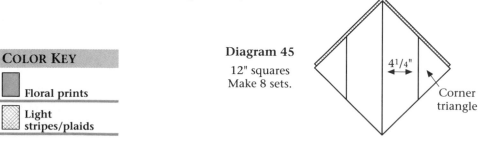

COLOR KEY

☐☐☐ **Floral prints**

▨ **Light stripes/plaids**

Diagram 45
12" squares
Make 8 sets.

4¹/₄"

Corner triangle

2. Sew bias strip pairs together in sets, using ¼"-wide seam allowances. Also sew the corner triangles together. Press seams toward the darker strips. Sew sets together.

3. Using the Bias Square ruler, cut 48 Square One units, each 4⅞" x 4⅞" (Diagram 46).

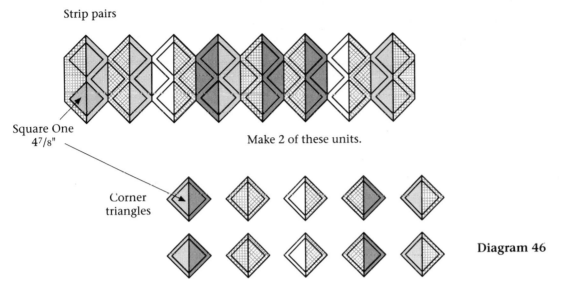

Strip pairs

Square One 4⅞"

Make 2 of these units.

Corner triangles

Diagram 46

Use as many corner triangles as needed.

4. To complete the 96 Square 1.5 units, place each of the 48 Square One units right sides together with 48 squares, each 4⅞" x 4⅞". Cut pairs diagonally and sew resulting triangle pairs, using ¼"-wide seam allowances (Diagram 47). Each pair will yield 2 Square 1.5 units that are mirror images. Press seams to one side. Check sewn units to make sure they measure 4½" x 4½" (cut edge to cut edge).

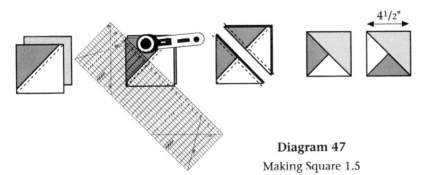

4½"

Diagram 47
Making Square 1.5

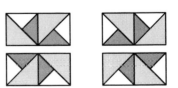

Diagram 48
Piecing Diagram
Pinwheel
8" block
Make 24.

Pinwheel Blocks

1. Piece 24 center pinwheels, following the piecing diagram (Diagram 48). When sewing the 2 halves of the block together, place a positioning pin (page 40) at the center for a precisely matched point.

   Note: Since the Square 1.5 units are mirror images, half of the pinwheels will spin in one direction, half in the other.

2. Add a large triangle (block corner) to each side of each completed Pinwheel block to complete the larger 11¼" block (Diagram 49). Press seams toward the large triangles.

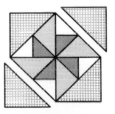

Diagram 49

Quilt Top Assembly

Join Flying Pinwheel blocks together in 6 rows of 4 blocks each, pressing for opposing seams from row to row. Sew rows together.

Borders

1. Sew the 2½"-wide light print inner border strips together, end to end, in sets of 2 to make 4 long strips. Measure the quilt top for borders as shown on page 46. Trim the border strips to correct length and stitch first to the sides of the quilt top. Press seams toward the borders. Then add border strips, trimmed to the correct length, to the top and bottom. Press seams toward the borders.

2. Trim the 6"-wide pastel stripe border strips to correct length after measuring the quilt top for borders as you did in step 1. Stitch to the sides of the quilt top first. Press seams toward the borders. Then add border strips, trimmed to the correct length, to the top and bottom. Press seams toward the borders.

Quilt Finishing

1. Layer the quilt top with batting and backing; baste.

2. Quilt in the design of your choice, or follow the Quilting Suggestion.

3. From the remaining pastel stripe, cut and piece 306" of 2½"-wide bias for binding, following the directions on pages 52–53. Bind the quilt edges.

Quilting Suggestion

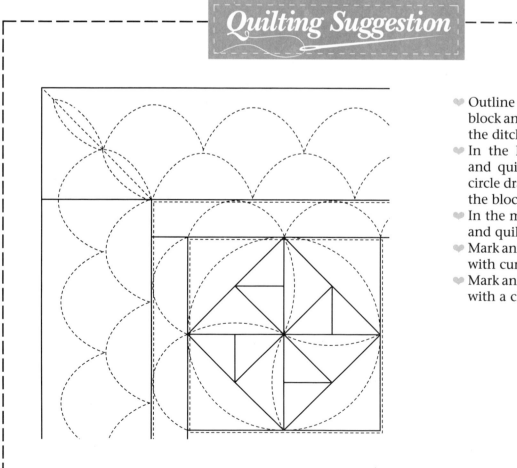

- Outline each Flying Pinwheel block and inner border with "in the ditch" quilting.
- In the largest triangles, mark and quilt a curve based on a circle drawn from the center of the block design.
- In the medium triangles, mark and quilt a curve as shown.
- Mark and quilt the inner border with curves as shown.
- Mark and quilt the outer border with a clamshell design.

Star Stairway

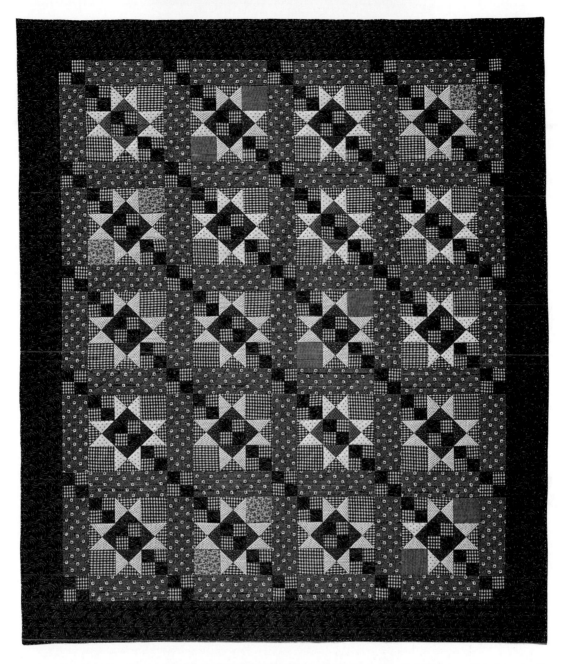

When I was choosing the fabrics for this quilt, I was thinking of a type of print popular during the late 1800s called "Shaker gray." These were actually black prints on a white ground that looked gray from a distance. The plaid fabric in this quilt has the same look; I chose it first. Then, I added the black print and the white one with little black figures.

Next, a purple "thirties" reproduction print just begged to be included. At home, I found three more purple prints in my fabric collection that "belonged" in this quilt. I pieced the quilt top over a quiet New Year's holiday while the rest of the family watched football.

Dimensions: *61" x 73"*

20 blocks, each 9" square,
set 4 across and 5 down;
lattice set with Four
Patch cornerstones;
5"-wide border

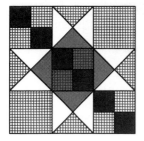

Star Stairway Block

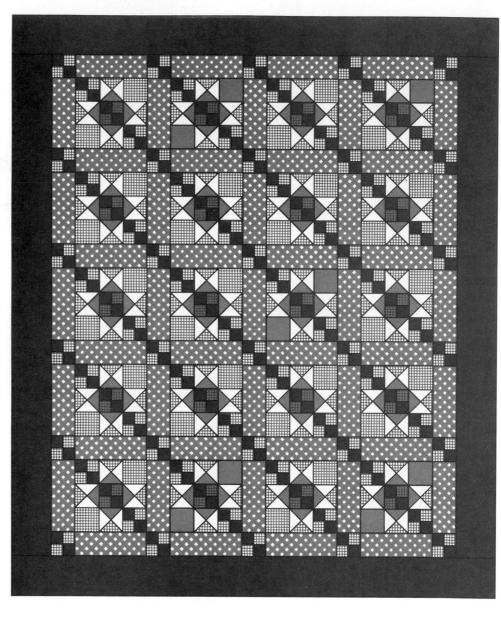

Materials: *44"-wide fabric*

Yardages listed are generous and are based on 44"-wide fabric that has been preshrunk. Strips cut across the fabric width should measure at least 42", as shown in the strip dimensions in the cutting chart.

- *½ yd. total assorted purple prints for block piecing
- 1½ yds. gray/white plaid for block piecing and cornerstones
- 2 yds. black print for border, piecing, and binding
- 1 yd. white print for piecing star points
- 1½ yds. purple print for lattices
- 4 yds. fabric of your choice for backing
- Batting and thread to finish

*Buy 3 different fat quarters, 18" x 22", or cut 3 different purple squares, each 14" x 14", from your fabric collection.

Cutting

All rotary-cutting dimensions include ¼"-wide seam allowances. Using a rotary cutter, rotary ruler, and cutting mat, cut the strips and squares as described in the chart. The strips and squares do not require additional cuts at this time so there is no second column.

Fabric	CUTTING	
	No. of Pieces	**Dimensions**
Black Print*	Border	
	4	5" x 72"
	Blocks and Four Patch Cornerstones	
	11	2" x 36"**
	*Set aside the remaining fabric for bias binding. See step 3, page 143.	
	**Cut from the lengthwise grain.	
Gray/White Plaid	Square Two Units	
	3	14" x 14"
	Blocks and Four Patch Cornerstones	
	11	2" x 36"*
	40	3½" x 3½"
	*Cut from the lengthwise grain.	
White Print	Square Two Units	
	6	14" x 14"
Purple Prints	3	14" x 14"*
	*Cut 1 square from each print.	
Purple Print	Lattices	
	49	3½" x 9½"

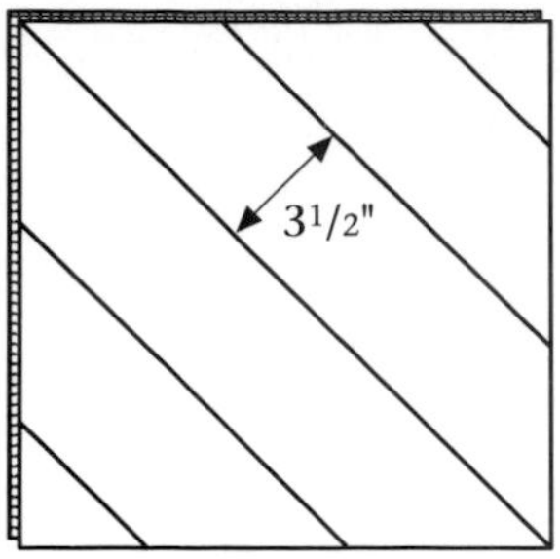

Diagram 50
14" squares
Make 3 sets.

Directions

Square Two Units

To make the Square Two units for the star points, use bias strip piecing.

1. Place three 14" squares of the white print and the three 14" squares of the gray/white plaid right sides together (3 sets). Cut diagonally, corner to corner, to establish the true bias (45° angle). Cut bias strips 3½" wide (Diagram 50).

2. Sew bias strip pairs together in sets, using ¼"-wide seam allowances. Press the seams toward the plaid strips. Sew sets together.

3. Using the Bias Square ruler, cut 40 Square One units, each 3⅞" x 3⅞" (Diagram 51).

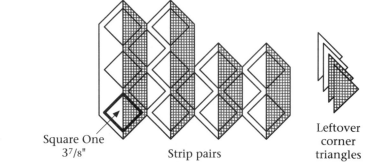

Diagram 51 Square One 3⅞" Strip pairs Leftover corner triangles

4. Place three 14" squares of the white print and the three 14" squares of purple prints right sides together. Repeat steps 1, 2, and 3, above, to make 40 Square One units, each 3⅞" x 3⅞".

5. To complete the 80 Square Two units for the star points, match pairs of Square One units (one of each color combination) right sides together, aligning opposing seams. Cut pairs diagonally and sew the resulting triangle pairs together, using ¼"-wide seam allowances to make star-point units (Diagram 52). Press seams to one side. Check completed units to make sure they measure 3½" x 3½" (cut edge to cut edge).

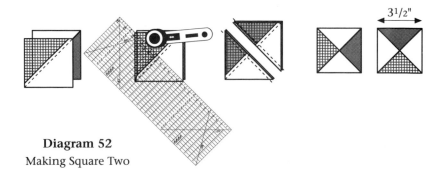

Diagram 52
Making Square Two

Four Patch Units

To make the 90 Four Patch units for the Star Stairway blocks and the cornerstones:

1. Sew together 11 sets of the 2"-wide strips of the black print and the gray/white plaid. Press seams toward the black strips.

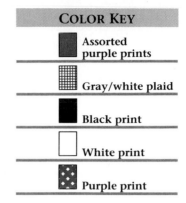

COLOR KEY

Assorted purple prints

Gray/white plaid

Black print

White print

Purple print

2. Place sets of strips right sides together, aligning opposing seams. Cut 90 segments, each 2" wide, as shown in Diagram 53. Sew each set together, using a ¼"-wide seam allowance. Press the seams on the resulting Four Patch cornerstones to one side.

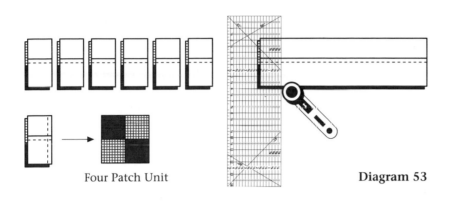

Four Patch Unit

Diagram 53

3. Assemble 20 Star Stairway blocks, following the piecing diagram (Diagram 54) and using 4 Square Two units, 3 Four Patch units, and 2 plaid 3½" squares in each. Press for opposing seams, row to row. Sew rows together.

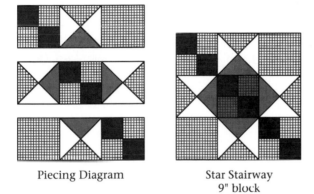

Piecing Diagram

Star Stairway
9" block
Make 20.

Diagram 54

Quilt Top Assembly

Referring to the quilt diagram on page 140, assemble the quilt top in rows of Star Stairway blocks, lattice strips, and Four Patch cornerstones. Press for opposing seams, row to row. Sew rows together.

Borders

Measure the quilt top for borders as shown on page 46. Trim the 5½"-wide black border strips to correct length and stitch first to the sides of the quilt top. Press the seams toward the borders. Then add border strips, trimmed to the correct length, to the top and bottom. Press the seams toward the borders.

Quilt Finishing

1. Layer the quilt top with batting and backing; baste.

2. Quilt in the design of your choice, or follow the Quilting Suggestion.

3. From the remaining black print, cut and piece 288" of 2½"-wide bias for binding, following the directions on pages 52–53. Bind the quilt edges.

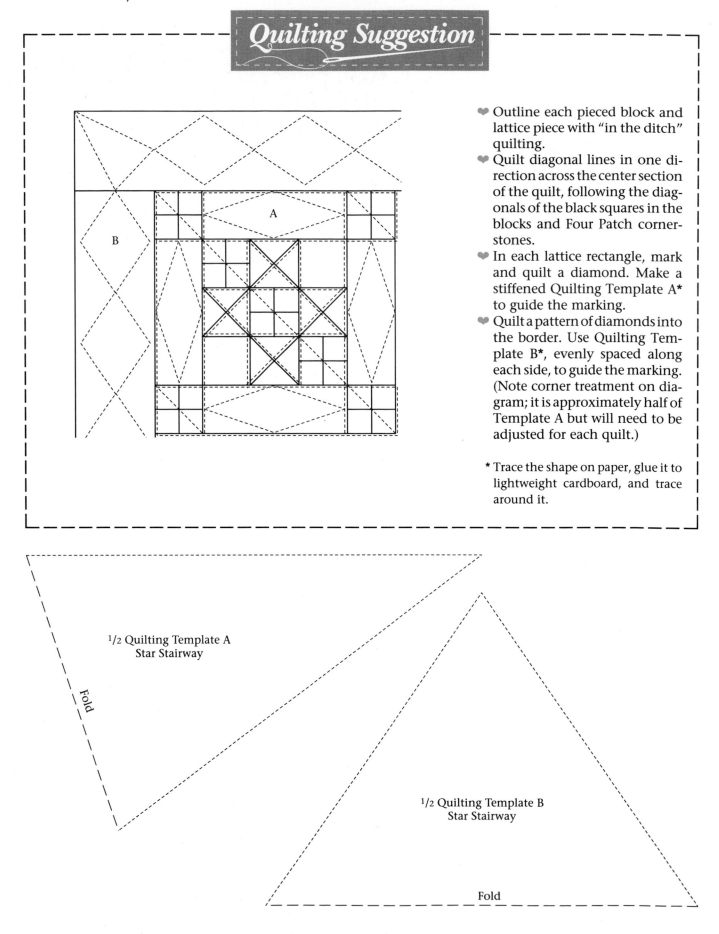

Quilting Suggestion

💜 Outline each pieced block and lattice piece with "in the ditch" quilting.

💜 Quilt diagonal lines in one direction across the center section of the quilt, following the diagonals of the black squares in the blocks and Four Patch cornerstones.

💜 In each lattice rectangle, mark and quilt a diamond. Make a stiffened Quilting Template A* to guide the marking.

💜 Quilt a pattern of diamonds into the border. Use Quilting Template B*, evenly spaced along each side, to guide the marking. (Note corner treatment on diagram; it is approximately half of Template A but will need to be adjusted for each quilt.)

* Trace the shape on paper, glue it to lightweight cardboard, and trace around it.

A

B

¹/2 Quilting Template A
Star Stairway

Fold

¹/2 Quilting Template B
Star Stairway

Fold

Fold

Hill and Valley

Hill and Valley is done in a "strippy" set. Unlike many traditional patchwork designs, this pattern is made of pieced rectangular units, sewn together in rows and joined by long lattice strips.

The Hill and Valley design unit is reminiscent of the traditional Flying Geese design but is pieced of Square Two and Square .5 units instead of Square One units. As you make your version of this quilt, I know you will enjoy playing with the blocks as much as I did—there are so many wonderful design arrangements possible.

Dimensions: *62" x 80"*

48 rectangular design units, each 4½" x 9", in a strippy set with lattices; 3½"-wide inner border; 3"-wide and 6"-wide pieced borders of Square One units; 4¼"-wide outer border

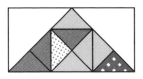

Hill and Valley Block

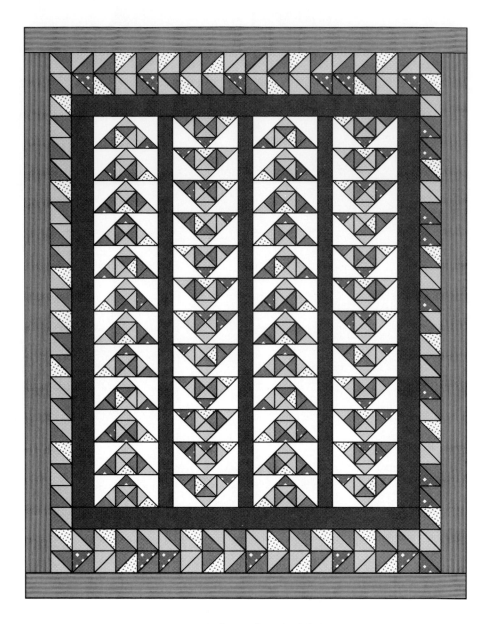

Materials: *44"-wide fabric*

Yardages listed are generous and are based on 44"-wide fabric that has been preshrunk. Strips cut across the fabric width should measure at least 42", as shown in the strip dimensions in the cutting chart.

- 1⅝ yds. brown floral print for inner border, long lattice strips, and bias strip piecing
- 2½ yds. total (or 10 fat quarters, each 18" x 22") of assorted rust, brown, and pink prints for bias strip piecing in blocks
- 2½ yds. total (or 10 fat quarters) assorted green prints for block piecing
- 1¼ yds. light-background print for block backgrounds
- 2⅜ yds. green stripe for outer border and binding

3¾ yds. fabric of your choice for backing

Batting and thread to finish

Cutting

> All rotary-cutting dimensions include ¼"-wide seam allowances. Using a rotary cutter, rotary ruler, and cutting mat, cut the strips and squares as described in the first column of the chart. Then from those squares, cut the pieces listed in the second column. Some strips and squares do not require additional cuts at this time so no directions appear in the second column.

Fabric	FIRST CUT No. of Pieces	FIRST CUT Dimensions	NEXT CUT No. of Pieces
Green Prints	Hill and Valley Units		
	14	14" x 14"	
	12	3" x 3"	24 ◩
Rust, Pink, and Brown	14	14" x 14"	
	12	3" x 3"	24 ◩
Light Background	48	5⅜" x 5⅜"	96 ◩
Brown Floral	Inner Border		
	4	3½" x 58½"	
	Lattices		
	3	2½" x 58½"	
Green Stripe*	Outer Border		
	4	4½" x 85½"	
	*Set aside the remaining striped fabric for bias binding. See step 3, page 150.		

◩ = Cut once diagonally to yield half-square triangles.

Directions

Bias Square Units

To make the Square One units for the pieced middle border and the Square Two and Square .5 units for the Hill and Valley units, use bias strip piecing.

1. Place each of the 14" green squares right sides together with one of the 14" squares of rust, pink, or brown (14 sets); cut diagonally, corner to corner, to establish the true bias (45° angle). Cut bias strips 3½" wide (Diagram 55).

2. Sew bias strip pairs together in sets, using the random-scrap setup described on page 110. Use ¼"-wide seam allowances. Press seams toward the darker strip in each pair. Sew sets together.

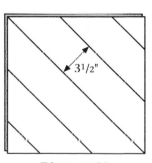

Diagram 55
14" squares
Make 14 sets.

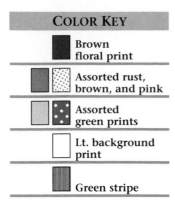

COLOR KEY
Brown floral print
Assorted rust, brown, and pink
Assorted green prints
Lt. background print
Green stripe

3. Using the Bias Square ruler, cut 96 Square One units, each 3⅞" x 3⅞" (Diagram 56). Save leftovers to cut 3½" Square One units for pieced border.

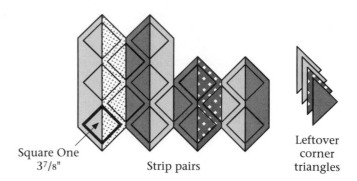

Diagram 56

Square One
3⅞" Strip pairs Leftover corner triangles

4. To obtain the required 48 Square Two units, place 24 pairs of Square One units right sides together, aligning opposing seams. Cut pairs diagonally and sew the resulting triangle pairs together, using ¼"-wide seam allowances (Diagram 57). Each pair will yield 2 Square Two units. Press seams to one side. Check completed units to make sure they measure 3½" x 3½" (cut edge to cut edge).

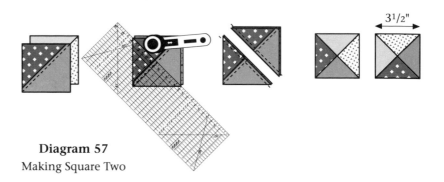

Diagram 57
Making Square Two

5. To complete the required 96 Square .5 units, cut 48 Square One units once diagonally (Diagram 58).

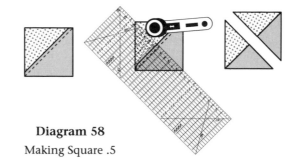

Diagram 58
Making Square .5

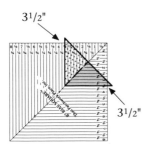

3½"

3½"

Diagram 59

Trimming Points
on Square .5

Trim points for matching at the 3½" marking on the Bias Square ruler (Diagram 59).

6. From the remaining bias strip pairs, cut 112 Square One units, 3½" x 3½" (Diagram 60) for the pieced middle border.

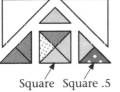

Diagram 60

Square One
3½" x 3½"
Make 112.

Hill and Valley Units

Follow the piecing diagram to assemble 48 Hill and Valley units, using 1 Square Two unit, 2 Square .5 units, 1 half-square triangle, and 2 light-background triangles in each unit (Diagram 61).

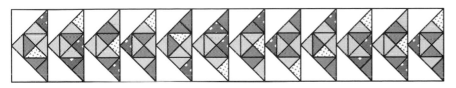

Square Square .5
Two

Hill and Valley
4½" x 9"
Make 48.

Diagram 61

Piecing Diagram

Quilt Top Assembly

1. Sew the 48 completed Hill and Valley units together in 4 rows of 12 each (Diagram 62).

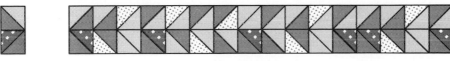

Diagram 62

Make 4 rows of 12
Hill and Valley units.

2. Referring to the quilt diagram on page 146, sew the 4 rows of Hill and Valley units together with the 2½"-wide brown floral lattice strips. Press seams toward the lattice strips.

Borders

1. Measure the quilt top for borders as shown on page 46. Trim the 3½"-wide brown floral border strips to correct length and stitch first to the sides of the quilt top. Press seams toward the borders. Then add border strips, trimmed to the correct length, to the top and bottom. Press the seams toward the borders.

2. Make the top and bottom pieced borders of Square One units, referring to the quilt photo on page 145 and the diagram on page 146. Sew 64 Square One units together to make 32 "Flying Geese" units. Sew Flying Geese units together into 2 rows of 16 units each. Sew to top and bottom of quilt top, with the "geese" flying "west" on the top edge of the quilt top and "east" on the bottom edge (Diagram 63).

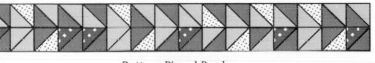

Flying Geese Unit
Make 32.

Top Pieced Border

Bottom Pieced Border

Diagram 63

3. Sew the remaining 48 Square One units together in 2 rows of 24 units each (Diagram 64). Sew to the sides of the quilt top as shown in the diagram on page 146.

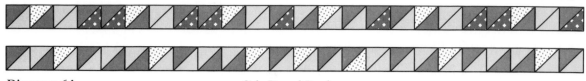

Diagram 64   Side Pieced Borders
                                          Make 2.

COLOR KEY	
■	Brown floral print
▨	Assorted rust, brown, and pink
▨	Assorted green prints
□	Lt. background print
▥	Green stripe

4. Measure the quilt top for borders as shown on page 46. Trim the 4½"-wide green striped outer border strips to the correct length and stitch first to the sides of the quilt top. Press seams toward the borders. Then add border strips, trimmed to the correct length, to the top and bottom. Press seams toward the borders.

Quilt Finishing

1. Layer the quilt top with batting and backing; baste.

2. Quilt in the design of your choice, or follow the Quilting Suggestion.

3. From the remaining green stripe, cut and piece 296" of 2½"-wide bias for binding, following the directions on pages 52–53. Bind the quilt edges.

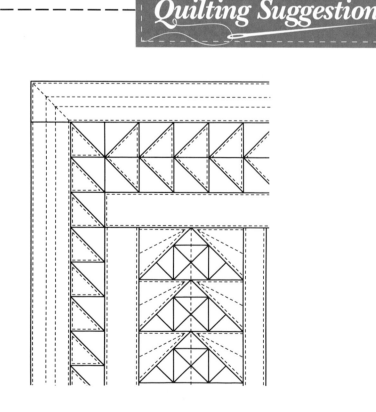

Quilting Suggestion

- ♥ Outline each Hill and Valley unit, lattice strip, and piece in the border designs with "in the the ditch" quilting.
- ♥ Quilt vertical lines through the center of the rows of Hill and Valley units.
- ♥ Quilt slanted lines in the large triangles of each block.
- ♥ Quilt two more lines in the border, spaced 1" apart and parallel to the outside edge of the quilt.

MEET
Mary Hickey
&
HER BIAS RECTANGLE
QUILTS

While I do not wish to go back as far as Adam and Eve to explain my passion for quilting, I must admit that my strongest feelings probably stem from an unfair rule in my kindergarten days.

Mrs. Craddock, our teacher, had a high chirping voice and walked with quick little steps, like a nervous bird. She carried a small speckled satchel and wore her gray hair in a large, disheveled bun that resembled an inverted bird's nest.

"The boys will play with the blocks on Monday, Wednesday, and Friday. The girls on Tuesday. We will have folk dancing on Thursdays," Mrs. Craddock squawked at us. Well, my five-year-old heart was outraged. You see, Mrs. Craddock's big blocks were painted in beautiful colors and were stored on a huge wagonlike box that could be rolled into the play corner. There were hundreds of squares, rectangles, triangles, cylinders, arches, and even a yellow stairway. We could make patterns to tiptoe across, or castles to live in, or forts to defend. Fairies could dance on the colored floors we created, and knights could ride over the roads we built. But the girls could only play with the blocks on Tuesday!

I appeared at breakfast one morning wearing my blue corduroy overalls and a St. Louis Cardinal's baseball cap, hoping that, at school, Mrs. Craddock might think I was a boy and let me play with the blocks. However, in the 1940s, girls wore dresses to school and the teacher's word was final. I was sent briskly back upstairs to put on my red plaid dress and told to play with the little stove and ironing board in the other corner of the classroom. It was not until I learned to make quilts that I really got over my irritation with Mrs. Craddock's "girls-on-Tuesday-only" rule.

Even though my mother and grandmothers were all expert seamstresses, none of them made quilts during my childhood. I feel a pang of envy when I see the quilts my friends have received or inherited. It's not the quilts I envy, but the sense of intimate connection to their past. I became an avid sewer at an early age, making dolls and their wardrobes, stuffed animals, and simple skirts and dresses. As a teenager, I made special dresses for school dances and for church events. I also learned to appliqué by stitching numbers and lightning bolts to the sails for our boat. I thought I was doing patchwork when I mended our old miners' tent with colorful patches.

I have always been drawn to the color and texture of cotton fabric. As a college student in color and design classes, I used cottons. No other medium seemed able to capture the light and create the surfaces and moods that cottons could. These design projects usually consisted of glued fabric collages, since in the college atmosphere of the sixties, sewing was an unacceptable art form.

When I was a school teacher, my fourth-grade students often played with a set of triangle tiles and design boards that my ever-supportive husband made in his workshop. The children developed wonderful patterns and made simple quilts, using their favorite designs. As a young mother, I made easy baby quilts as well as my children's clothing. However, it wasn't until 1975 that I started making quilts in earnest. While sorting used books for a charity sale, I bought a book called *The Perfect Patchwork Primer* by Beth Gutcheon. I spent many hours reading the book and planning my first real quilt. I carefully made the templates and drew around them with a pencil, following the directions in the book. I cut hundreds of triangles for an Ohio Star quilt, but, before long, I lost patience. So, I cut long strips of fabric and used a pencil and a right triangle ruler to divide the strips into triangles. While my methods were a bit crude, they were quick and accurate, and the quilt became a beloved "blankie" for its young owner.

I was completely smitten by quiltmaking, a love affair that has endured for the past eighteen years. My husband cheerfully overlooked the often-late and severely plain dinners that my Ohio Star quilt initiated, and he has heartily encouraged the making of hundreds more quilts.

I made many quilts in the years after the Ohio Star quilt—baby quilts, doll quilts, miniature quilts, hundreds of small, pieced wall hangings to sell at craft fairs, and one king-size monstrosity in bilious greens and poisonous purples that I eventually managed to wad up and stuff into a bag of blankets being sent to Biafra. During this period, I somehow lost my copy of *The Perfect Patchwork Primer* and I lost touch with traditional patchwork piecing. I started making pieced pictorial blocks, and instead of using three or four templates to make a block, I started making blocks with twenty-five or thirty separate templates. After I completed one quilt with pieced mallard ducks carrying pieced baby ducks on their backs, a block requiring more than twenty-five separate templates (Diagram 1), I decided it was time to get back to the basics.

That's when I signed up for a piecing class with Marsha McCloskey. By this time, I had a great deal of disorganized quilting knowledge and skill. However, Marsha's systematic methods and patient teaching helped me to organize that knowledge and return to the underlying geometric principles of quilting.

When I design quilts, I attempt to create several levels of pattern with the shapes and colors in the blocks. I prefer to have the block edges blur and the shapes on the edges connect in a way that creates a secondary design that is almost as obvious as the block. For this reason, I often make quilts that utilize two different block patterns. I try to develop quilting lines that continue to pull the block shapes out and connect the shapes in one block to the shapes in its neighboring blocks. It is this interplay of shapes, colors, and textures in one surface that appeals to me in quilts. I like to compare this to the mingling of the sounds of many musical instruments and melodies that create a symphony.

In 1985, I began teaching classes at In The Beginning, a quilt shop in Seattle.

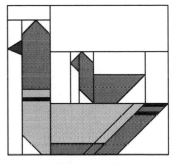

Diagram 1

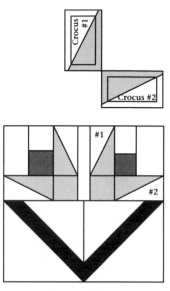

Crocus Block
Diagram 2

The patterns and handouts I used in my class on miniature quilts formed the basis of my first book, *Little by Little*, which was published by That Patchwork Place (1988).

The Crocus pattern in *Little by Little* included a tiny blossom made of long, thin triangles (Diagram 2). Because the pieces were so small, I cut narrow bias strips, sewed them together, and then used a tiny, rectangular template to cut the shapes. The result was an accurate way to cut and piece rectangles made of very narrow triangles.

Nancy Martin liked the method I had developed and encouraged me to expand the technique for use with larger quilts. This traditional shape, the long, thin triangle, has always been difficult and tedious to sew accurately. To expand the method given in *Little by Little*, I had to overcome three problems. First, the strips had to be cut so the points would not creep into the seam allowance; second, the strips had to be cut so the straight of grain would always be on the outside of the rectangle; and third, the strips had to be cut so half of the rectangles would have the darker color on the left and half of them would have it on the right.

My book *Angle Antics* and a companion rotary-cutting ruler called the BiRangle were the results of my efforts. I am continually amazed at the response to the techniques and the quilts. I was even more astonished and thrilled when I was invited to collaborate on this book. I felt that now, at last, I could play with blocks every day.

The process of combining and distilling the techniques and personalities of four ardent quilt designers and teachers has been rewarding and fascinating. So much so that as the process drew to a close I found I really missed the excitement of our meetings and exchanges. That's when I decided to name my four newly hatched chicks after the four authors of *Quick and Easy Quiltmaking*. I found great pleasure in watching the four little chicks charging around in their washtub home looking like muffins with legs. Each chick differed in every way from its companions, but the four moved together like a well-trained dance team. And the ardor with which they pecked for seeds was at least as strong as the passion with which the four of us pursued our quiltmaking. Nancy, Marsha, Sara, and Mary have become important members of our household, providing us with great amusement as they have grown to be creative and artistic chickens. You can see them visiting with me on our porch swing on page 151. (Mary is the one with dark hair).

♥

In the following section, you will find complete directions for making bias rectangles. I've also included my variation of Nancy Martin's method for making bias squares.

MAKING BIAS RECTANGLES

The quilts in this section of *Quick and Easy Quiltmaking* all include bias rectangles. With the techniques presented here, you will learn to make bias rectangles quickly and accurately. Once you have mastered the steps, you will be able to use the technique for other quilts containing this design element.

CUTTING THE STRIPS

1. Cut 10" x 42" pieces of the background fabric and the triangle fabric. **Note:** Always check the individual project for the size pieces to cut. The standard size is 10" x 42", but some projects require a different size.

2. Layer both fabrics *face down* on the cutting board.

3. Fold the fabrics in half, selvage to selvage (the way they are folded on the bolt). Cutting the strips with the fabrics folded creates rectangles with color on the left and rectangles with color on the right.

4. Place the fold on the right. Place the BiRangle ruler on the edge of the fabrics, with the long side on the selvages (Diagram 3).

Diagram 3

5. Place a large cutting ruler on the diagonal line of the BiRangle (Diagram 4).

6. Carefully slide the BiRangle out of the way.

7. Cut along the edge of the ruler (Diagram 5).

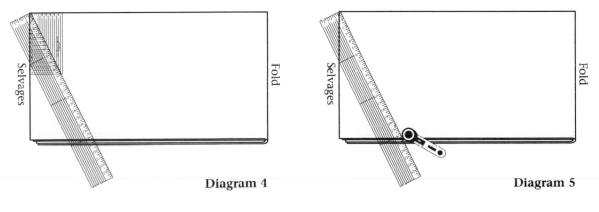

Diagram 4　　　　　　　　　　　　**Diagram 5**

8. Cut strips exactly parallel to the first cut (Diagram 6). Each quilt plan will tell you how wide to cut the bias strips.

9. Set aside the two large, leftover triangles.

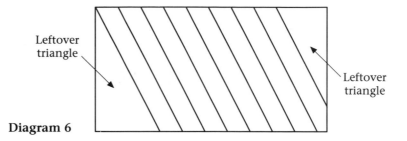

Leftover triangle

Leftover triangle

Diagram 6

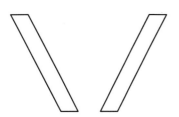

Left   Right
Diagram 7

10. Sort the strips into two sets, the ones that slant to the left and those that slant to the right (Diagram 7).

11. Set aside the strips that slant to the right (in another room or under your chair so you won't get them mixed up). You will find out what to do with them on page 159, under "Cutting the Other Set of Strips."

12. Arrange the strips that slant to the left in a unit, alternating the colors. Place the odd-shaped strips at the ends of the unit. The tops of the strips should form a straight line, not a zigzag line.

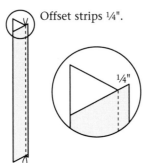

Offset strips ¼".

¼"

Diagram 8

13. Sew the strips together in pairs, offsetting the tops of the strips ¼" before stitching the seam as shown in Diagram 8. If you are not sure of the ¼", measure with your ruler. Eventually, it will become second nature.

14. Sew the pairs into a unit, again offsetting the tops ¼". Then sew the odd-shaped strips to the ends of the unit (Diagram 9).

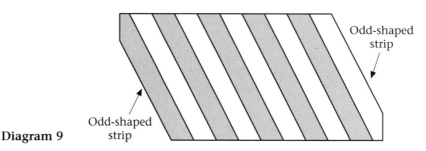

Odd-shaped strip

Diagram 9   Odd-shaped strip

15. Press the seams toward the darker color.

CUTTING THE SEGMENTS

1. Place the strip-pieced unit on the cutting mat, adjusting it so all or most of it is on the board. Depending on the size of the mat, it might fit better at an angle (Diagram 10).

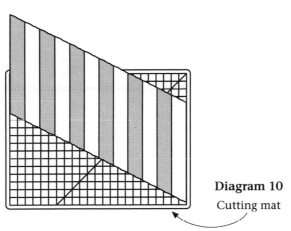

Diagram 10
Cutting mat

2. Place the BiRangle on top of the unit, aligning its diagonal line with one of the center seam lines. Place a rotary-cutting ruler against the top of the BiRangle.

3. Slide the two rulers toward the edge of the unit until the ruler is on the least amount of fabric possible and trim (Diagram 11). Only a few threads will need to be trimmed at one end while as much as ½" (sometimes more) will have to be trimmed from the other end. Maintain a positive attitude toward this step; it must be repeated every time you cut a segment and has a great impact on the accuracy of your bias rectangles.

4. Cut a segment of the width indicated in the specific quilt plan you are following (Diagram 12).

5. Repeat step 3, trimming the edge of the remaining strip-pieced unit before cutting the next segment (Diagram 13).

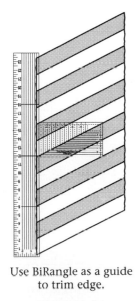

Use BiRangle as a guide
to trim edge.

Diagram 11

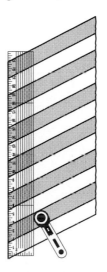

Diagram 12

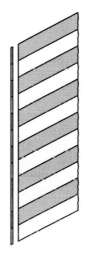

Trim edge of
strip-pieced unit.

Diagram 13

6. Cut another segment the proper size for the quilt plan you are making (Diagram 14).

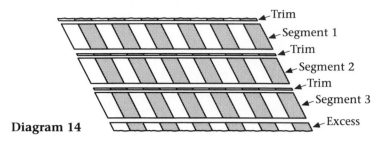

Diagram 14

(labels: Trim, Segment 1, Trim, Segment 2, Trim, Segment 3, Excess)

Note: You should be able to cut three segments from a 12" unit. However, the first time you make one of these bias strip-pieced units, you might only get two segments from the unit.

    This has to do with inexperience and inaccuracy when offsetting the tops of the strips ¼" as you sew them together. Don't feel you are the only one who has had this problem. The next one you make will be perfect!

CUTTING THE BIAS RECTANGLES

1. Align the bottom edge of the BiRangle ruler with the bottom edge of the strip-pieced segment.

2. Place the diagonal line of the BiRangle on the seam line.

3. Cut along the right edge of the BiRangle (Diagram 15).

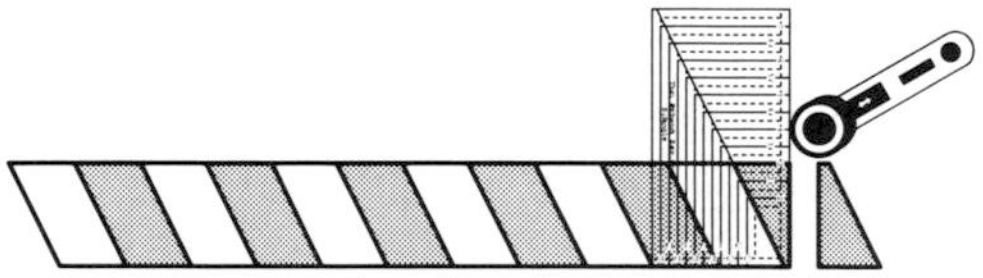

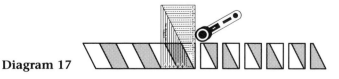

Diagram 15

4. Move the BiRangle to the next seam line. Make sure the bottom edge of the ruler is aligned with the bottom edge of the strip-pieced segment. Cut along the right edge (Diagram 16).

Diagram 16

5. Continue this process until you have made a cut to the right of each seam in the segment (Diagram 17).

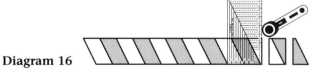

Diagram 17

6. Turn your cutting mat 180° so that the left sides of the rectangles are now on the right. These sides must be trimmed to complete the bias rectangles.

7. Position the BiRangle ruler so that the diagonal line is on the seam line and the bottom edge of the BiRangle is aligned with the bottom edge of the cut segment; trim the last side of each bias rectangle (Diagram 18).

Diagram 18

CUTTING THE OTHER SET OF STRIPS

1. Make strip-pieced units, using the strips that slant to the right and following the previous steps 1–7 (Diagram 19).

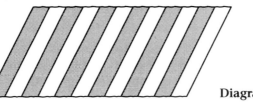

Diagram 19

2. Although it is a bit unorthodox, I recommend pressing all seams of these strips toward the lighter color. This makes it easier to match the angles when sewing the rectangles together.

3. After piecing the units, cut the segments and then the rectangles. Remember that these fabrics were facing down as you cut the strips, so to cut the segments and the rectangles, you will have to turn the fabrics face down and cut from the back (Diagram 20). Or, you can turn the BiRangle ruler over and work with the wrong side of it.

Diagram 20

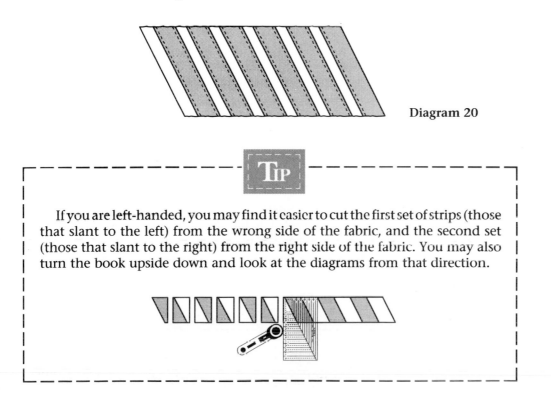

TIP

If you are left-handed, you may find it easier to cut the first set of strips (those that slant to the left) from the wrong side of the fabric, and the second set (those that slant to the right) from the right side of the fabric. You may also turn the book upside down and look at the diagrams from that direction.

DIAGONAL STRIP WIDTHS

The width to cut the strips for strip-pieced bias rectangles depends on the finished size of the rectangle you wish to make. Measure the short side of the finished rectangle and add 1". Cut strips this width.

The chart below is a quick reference for the standard-size bias rectangles you can strip piece and cut, using the BiRangle ruler.

DIMENSIONS OF FINISHED RECTANGLE		
Short Side	**Long Side**	**Diagonal Strip Width**
¾"	1½"	1¾"
1"	2"	2"
1¼"	2½"	2¼"
1½"	3"	2½"
1¾"	3½"	2¾"
2"	4"	3"
2¼"	4½"	3¼"
2½"	5"	3½"
2¾"	5½"	3¾"
3"	6"	4"
3¼"	6½"	4¼"
3½"	7"	4½"

BIAS RECTANGLE QUILTS

The designs for the quilt plans on pages 164–208 require bias rectangles. As you study the photographs and drawings, notice that sometimes the rectangles are joined on the long side, as in Starry Path (page 202) and Secret Gardens (page 170). Sometimes they are joined on the short side and the long side, as in Woodland Cottages (page 182), and sometimes they are joined to bias squares, as in Raven Dance (page 190). In other designs, such as Water Music (page 176) and Summer's End (page 196), they are separated by a strip of background fabric.

In Raven Dance and Summer's End, all of the triangles point in the same direction, while in all of the other quilts, the triangles point in two directions.

Each quilt plan tells how wide to cut the strips, segments, and bias rectangles, and whether or not to fold the fabrics. The fabric requirements are written very specifically. Feel free to substitute the colors and fabrics of your choice and do not hesitate to change the designs to suit your own creative desires.

Making Bias Squares

Bias strip piecing is by far the most accurate method for creating bias squares, squares made of two triangles. This method takes no longer than others, such as speed or sandwich piecing, but I find it much more accurate, so it saves time and frustration later when assembling the blocks. Strip-pieced bias squares are used in several of my quilts, so it is important to understand the basic technique described below before starting any of the quilts in this section.

There are several variations for making strip-pieced bias squares. My method is a variation of the ones shown on pages 59 and 108. I suggest you try each method and choose the one best suited to your stitching skills and personality.

Essentially, in each method, long bias strips are sewn together in pairs, and squares consisting of two triangles are cut from the bias-strip pairs.

I find it easiest to work with ⅓-yard pieces of fabric. The instructions for each quilt in this section indicate how many ⅓-yard pieces of each fabric to use and how many bias squares to cut.

> **Tip**
>
> Several fabrics can be layered at once for cutting the bias strips. When layering fabrics for cutting, place all fabrics face up (right side to wrong side).

Cutting the Strips

1. Layer the two fabrics for the bias squares, right side to wrong side (Diagram 21).

Diagram 21

Layer fabrics right side up.

2. Draw a true bias line (45° angle) on the top fabric. You can use the Bias Square ruler to establish this angle by aligning the diagonal line on the ruler with the long, straight edge of the fabric (Diagram 22).

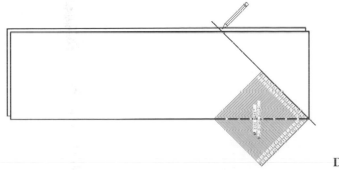

Diagram 22

In general, cut the strips for bias strip-pieced squares the same width as the finished size of the bias square plus ½". For example, for a finished bias square of 3", cut the strips 3½" wide.

3. Cut bias strips exactly parallel to the drawn line (Diagram 23). The instructions for each quilt indicate how many strips to cut and how wide to cut them.

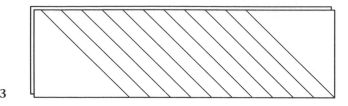

Diagram 23

4. Alternating the fabrics, sew the strips together into units made up of six to eight strips (Diagram 24). Press the seams toward the darker color.

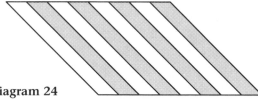

Diagram 24

CUTTING THE SEGMENTS

1. Place the strip-pieced unit on your cutting mat.

2. Position the Bias Square ruler with the diagonal line on a seam line and slide it toward the edge of the strip-pieced unit. Use the edge of the Bias Square to guide you in positioning your long cutting guide along the edge of the unit (Diagram 25). Trim the edge evenly. The trimmed edge should be at a perfect 45° angle to the seam lines.

3. Cut a segment parallel to the first cut (Diagram 26). Each quilt plan will tell you how wide to cut this segment. In general, always cut the segment the same width as the cut square required for the project.

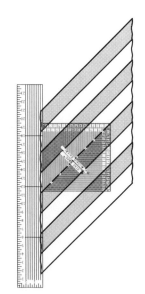

Diagram 25

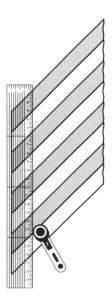

Diagram 26

4. Repeat step 2 to check and correct the angle along the top of the unit before cutting each segment (Diagram 27). Resist the temptation to skip the trimming step. Instead, try to view trimming as an opportunity to ensure success.

5. Continue cutting segments the width specified in the quilt instructions, making sure to check and correct the angle at the edge after each cut (Diagram 28).

Diagram 28

6. Sew the segments together, end to end, to create a long strip-pieced unit. Be careful not to stretch the bias. Seaming the segments together prevents wasting triangles at the end of the unit.

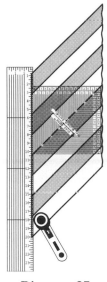

Diagram 27

CUTTING THE BIAS SQUARES

1. Place the unit on your cutting mat. Place the Bias Square ruler on the unit, with the diagonal line on a seam line and the edge of the Bias Square aligned with the bottom edge of the fabric (Diagram 29). (The printing on the Bias Square will be upside down and at an angle for this cut.) Cut along the right side of the Bias Square.

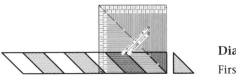

Diagram 29
First Position

2. Rotate the Bias Square ruler (so printing is right side up at an angle), reposition the diagonal line and cut along the left side of the Bias Square ruler (Diagram 30).

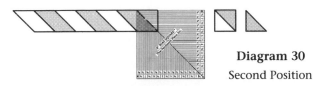

Diagram 30
Second Position

3. Continue to cut bias squares in this manner until you have the number specified in the directions for the quilt you are making.

WARM-UP Project

Williamsburg Star

*Colonial red fabric, depicting a bountiful Virginia harvest, frames
this simple quilt. Church-spire Star blocks form the centerpiece,
enclosed by the quiet Village Green blocks.*

Dimensions: *50" x 50"*

9 blocks, each 12"
square (4 Star blocks and
5 Village Green blocks), set
3 across and 3 down in an
alternating pattern;
2"-wide inner border;
5"-wide outer border

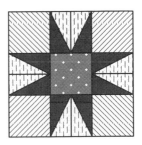

Star Block

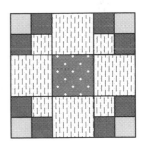

Village Green Block

Materials: *44"-wide fabric*

Yardages listed are generous and are based on 44"-wide fabric that has been preshrunk. Strips cut across the fabric width should measure at least 42", as shown in the strip dimensions in the cutting chart.

- 1 yd. background print fabric
- ⅓ yd. red print for stars
- ¼ yd. red floral print for block centers
- ⅓ yd. green stripe for corners of Star blocks (⅜ yd. if the squares are cut on the bias as shown in the quilt)
- ¼ yd. medium green for small squares
- ⅓ yd. dark green for small squares
- ⅓ yd. dark green for inner border
- ¾ yd. red floral for outer border
- 1¾ yds. fabric of your choice for backing
- ⅜ yd. red print for binding
- Batting and thread to finish

Cutting

All rotary-cutting dimensions include ¼"-wide seam allowances. Cut the bias strips for the bias rectangles first, following the directions below, and set aside any remaining fabric. Construct the bias rectangles and set aside. Then cut all remaining pieces as directed in the cutting chart. Some strips will not require additional cuts at this time so no directions appear in the second column.

Bias Rectangles

From the background fabric, cut 1 piece of fabric, 10" x 42".

From the red star fabric, cut 1 piece of fabric, 10" x 42".

Using these fabric pieces, follow the directions on pages 155–59, cutting the strips 3" wide, the strip-pieced segments 4½" wide, and the bias rectangles 2½" x 4½". You will need a total of 32 bias rectangles, 16 with red on the left and 16 with red on the right (Diagram 31).

Make 16.   Make 16.

Diagram 31

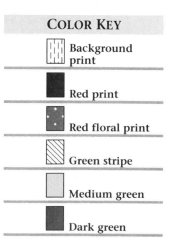

COLOR KEY

	Background print
	Red print
	Red floral print
	Green stripe
	Medium green
	Dark green

Fabric	FIRST CUT		ADDITIONAL CUTS	
	No. of Strips	Dimensions	No. of Pieces	Dimensions
Background Print	Village Green Blocks			
	3	4½" x 42"	20	4½" x 4½"
	2	2½" x 42"		
Dark Green	4	2½" x 42"		
Medium Green	2	2½" x 42"		
Red Floral	Centers of Village Green and Star Blocks			
	1	4½" x 42"	9	4½" x 4½"
Green Stripe	Corners of Star Blocks			
	2	4½" x 42"	16*	4½" x 4½"
*If you wish to cut these squares on the bias so that the stripes radiate from the stars as they do in the featured quilt, cut the strips on the bias so the cut squares will have stripes on the diagonal.				
Dark Green	Inner Border			
	4	2½" x 42"		
Red Floral	Outer Border			
	5	5¼" x 42"		

Directions

Village Green Blocks

1. Sew two 2½" x 42" strips of background print to two of the dark green strips (Diagram 32). Press the seams toward the dark green strips.

Diagram 32

2. Sew two 2½" x 42" strips of medium green to the two remaining dark green strips (Diagram 33). Press the seams toward the dark green strips.

Diagram 33

3. Crosscut the strip-pieced units into 2½"-wide segments, creating two-patch rectangles (Diagram 34). Cut 20 of each color combination.

2½"

Diagram 34

4. Sew the two-patch rectangles together to create the Four Patch units for the corners of the Village Green blocks (Diagram 35). Make 20 Four Patch units.

Diagram 35
Four Patch Unit
Make 20.

5. Assemble 5 Village Green blocks, following the piecing diagram (Diagram 36).

4½" square

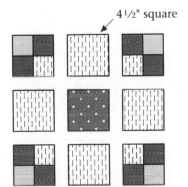 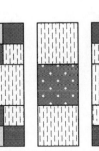 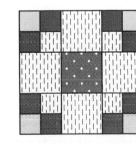

Diagram 36
Piecing Diagram
Village Green Block
Make 5.

Diagram 37

Sew bias rectangles
together in pairs.
Make 16.

Star Blocks

1. Sew pairs of bias rectangles together along the long side (Diagram 37). Press the seams open. You will need 16 pieced rectangle units.

2. Follow the piecing diagram to complete each of the 4 Star blocks (Diagram 38).

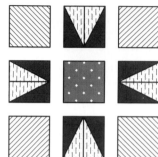

Diagram 38

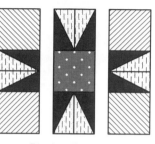

Piecing Diagram
Star Block
Make 4.

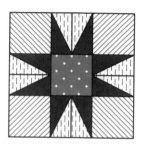

Quilt Top Assembly

1. Sew the blocks together in 3 rows of 3 blocks each (Diagram 39).

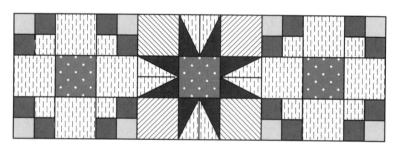

Make 2 rows.

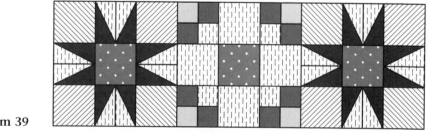

Diagram 39

Make 1 row.

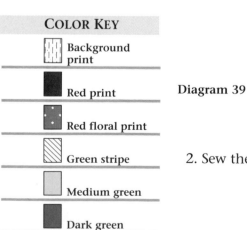

COLOR KEY

Background print

Red print

Red floral print

Green stripe

Medium green

Dark green

2. Sew the rows together, referring to the quilt plan on page 165.

Borders

1. Measure the quilt for borders as shown on page 46. Trim the 2½"-wide dark green border strips to correct length and stitch first to the sides of the quilt top. Press seams toward the borders. Then add border strips, trimmed to the correct length, to the top and bottom. Press seams toward the borders.

2. Add the 5¼"-wide red floral outer borders as described in step 1, stitching the outer border strips to the sides of the quilt top first and then to the top and bottom.

Quilt Finishing

1. Layer the quilt top with batting and backing; baste.

2. Quilt in the design of your choice, or follow the Quilting Suggestion.

3. From the red print for the binding, cut and piece 200" of 2½"-wide bias for binding, following the directions on pages 52–53. Bind the quilt edges.

Quilting Suggestion

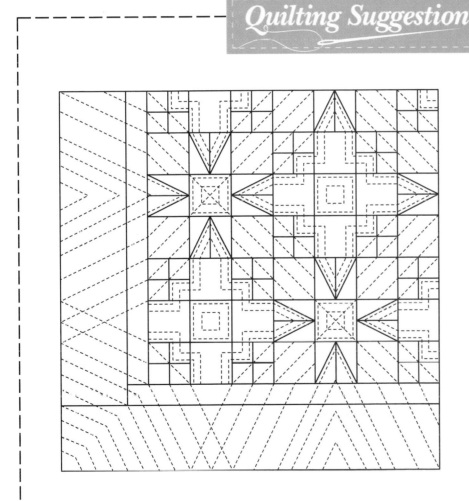

- Outline quilt in the background areas of the blocks ¼" and ¾" from the seams and inside the red floral squares.
- Stitch in the seams along the angled lines of the red stars, continuing this line through the dark squares of the Village Green blocks and out into the borders.
- Stitch diagonally across the Star blocks, continuing this line out into the borders.
- Stitch two lines parallel to each line in the borders, spacing the lines 1½" apart.

Secret Gardens

Daisy, tulip, and lily of the valley prints line the paths of this garden quilt. A simple Star block combined with a Garden Patch Block creates the suggestion of secret pathways winding from star to star across the surface of this beautiful quilt made in delicate shades of peach and green.

Dimensions: *84" x 108"*

35 blocks, each 12" square
(18 Star blocks and 17
Garden Patch blocks),
set 5 across and 7 down;
2"-wide inner border;
1"-wide middle border;
9"-wide outer border

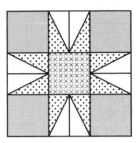

Star Block

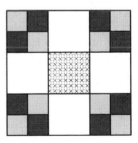

Garden Patch Block

Materials: *44"-wide fabric*

Yardages listed are generous and are based on 44"-wide fabric that has been preshrunk. Strips cut across the fabric width should measure at least 42", as shown in the strip dimensions in the cutting chart.

- ☐ 2½ yds. white print for background
- ▨ 1¾ yds. light green for squares
- ■ ¾ yd. dark green for squares
- ⬚ 1⅓ yds. assorted peaches for stars (Each piece must be at least 10" x 42".)
- ▨ ⅝ yd. floral print for block centers
- ■ ⅝ yd. dark green for inner border
- ⬚ ⅜ yd. peach for middle border
- ▨ 2⅔ yds. floral print for outer border
- ¾ yd. peach for binding
- 6¼ yds. fabric of your choice for backing
- Batting and thread to finish

Cutting

All rotary-cutting dimensions include ¼"-wide seam allowances. Cut the bias strips for the bias rectangles first, following the directions below, and set aside any remaining fabric. Construct the bias rectangles and set aside. Then cut all remaining pieces as directed in the cutting chart. Some strips will not require additional cuts at this time so no directions appear in the second column.

Bias Rectangles

From the white background print, cut 4 pieces of fabric, each 10" x 42".

From the assorted peaches for stars, cut 4 pieces of fabric, each 10" x 42".

Using these fabric pieces, follow the directions on pages 155–59, cutting the strips 3" wide, the strip-pieced segments 4½" wide, and the bias rectangles 2½" x 4½". You will need a total of 144 bias rectangles for the stars, 72 with peach on the left and 72 with peach on the right (Diagram 40).

Make 72.   Make 72.

Diagram 40

| Fabric | FIRST CUT | | ADDITIONAL CUTS | |
	No. of Strips	Dimensions	No. of Pieces	Dimensions
White Background Print	Garden Patch Blocks			
	8	4½" x 42"	68	4½" x 4½"
Dark Green	9	2½" x 42"		
Light Green	Garden Patch Blocks and Star Blocks			
	9	2½" x 42"		
	8	4½" x 42"	72	4½" x 4½"
Floral Print	Block Centers			
	4	4½" x 42"	35	4½" x 4½"
Dark Green	Inner Border			
	8	2½" x 42"		
Peach	Middle Border			
	8	1½" x 42"		
Floral Print	Outer Border			
	4	9¼" x 96"*		
*Cut strips from the lengthwise grain.				

Directions

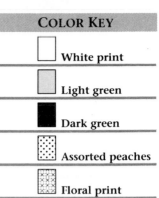

COLOR KEY	
	White print
	Light green
	Dark green
	Assorted peaches
	Floral print

Garden Patch Blocks

1. Sew each of the 2½" x 42" strips of light green to a 2½" x 42" strip of dark green. Press seams toward the dark green strips. Make 9 strip-pieced units. Crosscut the sewn units into 2½"-wide segments, creating two-patch rectangles (Diagram 41).

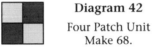

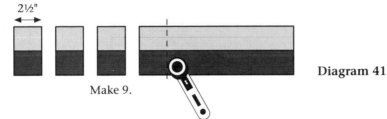

Diagram 41

Make 9.

2. Sew the two-patch rectangles together in pairs as shown in Diagram 42 to create the Four Patch units for the corners of the Garden Patch blocks. Make 68 Four Patch units.

Diagram 42
Four Patch Unit
Make 68.

3. Assemble 17 Garden Patch blocks, following the piecing diagram (Diagram 43).

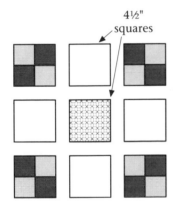

4½"
squares

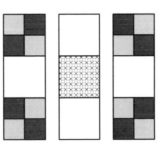

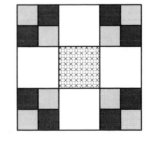

Diagram 43

Piecing Diagram
Garden Patch Block
Make 17.

Star Blocks

1. Sew pairs of the peach-and-white bias rectangles together along the long white side (Diagram 44). Press the seams open. You will need 72 pieced rectangle units.

Diagram 44

Sew bias rectangles
together in pairs.
Make 72.

2. Follow the piecing diagram to complete each of the 18 Star blocks (Diagram 45).

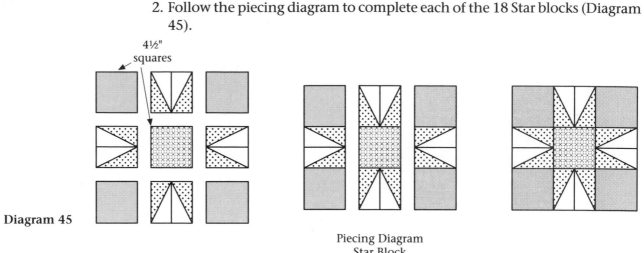

Diagram 45

Piecing Diagram
Star Block
Make 18.

Quilt Top Assembly

1. Sew the blocks together in rows of 5 blocks each (Diagram 46).

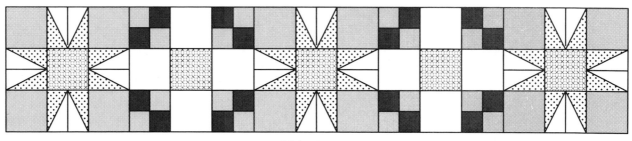

Make 4 rows.

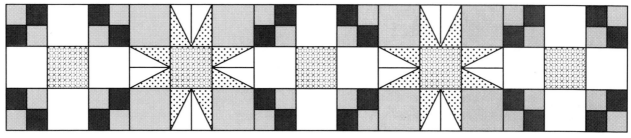

Make 3 rows.

Diagram 46

2. Sew the rows together, referring to the quilt plan on page 171.

Borders

1. Piece together the 2½"-wide dark green strips for the inner borders. Measure the quilt for borders as shown on page 46. Trim the inner side border strips to correct length and stitch first to the sides of the quilt top. Press seams toward the borders. Then add the top and bottom dark green borders to fit, and stitch to the quilt top. Press seams toward the borders.

2. Measure the quilt top and piece the middle borders from the 1½"-wide peach strips. Stitch to the sides and then to the top and bottom edges of the quilt top. Repeat with the 9¼"-wide outer floral print border strips.

Quilt Finishing

1. Layer the quilt top with batting and backing; baste.

2. Quilt in the design of your choice, or follow the Quilting Suggestion.

3. From the peach fabric for the binding, cut and piece 384" of 2½"-wide bias for binding, following the directions on pages 52–53. Bind the quilt edges.

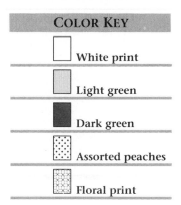

COLOR KEY	
	White print
	Light green
	Dark green
	Assorted peaches
	Floral print

Quilting Suggestion

- Outline quilt in the background areas of the blocks ¼" and ½" from the seams and ½" inside the floral squares.
- Outline quilt ¼" inside the star points, inside the large squares in the Star blocks, and inside the large and small squares of the Garden Patch blocks.
- In the border, quilt parallel diagonal lines 1½" apart as shown.

Water Music

The softly curved patterns flowing across the surface of this quilt are reflected in the rippling movement of the background fabric and in the waving blue leaves in the fabric used for the "chain" that connects the blocks. The illusion of curves is created where the tips of the thin triangles in the Star blocks join the points of the wide triangles in the Snowball blocks.

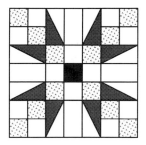

Star Block

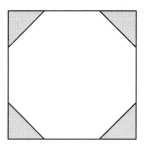

Snowball Block

Dimensions: *70" x 91"*

35 blocks, each 10½"
square (18 Star blocks and
17 Snowball blocks),
set 5 across and 7 down;
2¼"-wide inner border;
¾"-wide middle border;
5¾"-wide outer border

Materials: *44"-wide fabric*

Yardages listed are generous and are based on 44"-wide fabric that has been preshrunk. Strips cut across the fabric width should measure at least 42", as shown in the strip dimensions in the cutting chart.

- ☐ 3½ yds. light background print
- ▨ ¾ yd. navy for triangles
- ▨ ⅝ yd. blue print for squares
- ■ ⅛ yd. magenta for squares
- ▨ ⅝ yd. pastel blue for snowball triangles
- ▨ ⅝ yd. blue print for inner border
- ▬ ⅓ yd. magenta for middle border
- ▬ 1⅓ yds. navy for outer border
- 5⅓ yds. fabric of your choice for backing
- ⅝ yd. navy for binding
- Batting and thread to finish

Cutting

All rotary-cutting dimensions include ¼"-wide seam allowances. Cut the bias strips for the bias rectangles first, following the directions below, and set aside any remaining fabric. Construct the bias rectangles and set aside. Then cut all remaining pieces as directed in the cutting chart. Some strips will not require additional cuts at this time so no directions appear in the second column.

Bias Rectangles

From the light background print, cut 2 pieces of fabric, each 12" x 42".

From the navy for triangles, cut 2 pieces of fabric, each 12" x 42".

Using these fabric pieces, follow the directions on pages 155–59, cutting the strips 2½" wide, the strip-pieced segments 3½" wide, and the bias rectangles 2" x 3½". You will need a total of 144 bias rectangles, 72 with navy on the left and 72 with navy on the right (Diagram 47).

Make 72.   Make 72.

Diagram 47

COLOR KEY	
□	Light background print
■	Navy
▨	Blue print
■	Magenta
□	Pastel blue

Fabric	FIRST CUT		ADDITIONAL CUTS	
	No. of Strips	Dimensions	No. of Pieces	Dimensions
Light Background Print	Snowball Blocks			
	6	11" x 42"	17	11" x 11"
Pastel Blue	6	3½" x 42"	68	3½" x 3½"
Light Background Print	Star Blocks			
	17*	2" x 42"	72	2" x 3½"
	*Set aside 11 strips for Star block units.			
Blue Print	11	2" x 42"		
Magenta	2	2" x 42"		
Blue Print	Inner Border			
	8	2¾" x 42"		
Magenta	Middle Border			
	8	1¼" x 42"		
Navy	Outer Border			
	8	6" x 42"		

Directions

Star Blocks

1. Sew each of 7 of the 2" x 42" light background strips to a 2" x 42" strip of the blue print. Crosscut the sewn units into 2"-wide segments, creating 144 two-patch rectangles (Diagram 48).

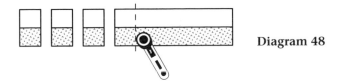

Diagram 48

2. Sew the two-patch rectangle pairs together to create 72 Four Patch units for the corners of the Star blocks (Diagram 49).

Diagram 49
Four Patch Unit
Make 72.

3. Make two strip-pieced units, each made of 2 blue print 2" x 42" strips and 1 light background 2" x 42" strip. From these 2 units, crosscut 36 segments, each 2" wide (Diagram 50).

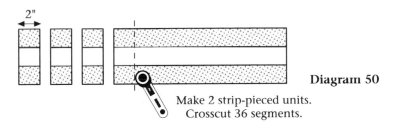

2"

Diagram 50

Make 2 strip-pieced units.
Crosscut 36 segments.

4. Sew 2 light background strips, each 2" x 42", to a 2" x 42" magenta strip. Crosscut 18 segments, each 2" wide (Diagram 51).

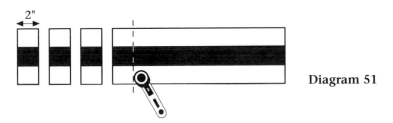

2"

Diagram 51

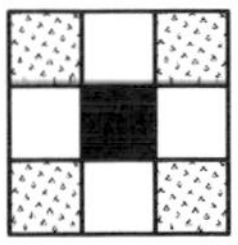

5. Stitch the three-patch segments together, creating 18 Ninepatch units (Diagram 52).

6. Assemble 18 Star blocks, following the piecing diagram (Diagram 53).

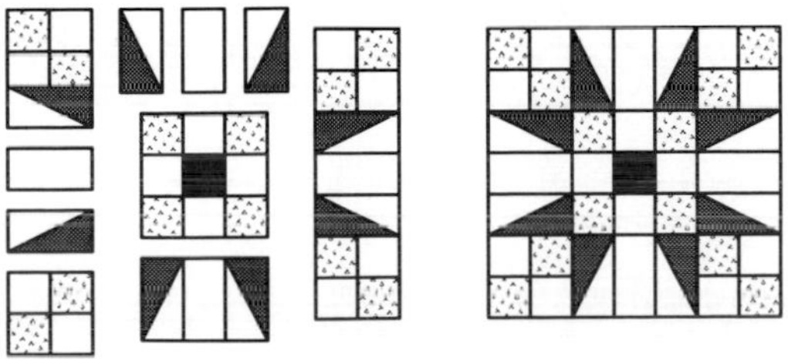

Diagram 52
Ninepatch Unit
Make 18.

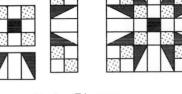

Diagram 53

Piecing Diagram
Star Block
Make 18.

Snowball Blocks

Assemble 17 Snowball blocks, using the pastel blue 3½" squares and the 11" light background squares.

Right side of square

Diagram 54

For each block, repeat steps 1–4:

1. Fold 4 of the 3½" pastel blue squares in half on the diagonal, wrong sides together (Diagram 54). Press a crease along each fold.

2. Open out the pressed squares and place one on each corner of an 11" background square with right sides together. Stitch on each crease (Diagram 55).

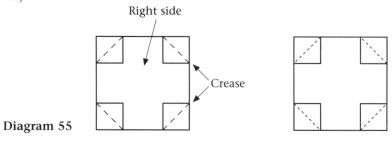

Right side

Crease

Diagram 55

3. Trim corners ¼" from stitching (Diagram 56). Press seams toward the triangle in each corner of the block.

> ### Tip
>
> Before trimming each corner, sew a second row of stitching, ½" from the first row of stitches. Then, cut between the two rows of stitching. The cut-away triangle shapes at each corner are actually small bias squares, which you can save for future quilting projects.
>
> Rows of stitching ½" apart
>
> Cut between rows of stitching.

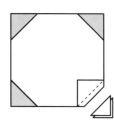

Diagram 56

Trim corners.

Snowball Block
Make 17.

Quilt Top Assembly

1. Sew the blocks together in rows of 5 blocks each, alternating the Star and Snowball blocks as shown in Diagram 57.

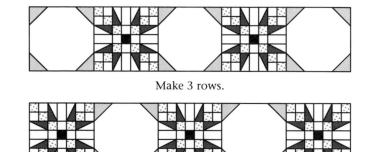

Make 3 rows.

Diagram 57

Make 4 rows.

2. Sew the rows together, referring to the quilt plan on page 177.

Borders

1. Piece together the 2¾"-wide blue print border strips for the inner borders. Measure the quilt top for borders as shown on page 46. Trim the inner side borders to correct length and stitch first to the sides of the quilt top. Press seams toward the borders. Then add the top and bottom blue print borders to fit and stitch to the quilt top. Press seams toward the borders.

2. Measure the quilt top and piece the middle borders from the 1¼"-wide magenta strips. Stitch to the sides and then to the top and bottom edges of the quilt top. Repeat with the 6"-wide navy outer border strips.

Quilt Finishing

1. Layer the quilt top with batting and backing; baste.

2. Quilt in the design of your choice, or follow the Quilting Suggestion.

3. From the navy fabric for binding, cut and piece 322" of 2½"-wide bias for binding, following the directions on pages 52–53. Bind the quilt edges.

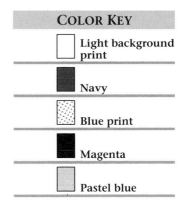

COLOR KEY	
▢	Light background print
▨	Navy
▤	Blue print
■	Magenta
▨	Pastel blue

Quilting Suggestion

- Outline quilt ¼" inside the shapes in the Star blocks and inside the Snowball triangles.
- Quilt a feathered wreath in the background areas of the Snowball blocks.
- Use a small cable in the inner border and stitch ¼" inside the middle border seams.
- Quilt a large cable in the outer border as shown.

Woodland Cottages

Building a house or cabin was the first task early settlers faced. A home provided safety, warmth, and permanence for families struggling to cope with nature and separation from their homeland. The image of a house became identified with the circle of the family and community. The houses in this quilt, made of bias rectangles and fabric strips, are clustered in a circle of protecting trees.

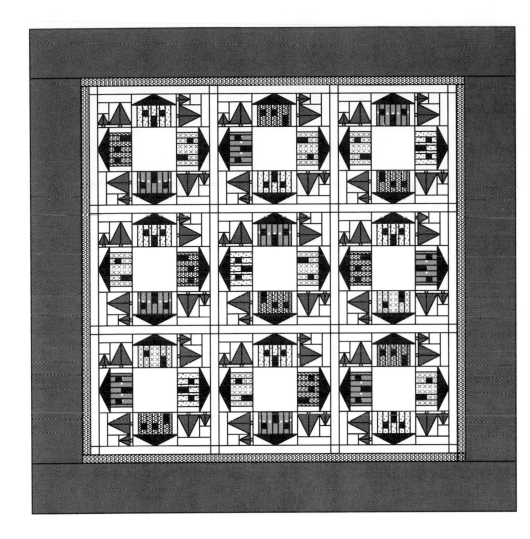

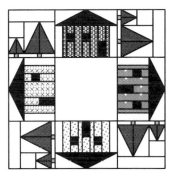

Woodland Cottage Block

Dimensions: 90" x 90"

9 blocks, each 20" square (and each containing 4 houses, 4 small trees, and 4 large trees), set 3 across and 3 down; 2"-wide sashing; 2"-wide inner border and 9"-wide outer border

Materials: 44"-wide fabric

Yardages listed are generous and are based on 44"-wide fabric that has been preshrunk. Strips cut across the fabric width should measure at least 42", as shown in the strip dimensions in the cutting chart.

Note: Solids or non-directional prints are the most suitable fabrics for the houses. Also, if you want to use several different backgrounds, be sure that four of them each measure 10" x 42" for strip piecing.

- ☐ 4 yds. assorted beiges for background or 3⅝ yds. if using only one beige
- ■ ⅝ yd. black for roofs
- ▨ ⅝ yd. green print for large trees
- ▦ ¼ yd. green print for small trees
- ▩ ⅓ yd. red for houses
- ▨ ⅓ yd. light green for houses
- ▦ ⅓ yd. dark green for houses
- ▨ ⅓ yd. blue for houses
- ■ ⅓ yd. black for windows and doors
- ▨ ⅛ yd. brown for tree trunks
- ▦ ⅔ yd. red for inner border
- ▨ 2⅝ yds. green print for outer border
- ¾ yd. green print for binding
- 6 yds. fabric of your choice for backing
- Batting and thread to finish

Cutting

COLOR KEY

☐ Assorted beiges

■ Black

■ Green print (large trees)

■ Green print (small trees)

▨ Red

▨ Light green

▨ Dark green

▨ Blue

▨ Brown

All rotary-cutting dimensions include ¼"-wide seam allowances. Cut the bias strips for the bias rectangles first, following the directions below, and set aside any remaining fabric. Construct the bias rectangles and set aside. Then cut all remaining pieces as directed in the cutting chart. Some strips will not require additional cuts at this time so no directions appear in the second column.

Bias Rectangles

From the beige background fabric, cut 4 pieces of fabric, each 10" x 42", and 1 piece, 9" x 42".

From the black roof fabric, cut 2 pieces of fabric, each 10" x 42".

From the green for large trees, cut 2 pieces of fabric, each 10" x 42".

From the green for small trees, cut 1 piece of fabric, 9" x 42".

Using the 10"-wide fabric pieces, follow the directions on pages 155–59, cutting the strips 3" wide, the strip-pieced segments 4½" wide, and the bias rectangles 2½" x 4½". You will need a total of 72 beige/black bias rectangles for the roofs and 72 beige/green bias rectangles for the large trees (Diagram 58).

Diagram 58   Make 36.   Make 36.   Make 36.   Make 36.

Make 36.   Make 36.

Diagram 59

Using the 9"-wide fabric pieces of beige and green, cut the strips 2" wide, the strip-pieced segments 2½" wide, and the bias rectangles 1½" x 2½". You will need a total of 72 bias rectangles for the small trees (Diagram 59).

Fabric	FIRST CUT		ADDITIONAL CUTS	
	No. of Strips	Dimensions	No. of Pieces	Dimensions
Blue	Houses			
	4	1½" x 42"		
	2	2½" x 42"		
Red, Light Green, Dark Green	Cut the following from each of the 3 House fabrics. For speedier cutting, layer the 3 fabrics and cut all strips at once.			
	2	1" x 42"		
	3	1½" x 42"		
	1	2½" x 42"		

(CONTINUED)

Cutting (CONTINUED)

Fabric	FIRST CUT		ADDITIONAL CUTS	
	No. of Strips	Dimensions	No. of Pieces	Dimensions
Black	Windows			
	4	1½" x 42"		
Black	Doors			
	2	2½" x 42"		
Brown	Tree Trunks			
	2	1" x 42"		
Assorted Beiges	Background Strip on Each Side of Each House			
	8	1½" x 42"		
	Piece #1 in Tree Section of House Blocks			
	6	2" x 42"	36	2" x 6½"
	Piece #2 in Tree Section of House Blocks			
	2	2½" x 42"	36*	2½" x 2½"
	*Cut 2 of these squares from leftover scraps of beige, as you cannot cut all 36 from 2 strips.			
	Background Spaces between Tree Trunks			
	1	1¼" x 42"		
	1	3" x 42"		
	1	2¼" x 42"		
	Sashing and Set Squares			
	13	2" x 42"	24	2" x 20½"
			16	2" x 2"
Assorted Beiges	Center Squares in House Blocks			
	2	8½" x 42"	9*	8½" x 8½"
	*Cut one of these squares from scrap if you cannot get all 9 from the 2 strips. If you would rather make each of the block centers from 4 quarter-square triangles, cut 9 squares, each 9¼" x 9¼". Layer the squares into two piles and cut twice diagonally for a total of 36 triangles. Then join 4 triangles to make each of the 9 center squares required.			
Red	Inner Border			
	8	2½" x 42"		
Green Print	Outer Border			
	4	9¼" x 94"*		
	*Cut strips from the lengthwise grain.			

Large Tree
Make 36.

Small Tree
Make 36.

Diagram 60

Directions

Tree Sections

1. Sew 36 pairs of bias rectangles together for the large trees as shown in Diagram 60. Repeat with 36 pairs of bias rectangles for the small trees.

2. Sew a 2½" background square (Piece #2), to the top of each small tree; then sew each small tree unit to a large tree and press the seam toward the large tree. Sew a 2" x 6½" background strip (Piece #1) to the top of each pair of trees (Diagram 61).

Tree Sections
Make 36.

Diagram 61

3. To form the tree trunk segments, sew strips together as shown in Diagram 62. Press all seams toward the brown strips. Crosscut the strip-pieced unit into 36 tree trunk segments, each 1" wide.

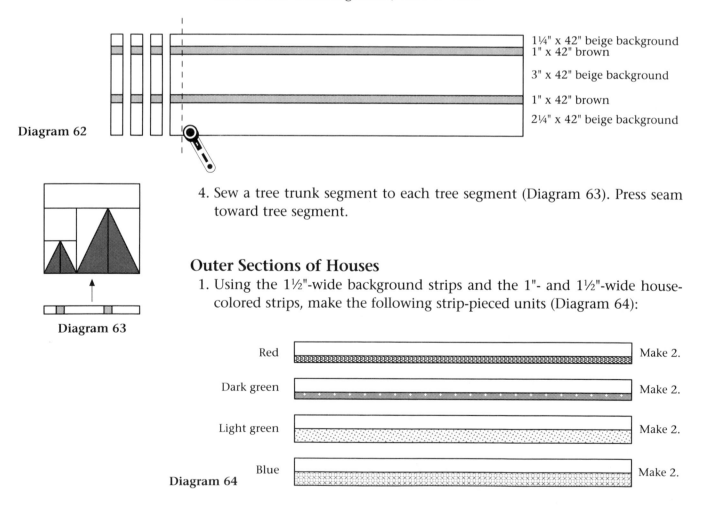

1¼" x 42" beige background
1" x 42" brown

3" x 42" beige background

1" x 42" brown

2¼" x 42" beige background

Diagram 62

4. Sew a tree trunk segment to each tree segment (Diagram 63). Press seam toward tree segment.

Diagram 63

Outer Sections of Houses

1. Using the 1½"-wide background strips and the 1"- and 1½"-wide house-colored strips, make the following strip-pieced units (Diagram 64):

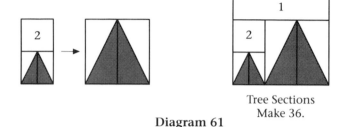

Red — Make 2.

Dark green — Make 2.

Light green — Make 2.

Blue — Make 2.

Diagram 64

2. Layer the strip-pieced units in stacks of 4 to 6 each and crosscut into 4½"-long segments (Diagram 65).

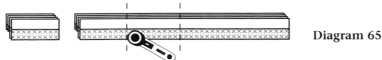

Diagram 65

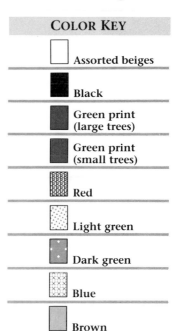

3. Layer the following strips and cut them into 4½"-long segments, 36 of each color:

　　2 red strips, each 1" x 42"　　　　2 blue strips, 1½" x 42"

　　2 dark green strips, each 1" x 42"　　2 light green strips, each 1" x 42"

4. Sort the segments into groups by color.

House Sections with Windows and Doors

1. Layer 1 strip, 1½" x 42", of each house color and crosscut into 2 sections, one 14" long and one 28" long.

2. Layer 1 strip, 2½" x 42", of each house color and cut into 2 sections, one 14" long and one 28" long.

3. Layer the black window strips and the black door strips and cut into 2 sections, one 14" long and one 28" long.

4. From each of the house colors, strip piece a unit as shown. Crosscut into 1½"-wide segments (Diagram 66).

1½"

1½" x 28" house color
1½" x 28" black
2½" x 28" house color

Diagram 66

5. From each of the house colors, strip piece a unit as shown. Crosscut into 1½"-wide pieces (Diagram 67).

1½"

2½" x 14" black

2½" x 14" house color

Diagram 67

House Block Assembly

1. Arrange the strip-pieced units for each color house on your work surface as shown in Diagram 68.

2. Sew the strip-pieced units together to form the base of only one house. Since the roof section of the house has only one vertical seam and the base of the house has eight vertical seams, there is a possibility that the house will be a little wider or narrower than the roof section.

Diagram 68

After you have sewn the base of one house, check to see if it will fit your roof sections. If it is too wide or too narrow, adjust the size of the seam allowances to make the base of the house fit the roof section. After adjusting seams so that the bases fit the roofs, sew all of the house bases.

3. Sew a roof to each house (Diagram 69).

Diagram 69

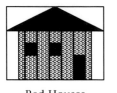

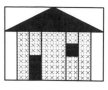

Red Houses
Make 9.

Dark Green Houses
Make 9.

Light Green Houses
Make 9.

Blue Houses
Make 9.

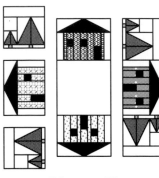

Diagram 70

Piecing Diagram
House Block
Make 9.

4. To assemble the House blocks, refer to the color photo on page 182 and arrange each block with 1 house of each color, 4 tree units, and 1 large background square (8½" x 8½"). Sew blocks together, following the piecing diagram (Diagram 70).

Quilt Top Assembly

1. Sew the blocks together in 3 rows of 3 blocks each, with sashing strips and set squares as shown in Diagram 71.

Set squares

Sashing

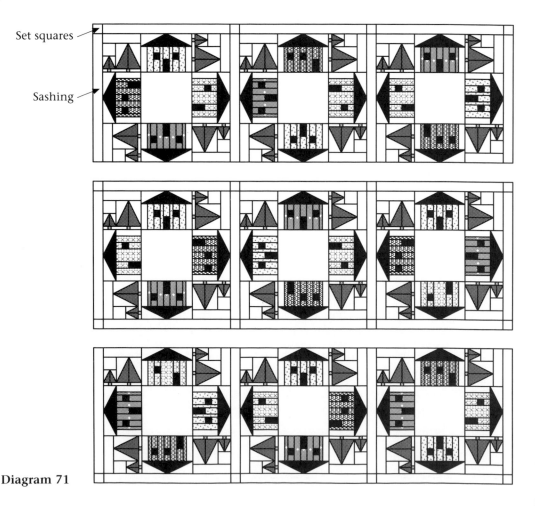

Diagram 71

2. Sew the rows together, referring to the quilt plan on page 183.

referring to the quilt plan on page 183.

Borders

1. Piece together the 2½"-wide red border strips for the inner border. Measure the quilt top for borders as shown on page 46. Trim the 2½"-wide red border strips to correct length and stitch first to the sides of the quilt top. Press seams toward the borders. Then add border strips, trimmed to the correct length to the top and bottom. Press seams toward the borders.

2. Piece together the 9¼"-wide green strips for the outer border. Trim to correct length after measuring the quilt top for borders as you did in step 1. Stitch to the sides of the quilt top first. Press seams toward the borders. Then add border strips, trimmed to the correct length, to the top and bottom. Press seams toward the borders.

Quilt Finishing

1. Layer the quilt top with batting and backing; baste.

2. Quilt in the design of your choice, or follow the Quilting Suggestion.

3. From the green print for the binding, cut and piece 360" of 2½"-wide bias for binding, following the directions on pages 52–53. Bind the quilt edges.

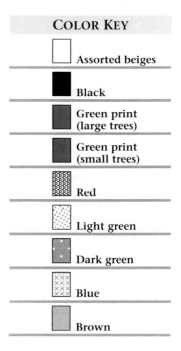

COLOR KEY	
	Assorted beiges
	Black
	Green print (large trees)
	Green print (small trees)
	Red
	Light green
	Dark green
	Blue
	Brown

Quilting Suggestion

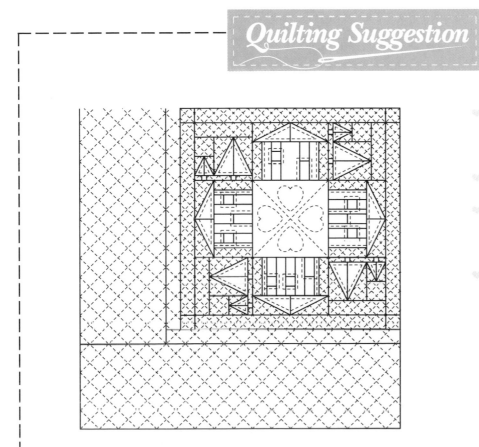

- Outline quilt ¼" from the seams inside the sides of the houses, roofs, and trees, and outside the windows and doors.
- Use a four-heart design in the area between the houses.
- Stitch a 1" diagonal grid in the background spaces around houses and trees and between the blocks.
- Stitch a 2" diagonal grid in the borders.

Raven Dance

Every spring the Indians of the Queen Charlotte Islands in Canada hold a ceremony during which they perform a hauntingly beautiful dance to the ancient rhythms of their shallow drums. This quilt, with black pinwheels twisting to the left and red pinwheels twirling to the right, pays homage to their beautiful Raven Dance. The black pinwheels in the center of each block are formed with bias squares and bias rectangles. Red pinwheels form where the red triangles in the corners of the blocks meet the triangles of neighboring blocks.

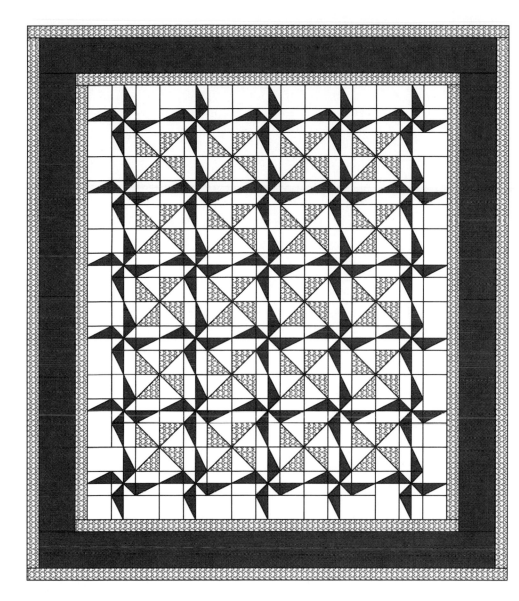

Dimensions: *80" x 92"*

30 blocks, each 12"
square, set side by side,
5 across and 6 down;
2"-wide inner border;
6"-wide middle border;
2"-wide outer border

Pinwheel I Block

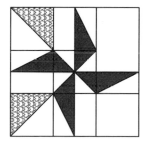

Pinwheel II Block

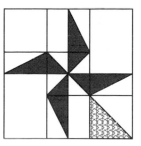

Pinwheel III Block

Materials: *44"-wide fabric*

Yardages listed are generous and are based on 44"-wide fabric that has been preshrunk. Strips cut across the fabric width should measure at least 42", as shown in the strip dimensions in the cutting chart.

- ☐ 4½ yds. tan for background
- ■ 1⅜ yds. black for bias squares and bias rectangles
- ▨ 1¼ yds. red for bias squares
- ▨ 1¼ yds. red for inner and outer borders
- ■ 1½ yds. black for middle border
- 5¼ yds. fabric of your choice for backing
- ⅝ yd. red for binding
- Batting and thread to finish

Cutting

COLOR KEY

☐ Tan

■ Black

▨ Red

All rotary-cutting dimensions include ¼"-wide seam allowances. Cut the bias strips for the bias rectangles first, following the directions below, and set aside any remaining fabric. Construct the bias rectangles and set aside. Then cut all remaining pieces as directed in the cutting chart. Some strips will not require additional cuts at this time so no directions appear in the second column.

Make 120.

Diagram 72

Bias Rectangles

From the tan background fabric, cut 3 pieces of fabric, each 10" x 42".

From the black for bias rectangles, cut 3 pieces of fabric, each 10" x 42".

Using these fabric pieces, follow the directions on pages 155–59, cutting the strips 3" wide, the strip-pieced segments 4½" wide, and the bias rectangles 2½" x 4½". Cut all strips with both fabrics face up. Do not fold the fabrics. You will need a total of 120 bias rectangles with black on the left (Diagram 72).

Bias Squares

From the tan background fabric, cut 2 pieces of fabric, each 12" x 42".

From the black for bias squares, cut 2 pieces of fabric, each 12" x 42".

Make 120.

Diagram 73

Using these fabric pieces, follow the directions on pages 155–59, cutting the strips 2½" wide, the strip-pieced segments 2½" wide, and the bias squares 2½" x 2½". You will need a total of 120 bias squares, each 2½" x 2½" (Diagram 73).

From the tan background fabric, cut 3 pieces of fabric, each 10" x 42".

From the red for bias squares, cut 3 pieces of fabric, each 10" x 42".

Make 80.

Diagram 74

Using these fabric pieces, follow the directions on pages 155–59, cutting the strips 4½" wide, the strip-pieced segments 4½" wide, and the bias squares 4½" x 4½". You will need a total of 80 bias squares, each 4½" x 4½" (Diagram 74).

Fabric	FIRST CUT		ADDITIONAL CUTS	
	No. of Strips	Dimensions	No. of Pieces	Dimensions
Tan Background	Pinwheel Blocks			
	11	2½" x 42"	98	2½" x 4½"
	2	4½" x 42"	18	4½" x 4½"
	4	4½" x 42"	22	4½" x 6½"
Red	Inner and Outer Borders			
	8	2½" x 42"		
	8	2¼" x 42"		
Black	Middle Border			
	8	6½" x 42"		

Directions

Pinwheel Blocks

1. Sew the black/tan bias squares together to create the black center pinwheels (Diagram 75). Press the seams open for easier construction.

2. Sew each of the tan 2½" x 4½" rectangles to the long black edge of a black/tan bias rectangle (Diagram 76). You will have 22 bias rectangles left over to use in step 4, below.

Diagram 75
Pinwheel Unit
Make 30.

Diagram 76
Bias Rectangle Unit
Make 98.

3. Sew a bias rectangle unit to opposite sides of each pinwheel unit (Diagram 77).

4. Using the remaining bias rectangles, bias squares, cut pieces, and bias rectangle units, assemble 12 Pinwheel I blocks as shown in Diagram 78, 14 Pinwheel II blocks as shown in Diagram 79, and 4 Pinwheel III blocks as shown in Diagram 80.

Diagram 77
Make 30.

Diagram 78
Piecing Diagram
Pinwheel I Block
Make 12.

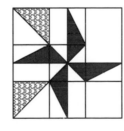

Diagram 79
Piecing Diagram
Pinwheel II Block
Make 14.

Diagram 80
Piecing Diagram
Pinwheel III Block
Make 4.

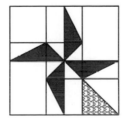

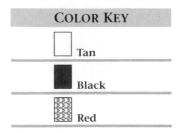

COLOR KEY

Tan

Black

Red

Quilt Top Assembly

1. Sew the blocks together in rows as shown in Diagram 81.

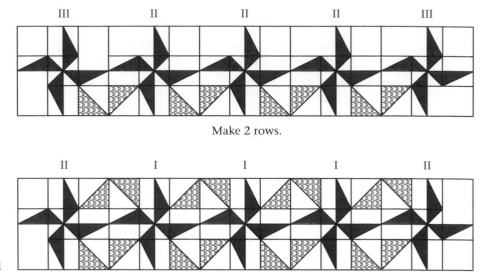

Diagram 81

2. Sew the rows together, referring to the quilt plan on page 191.

Borders

1. Piece together the 2½"-wide red strips for the inner border. Measure the quilt top for borders as shown on page 46. Trim the border strips to correct length and stitch first to the sides of the quilt top. Press seams toward the borders. Then add border strips, trimmed to the correct length, to the top and bottom. Press seams toward the borders.

2. Measure the quilt top and add the 6½"-wide black strips for the middle border as described in step 1, stitching them to the sides of the quilt top first and then to the top and bottom.

3. Repeat with the 2¼"-wide red strips for the outer border.

Quilt Finishing

1. Layer the quilt top with batting and backing; baste.

2. Quilt in the design of your choice, or follow the Quilting Suggestion.

3. From the binding fabric, cut and piece 344" of 2½"-wide bias for binding, following the directions on pages 52–53. Bind the quilt edges.

Quilting Suggestion

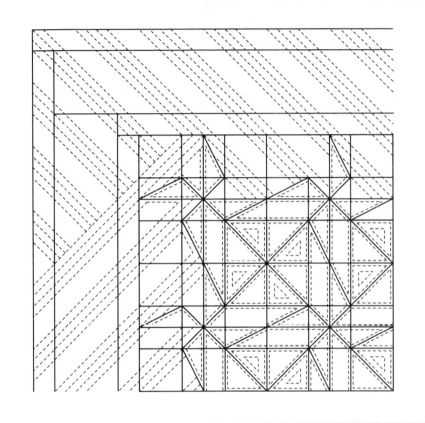

- Outline quilt in the red/tan bias squares ¼" and ¾" from the seams.
- Outline quilt in the background areas surrounding the black pinwheels as shown.
- Quilt diagonally in parallel rows spaced 1" apart, extending the quilting into the borders as shown.

Summer's End

The fragrance of the last roses on the trellis, the gentle creaking of the porch swing, and the soft warmth of the September sun are enchanting visions created by this lovely quilt. Occasionally, the dynamic elements of a quilt design occur in the sashing rather than in the blocks. In Summer's End, two simple blocks, one pieced and one unpieced, are separated by triangular sashing pieces that produce a lovely rhythm.

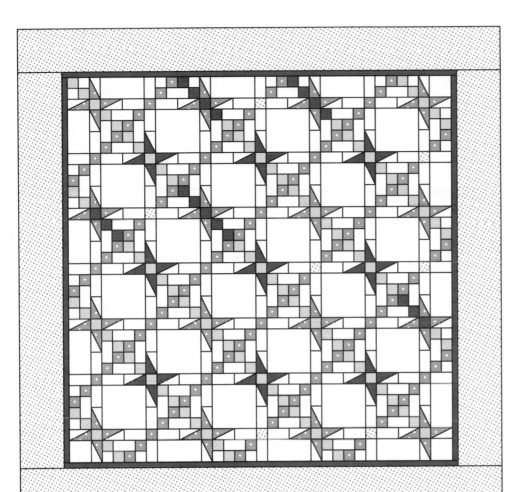

Materials: *44"-wide fabric*

Yardages listed are generous and are based on 44"-wide fabric that has been preshrunk. Strips cut across the fabric width should measure at least 42", as shown in the strip dimensions in the cutting chart.

- ☐ 3¾ yds. light pink for background
- ▦ ⅔ yd. red for triangles
- ■ ⅓ yd. dark purple for triangles
- ▨ ⅔ yd. red for squares
- ☐ ⅔ yd. light purple for squares
- ■ ⅜ yd. dark purple for inner border
- ▦ 2½ yds. floral print for outer border
- ¾ yd. floral print for binding
- 6 yds. fabric of your choice for backing
- Batting and thread to finish

Dimensions: *88" x 88"*

18 Stepping Stone blocks and 18 unpieced blocks, each 8" square, set 6 across and 6 down; 2"-wide, pieced sashing strips; blocks and sashing surrounded by half blocks; 1"-wide inner border; 8"-wide outer border

Stepping Stone Block

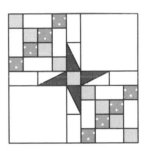

Stepping Stone Blocks with Alternate Blocks, Sashing, and Set Squares

Cutting

> All rotary-cutting dimensions include ¼"-wide seam allowances. Cut the bias strips for the bias rectangles first, following the directions below, and set aside any remaining fabric. Construct the bias rectangles and set aside. Then cut all remaining pieces as directed in the cutting chart. Some strips will not require additional cuts at this time so no directions appear in the second column.

Bias Rectangles

From the light pink background, cut 3 pieces of fabric, each 10" x 42".

From the red for triangles, cut 2 pieces of fabric, each 10" x 42".

From the dark purple for triangles, cut 1 piece of fabric, 10" x 42".

Using these fabric pieces, follow the directions on pages 155–59, cutting the strips 3" wide, the strip-pieced segments 4½" wide, and the bias rectangles 2½" x 4½". Cut all strips with both fabrics face up. Do not fold the fabrics (Diagram 82).

Make 64.   Make 36.

Diagram 82

Fabric	FIRST CUT		ADDITIONAL CUTS	
	No. of Strips	Dimensions	No. of Pieces	Dimensions
Light Pink Background	Unpieced Blocks			
	5	8½" x 42"	18	8½" x 8½"
	Half Blocks			
	5*	4½" x 42"	12**	4½" x 8½"
	*Set aside 3 of these strips for the Stepping Stone blocks. **Cut 4 of these from the large scraps at the end of the strips.			
			2***	4½" x 4½"
	***Cut these from the scraps.			
	2	2½" x 42"	24	2½" x2½"
	Stepping Stone Blocks and Sashing			
	14	2½" x 42"	132*	2½" x 4½"
	*Use 36 for the Stepping Stone blocks and 96 for the sashing.			
Red	Sashing Squares			
	8*	2½" x 42"	24	2½" x2½"
	*Set aside 6 of these strips for the Stepping Stone blocks.			
Light Purple	8**	2½" x 42"	25	2½" x2½"
	**Set aside 6 of these strips for the Stepping Stone blocks.			
Dark Purple	Inner Border			
	8	1½" x 42"		
Floral Print	Outer Border			
	4	8¼" x 90"		

COLOR KEY

☐ Light pink

▨ Red triangles

■ Dark purple

▨ Red squares

▨ Light purple

Directions

Stepping Stone Blocks and Half Blocks

1. Sew 3 red and 3 light purple strips together in pairs. Crosscut the strip-pieced units into 2½"-wide segments, creating 48 two-patch rectangles (Diagram 83).

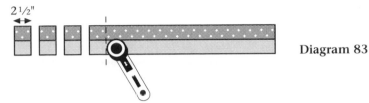

2½"

Diagram 83

2. Sew 36 of the two-patch rectangles together to create 18 Four Patch units (Diagram 84). Set aside 12 of the remaining two-patch rectangles for the half blocks on the outer edges of the quilt.

3. Arrange the Four Patch units in a stack, with a red square in the upper right corner of each Four Patch unit. Stitch a 2½" x 4½" pink rectangle to the top and bottom edges of each Four Patch unit. As you stitch these pieces together, be careful to keep the red in the upper right corner (Diagram 85).

4. Make 3 strip-pieced units, each using one 2½"-wide red strip, one 4½"-wide pink strip, and one 2½"-wide light purple strip (Diagram 86).

Diagram 86

Make 3.

5. Crosscut the strip-pieced units into 2½"-wide segments (Diagram 87). You need 36 for the Stepping Stone blocks and 12 for the half blocks at the outer edge of the quilt.

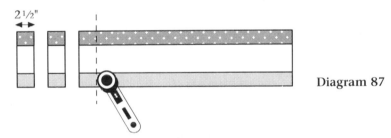

2½"

Diagram 87

6. Assemble 18 Stepping Stone blocks, following the piecing diagram. As you stitch these pieces together, be sure to position the red squares in the upper right and lower left corners (Diagram 88).

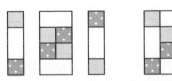

Diagram 88

Piecing Diagram
Stepping Stone Block
Make 18.

7. Assemble 6 of Half Block A and 6 of Half Block B (Diagram 89).

Diagram 84

Four Patch Unit
Make 18.

Red in upper right-hand corner

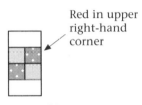

Diagram 85

Half Block A   Half Block B
Make 6.   Make 6.

Diagram 89

Diagram 90
Make 48.

Diagram 91
Make 36.

Sashing Strips

1. Sew 48 pink rectangles to the short pink edge of 48 pink/red bias rectangles (Diagram 90). You should have 16 pink/red bias rectangles remaining to use in the sashing.

2. Sew 36 pink rectangles to the short pink edge of 36 pink/dark purple bias rectangles (Diagram 91).

Quilt Top Assembly

1. Sew the sashing, blocks, half blocks, remaining bias rectangles, and cut pieces together in rows as shown in Diagram 92.

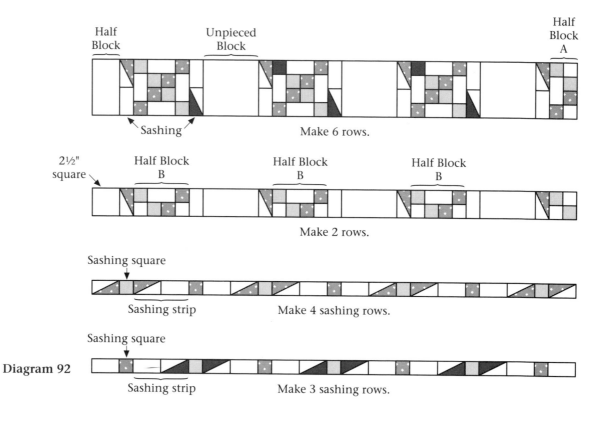

Half
Block

Unpieced
Block

Half
Block
A

Sashing

Make 6 rows.

2½"
square

Half Block
B

Half Block
B

Half Block
B

Make 2 rows.

Sashing square

Sashing strip   Make 4 sashing rows.

Sashing square

Diagram 92

Sashing strip   Make 3 sashing rows.

2. Referring to the quilt plan on page 197, sew the rows together to complete the quilt top.

Borders

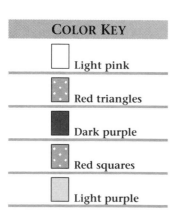

COLOR KEY
☐ Light pink
▨ Red triangles
■ Dark purple
▨ Red squares
▨ Light purple

1. Piece together the 1½"-wide dark purple strips for the inner border. Measure the quilt for borders as shown on page 46. Trim the border strips to correct length and stitch first to the sides of the quilt top. Press seams toward the borders. Then add border strips, trimmed to the correct length, to the top and bottom. Press seams toward the borders.

2. Measure the quilt top and add the 8¼"-wide floral print strips for the outer border as described in step 1, stitching them to the sides first and then to the top and bottom. Press seams toward the borders.

Quilt Finishing

1. Layer the quilt top with batting and backing; baste.

2. Quilt in the design of your choice, or follow the Quilting Suggestion.

3. From the floral print for the binding, cut and piece 352" of 2½"-wide bias for binding, following the directions on pages 52–53. Bind the quilt edges.

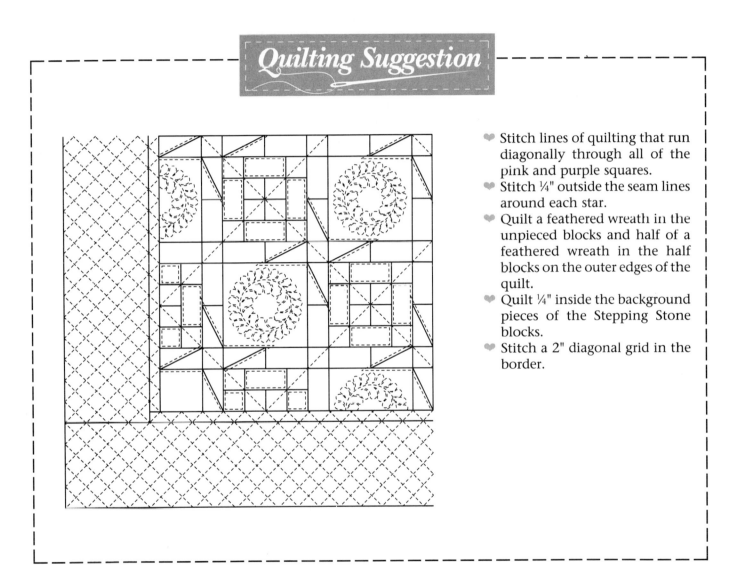

Quilting Suggestion

- Stitch lines of quilting that run diagonally through all of the pink and purple squares.
- Stitch ¼" outside the seam lines around each star.
- Quilt a feathered wreath in the unpieced blocks and half of a feathered wreath in the half blocks on the outer edges of the quilt.
- Quilt ¼" inside the background pieces of the Stepping Stone blocks.
- Stitch a 2" diagonal grid in the border.

Starry Path

Stars, a much-beloved image in quiltmaking, are the focus of this lively quilt.
Forty-nine simple Star blocks take on a complex appearance when their
corners link to produce the illusion of a curving blue trellis where the wide blue
triangles meet the thin blue triangles. Omitting the triangles and Four Patch
units in the outer corners of the blocks in the outside rows makes the stars and
trellis seem to float on the background fabric.

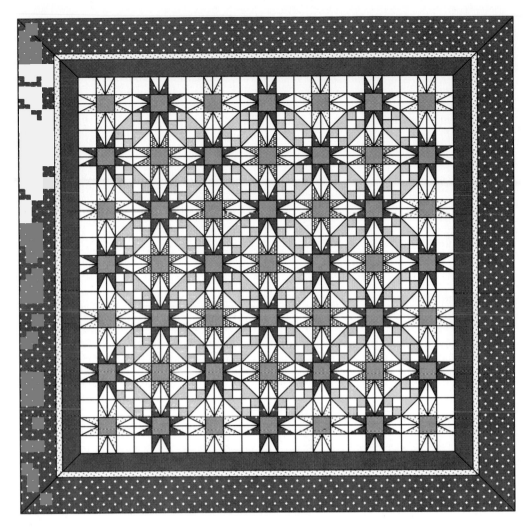

Dimensions: *83½" x 83½"*

49 blocks, each 9" square, set 7 across and 7 down. The pink and blue stars on the outer rows of the quilt have plain corners on their outside edges, and either bias squares or Four Patch units on their inside edges. The 12 blue stars in the center of the quilt have Four Patch units in each corner. The 13 red stars have bias squares in each corner; 3"-wide inner border; 1"-wide middle border; 6¼"-wide outer border. Borders are mitered.

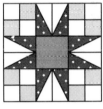

Star I Block

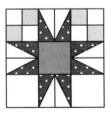

Star II Block

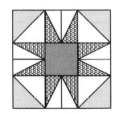

Star III Block

Materials: *44"-wide fabric*

Yardages listed are generous and are based on 44"-wide fabric that has been preshrunk. Strips cut across the fabric width should measure at least 42", as shown in the strip dimensions in the cutting chart.

- ☐ 4⅛ yds. light print for background
- ▪ 1⅛ yds. dark blue for stars
- ▨ ¾ yd. red for stars
- ▨ ¾ yd. pink for stars
- ▨ 1¼ yds. light blue for Four Patch units and bias squares
- ▨ ½ yd. floral print for star centers
- ▪ 1 yd. blue floral for inner border or 2⅛ yds. if using a lengthwise stripe
- ▨ ⅜ yd. pink for middle border
- ▪ 1⅝ yds. dark blue for outer border
- ⅝ yd. blue for binding
- 5 yds. fabric of your choice for backing
- Batting and thread to finish

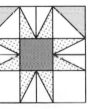

Star IV Block

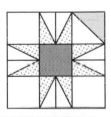

Star V Block

Cutting

COLOR KEY	
□	Light print
▨	Dark blue
▨	Red
▨	Pink
▨	Light blue
▨	Floral print

All rotary-cutting dimensions include ¼"-wide seam allowances. Cut the bias strips for the bias rectangles first, following the directions below, and set aside any remaining fabric. Construct the bias rectangles and set aside. Then cut all remaining pieces as directed in the cutting chart. Some strips will not require additional cuts at this time so no directions appear in the second column.

Bias Rectangles

From the light print, cut 7 pieces of fabric, each 12" x 42".

From the dark blue for stars, cut 3 pieces of fabric, each 12" x 42".

From the red for stars, cut 2 pieces of fabric, each 12" x 42".

From the pink for stars, cut 2 pieces of fabric, each 12" x 42".

Using these fabric pieces, follow the directions on pages 155–59, cutting the strips 2½" wide, the strip-pieced segments 3½" wide, and the bias rectangles 2" x 3½". You will need a total of 192 dark blue/light print bias rectangles, 104 red/light print bias rectangles, and 96 light print/pink bias rectangles (Diagram 93).

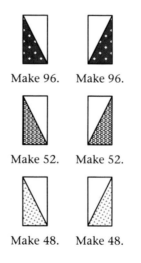

Make 96.   Make 96.

Make 52.   Make 52.

Diagram 93   Make 48.   Make 48.

Bias Squares

From the light print for the background, cut 2 pieces of fabric, each 12" x 42".

From the light blue for the Four Patch units and bias squares, cut 2 pieces of fabric, each 12" x 42".

Using these fabric pieces, follow the directions on pages 155–59, cutting the strips 3½" wide, the strip-pieced segments 3½" wide, and the bias squares 3½" x 3½". You will need a total of 72 bias squares (Diagram 94).

Diagram 94
Make 72.

Fabric	FIRST CUT		ADDITIONAL CUTS	
	No. of Strips	Dimensions	No. of Pieces	Dimensions
Light Print	Star Block Backgrounds			
	5	3½" x 42"	52	3½" x 3½"
	7	2" x 42"		
Floral Print	Star Centers			
	4	3½" x 42"	49*	3½" x 3½"
	*Cut 1 square from scraps if necessary.			
Light Blue	Star Blocks			
	7	2" x 42"		
Blue Floral	Inner Border			
	8	3½" x 42"*		
	*If you are using a striped fabric, cut 4 strips 3½" wide and the length of the fabric (approximately 76").			
Pink	Middle Border			
	8	1½" x 42"		
Dark Blue	Outer Border			
	8	6½" x 42"		

Directions

Star Blocks

1. Sew 196 pairs of bias rectangles together for the stars (Diagram 95).

Diagram 95
Make 196.

2. Sew the 2"-wide light print strips to the 2"-wide light blue strips in pairs. Crosscut the strip-pieced units into 2"-wide segments, creating 144 two-patch rectangles (Diagram 96).

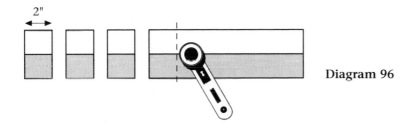

2"

Diagram 96

3. Sew the two-patch rectangles together as shown in Diagram 97. Make 72 Four Patch units.

Diagram 97
Four Patch Unit
Make 72.

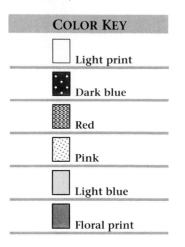

COLOR KEY

Light print

Dark blue

Red

Pink

Light blue

Floral print

4. Assemble 12 blue Star I blocks, following the piecing diagram (Diagram 98). Press the seams toward the outer edges of the blocks.

Diagram 98

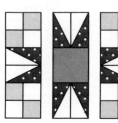
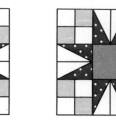

Piecing Diagram
Star I Block
Make 12.

5. Assemble 12 blue Star II blocks, following the piecing diagram (Diagram 99). Press the seams toward the outer edges of the blocks.

Diagram 99

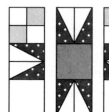
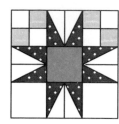

Piecing Diagram
Star II Block
Make 12.

6. Assemble 13 red Star III blocks, following the piecing diagram (Diagram 100). Press the seams toward the centers of the blocks.

Diagram 100

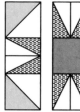
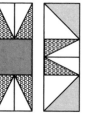
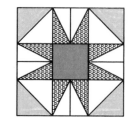

Piecing Diagram
Star III Block
Make 13.

7. Assemble 8 pink Star IV blocks as shown in Diagram 101. Press the seams toward the centers of the blocks.

Diagram 101

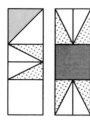
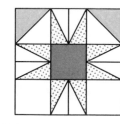

Piecing Diagram
Star IV Block
Make 8.

8. Assemble 4 pink Star V blocks, following the piecing diagram (Diagram 102). Press the seams toward the centers of the blocks.

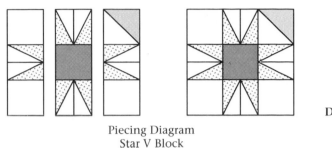

Piecing Diagram
Star V Block
Make 4.

Diagram 102

Quilt Top Assembly

1. Sew the blocks together into rows as shown in Diagram 103.

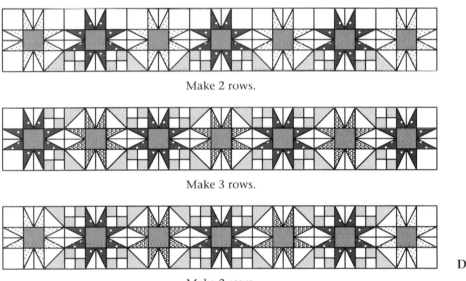

Make 2 rows.

Make 3 rows.

Make 2 rows.

Diagram 103

2. Referring to the quilt plan on page 203, sew the rows together to complete the quilt top.

Borders

1. Piece the 3½"-wide blue floral border strips together to make 4 strips, each 3½" x 84", for the inner border. Repeat with the 1½"-wide pink strips for the middle border and the 6½"-wide dark blue strips for the outer border.

2. Make 4 strip-pieced borders, using 1 each of the inner, middle, and outer borders (Diagram 104).

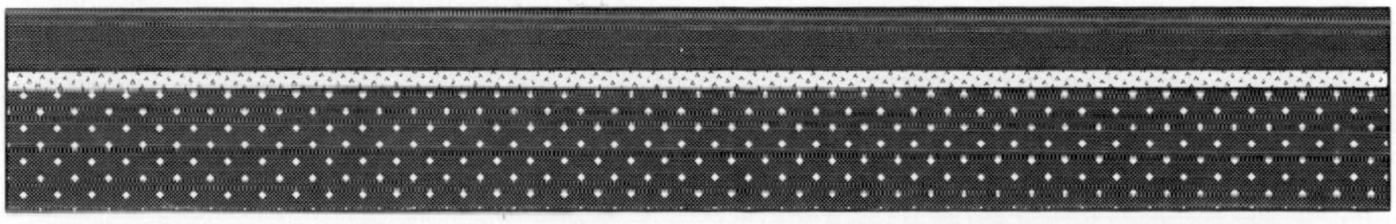

Blue floral (inner)
Pink (middle)

Dark blue (outer)

Diagram 104

3. Stitch the borders to the quilt top, mitering the corners as shown on pages 47–48.

Quilt Finishing

1. Layer the quilt top with batting and backing; baste.

2. Quilt in the design of your choice, or follow the Quilting Suggestion.

3. From the blue for the binding, cut and piece 334" of 2½"-wide bias for binding, following the directions on pages 52–53. Bind the quilt edges.

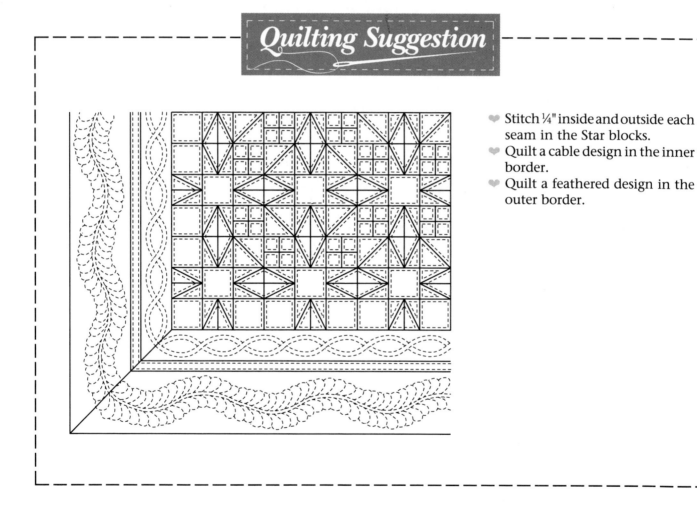

Quilting Suggestion

- Stitch ¼" inside and outside each seam in the Star blocks.
- Quilt a cable design in the inner border.
- Quilt a feathered design in the outer border.

MEET
Sara Nephew
&
HER EQUILATERAL
TRIANGLE QUILTS

I made my first "quilt" from 4" squares of corduroy cut from my daughter Elizabeth's outgrown rompers. That was twenty-five years ago. I never quilted the completed corduroy patchwork, but did use it to add color to Elizabeth's bed. When our family moved to three acres in the country, some of these squares were included in two more corduroy quilts, one with a Blazing Star center and one with a Wild Goose Chase border. I began hand quilting the Star quilt but quickly learned how difficult it is to hand stitch through corduroy. I finished it with machine quilting and tied the second corduroy quilt, which was an even faster and easier way to finish it.

My next venture into quilting was inspired by a book club offer. *The Perfect Patchwork Primer* by Beth Gutcheon was one of the first four books that I ordered. It inspired me to try many different blocks and methods. This experimentation drew me even further into the world of quilting.

Next, I joined a quilt guild, and the monthly exposure to other quiltmakers and their quilts helped me develop my quiltmaking skills so much that when two of our children were getting ready to go off to college, I started a business making and repairing quilts to raise a little extra money.

Soon, I was producing quantities of wall hangings to sell, using miniature Log Cabin blocks. Trying variations of this, I experimented with Log Cabin designs based on diamonds. One day while I was trying to sew 60° Log Cabin diamonds into a star design with set-in seams, I realized the task would be much easier if the diamond shapes were made up of triangles instead.

How exciting it was to discover all kinds of things about the 60° triangle! Quilt designs flew around in my head. I sewed strips together and cut triangles out of them. To make the cutting easier, I taped together two little triangles purchased at a local stationery store and then scratched a series of lines for measuring into the surface. Voila! A new rotary-cutting tool, the Clearview Triangle, was born. Before I knew it, I was teaching classes on my new cutting techniques, and my first book, *Quilts from a Different Angle*, was being published by That Patchwork Place.

The book was an introduction to quilts made with 60° triangles. Since its publication, I have written four more books. *My Mother's Quilts: Designs from the Thirties* was about the fabrics and quilt patterns of the 1930s, when quilting became very popular. *Stars and Flowers: Three-Sided Patchwork* shows how to rotary cut 60° shapes for pieced quilts that look like floral appliqué. *Building Block Quilts* and *Building Block Quilts 2*, my most recent books, are about achieving a three-dimensional look in patchwork, once again using my favorite angles. All of my 60° triangle books are based on easy rotary-cutting techniques.

The result of all my experimentation and teaching is that I have a home-based business centered around my tools and books, which are sold internationally. My teaching takes me to all kinds of interesting places. And I'm having lots of fun piecing and quilting new designs.

I firmly believe that quilting should always be fun. I love using rotary-cutting techniques because they're fast and accurate; before I know it, I can cut and piece a block to see how a design looks in fabric. My specialized cutting techniques using the Clearview Triangle are shown in detail on pages 213–218.

In addition to developing my cutting and piecing methods and tools, I've discovered lots of tricks and tips that might help you as you explore the wonderful world of quiltmaking. As in any other creative medium, it's important to stay open to new ideas and techniques.

For example, when choosing fabrics for a quilt, many quiltmakers agonize over each choice, trying to make all of the colors match and blend. If this sounds like you, give yourself permission to play with color a bit. Even when a quilt relies on shades of a single color, such as Sailing on page 237, the results will be more interesting if you let yourself go a little. When I chose the fabrics for Sailing, I started with blue fabrics printed with nautical designs and aquatic patterns. I made sure to select a variety of values from very light to very dark.

For added interest, I threw in a visual twist by allowing my color choices to slide a little in both directions from the position of blue on the color wheel. Sliding toward red meant I could use a little purple and lavender, and sliding toward yellow added a little blue-green to my choices. Then I really let myself go and added a red accent here and there for sparkle. As you examine the color photo of this quilt, try to imagine it without the purple, blue-green, and red shades. It would be a little boring, to be sure!

Purchase the best materials you can afford. Support your local quilt shop, where you'll find the best fabrics for quilting, plus the assistance you need to get started on your next project. (In addition, I often find wonderful cotton fabrics at garage sales for bargain prices.)

When I'm making a quilt, particularly a large one, the sewing can become tedious. To eliminate boredom, I often divide cutting, sewing, and pressing into bite-size pieces. I cut for awhile, then sew for awhile, then press for awhile. This helps prevent physical aches and pains from doing one thing over and over again for long periods of time, and the work seems to go more quickly. Stop if you get tired because there's a mistake out there just waiting to happen when you're not quite up to par!

It is important to develop good pressing habits. Each quiltmaker develops her own method for accurate pressing. I press with a dry iron, making sure to press each seam in the desired direction, before it is crossed with another seam. When I complete a

TIP

If you really like a fabric, buy more than you will need for a specific project. Having a selection of fabrics on your shelf eliminates emergency shopping trips and the frustration that comes when you underestimate your needs or change your mind midstream and need more fabric, ultimately robbing you of your time to piece and quilt.

block, I place a damp press cloth (an old piece of cotton sheeting or muslin) over the block and press to just dampen the patchwork piece. After removing the damp press cloth, I final press the piece, being careful not to stretch or distort it in any way. I find this method of pressing results in smooth, flat blocks and, ultimately, a smooth, flat quilt top.

Get some distance from your work to examine your progress and to make design changes as you go along. Some quilters work on a wall covered with a piece of fleece, but since I do not have a "quilt wall," I lay my completed blocks on the floor in the desired arrangement and then back away a bit to squint at it. (You can even stand on a chair to get farther away. Just beware of ceiling light fixtures!) Squinting from a distance allows the eye to mix and compare colors, to see the overall pattern of light and dark, and to judge how the design is turning out. Practice makes this easier and easier. You will be amazed at the value of this exercise in training your eye to judge color relationships in your quilts!

As I developed new techniques and wrote my last two books on using 60° shapes to create three-dimensional illusions in my quilts, I learned a lot about color and value. When choosing fabrics for a complex quilt, I now make a color value chart to guide me. Some quilts with three-dimensional illusions require a wide range of colors. To keep track of all the prints and colors, I cut a 1" x 5" strip of each fabric and glue the strips to a piece of lightweight cardboard, placing them in order by value from light to dark. Then I can evaluate the entire group of fabrics chosen, to make sure I have enough lights, mediums, and darks and a pleasing color scheme, making changes as needed before I start to cut the pieces.

If I need additional fabrics that do not exist in my fabric collection, it's easy to carry my color chart to the fabric store so I can choose the perfect fabric(s) to make the quilt "work." And, when all the fabric pieces get tumbled into tangled piles during the cutting and sewing process, the color chart comes in very handy as a reference.

Now it is time to acquaint yourself with my rotary-cutting techniques for 60° shapes. Following the section on cutting my quilts, you will find complete instructions for seven quilts. Among them, I hope you find a quilt that you can hardly wait to piece.

TIP

If you are able, join a quilt guild. The support, encouragement, and inspiration you will receive from other quilters is truly amazing. Show-and-tell sessions are often so exciting that you can hardly wait to get home to start a new quilt!

HOW TO CUT 60° TRIANGLES AND RELATED SHAPES

Grouped for your review on the following pages are cutting methods suitable only for quilts made with 60°-angle shapes. Specific measurements are not given, as these change depending on the scale chosen for the quilt design. Following the cutting directions, I've included some helpful tips to make your quiltmaking adventure worry-free.

The basic rule to remember when cutting 60° triangles is that the width of the fabric strip must equal the height (perpendicular measurement) from the tip to the base of the triangle required (Diagram 1). Therefore, if the quilt directions require a 3" triangle, you would first cut fabric strips 3" wide.

1. Position the tip of the Clearview Triangle at one edge of the fabric strip and the ruled line that marks the triangle measurement given in the pattern at the other edge of the strip. Rotary cut along both sides of the triangle (Diagram 2).

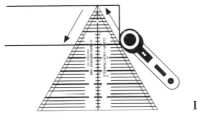

Diagram 2

2. Move the triangle ruler along the bottom edge of the fabric strip to position it for the next cut, which will yield two more 60° triangles (Diagram 3). Continue in this manner until you've reached the end of the strip.

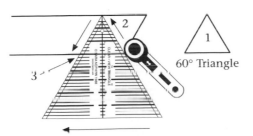

Move triangle ruler along edge of fabric strip. **Diagram 3**

CUTTING 60° TRIANGLES

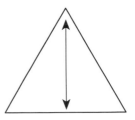

Diagram 1
60° Equilateral Triangle
Arrow indicates
height of triangle.

TIP

When you cut shapes with 60° angles, strips may be layered up to six thicknesses and cut at once to save time.

CUTTING 60° DIAMONDS

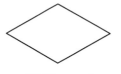

60° Diamond

1. To make the first cut, position one side of the Clearview Triangle along one edge of the strip. Rotary cut to trim the end of the strip to a 60° angle as shown in Diagram 4.

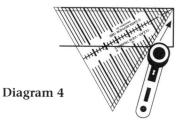

Diagram 4

Cut 60° angle at end of strip.

2. Position the ruler as if you were going to cut a triangle, with the tip at one edge of the strip and a ruled line at the other. One edge of the ruler should intersect the point at the bottom edge of the strip (Diagram 5). Cut along the opposite edge of the triangle. This cut becomes the first cut for the next diamond you will cut.

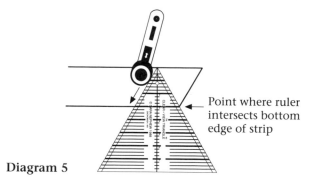

Point where ruler intersects bottom edge of strip

Diagram 5

3. As you continue to cut diamonds, move the tool along the bottom edge of the strip and cut only along the edge of the triangle that is opposite the first cut (Diagram 6).

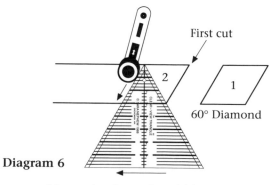

First cut

60° Diamond

Diagram 6

Move ruler along edge of fabric strip.

1. Place the Clearview Triangle on the fabric strip, lining up the triangle on the bottom edge of the strip at the measurement given in the quilt directions. Rotary cut along both edges of the triangle (Diagram 7).

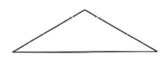

Flat Pyramid

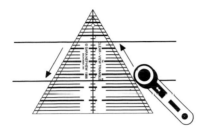

Diagram 7

2. Rotate (do not flip over) the triangle and line it up along the other edge of the fabric strip to cut the next flat pyramid (Diagram 8).

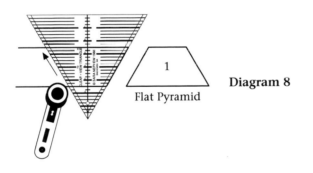

1

Flat Pyramid

Diagram 8

CUTTING DIAMOND HALVES

1. Line up the center line of the Clearview Triangle with one edge of the fabric strip. (Strip width is given in pattern directions.) Cut along one side of the triangle (Diagram 9).

2. Turn the tool, line up the center line with the edge of the strip again, and rotary cut along the other side (Diagram 10). One edge of ruler should intersect the point at the top edge of the strip.

Diamond Half

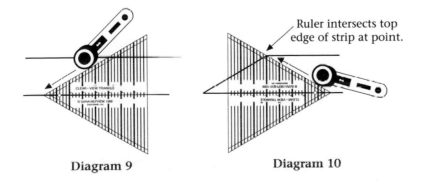

Ruler intersects top edge of strip at point.

Diagram 9   Diagram 10

CUTTING
TRIANGLE
HALVES

Triangle Half

1. Cut 60° triangles according to the measurement given in the quilt pattern (Diagram 11).

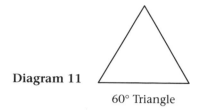

Diagram 11

60° Triangle

2. Line up the side of the fabric triangle with the center line of the Clearview Triangle and rotary cut along the edge of the triangle ruler (Diagram 12).

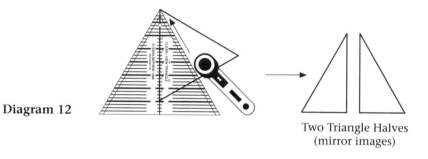

Diagram 12

Two Triangle Halves
(mirror images)

You can use this alternate method to cut triangle halves:

1. Cut a rectangle whose length is equal to the height given for the triangle half and whose width is equal to half the width of the base. (Dimensions for the rectangle will be given in quilt patterns where required.)

2. Position a rotary ruler on the rectangle, placing it diagonally from corner to corner. Rotary cut. This will yield two identical triangle halves (Diagram 13).

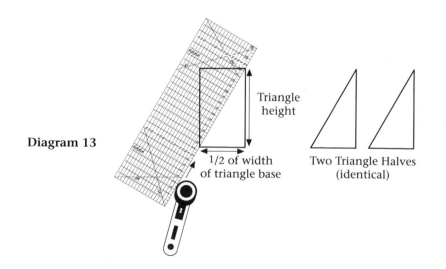

Diagram 13

Triangle height

1/2 of width
of triangle base

Two Triangle Halves
(identical)

SANDWICH PIECING 60° UNITS

It is possible to speed up the cutting and sewing of many of the units in my quilts by using sandwich piecing.

Sandwich Piecing Triangle Pairs

1. Cut a strip of each of two different fabrics the width given in the directions for the quilt you are making. Place strips right sides together with raw edges even. Stitch ¼" from both long edges.

2. Cut 60° triangles from the paired strips, following the directions for cutting triangles on page 213. Gently pull tips of seamed triangles apart to remove the stitches; press seam toward darker triangle (Diagram 14).

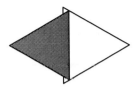

Sandwich-Pieced
Triangle Pairs

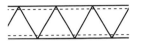 Pull apart here to
remove stitch and
open triangle pair. **Diagram 14**

Sandwich Piecing Triangle Halves

1. Cut a strip of each of two different fabrics the width given in the directions for the quilt you are making. Place strips right sides together with raw edges even. Stitch ¼" from both long edges.

Triangle Halves

2. Cut these strips into rectangular sections according to the measurements given for the quilt you are making (Diagram 15).

 **Diagram 15**

3. Line up the side of the fabric rectangle with the center line of the Clearview Triangle, placing the tip of the triangle at the upper corner. Rotary cut along the edge of the triangle (Diagram 16). Turn the ruler to check the accuracy of the remaining part of the rectangle. Gently pull the tips of the seamed triangles apart to remove the stitches and press the seam toward the darker triangle. From each rectangle you cut, you will produce a pair of pieced half triangles. To create triangles that are identical, be sure to cut all rectangles with the same color fabric on top. If you turn some of the rectangles over to cut, the color placement in the resulting triangles will be reversed (Diagram 16).

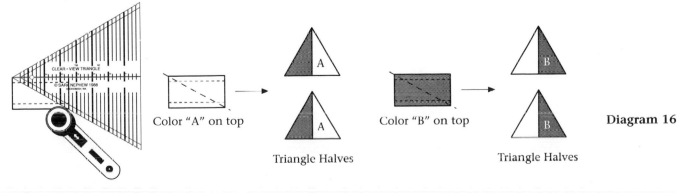

Color "A" on top

Triangle Halves

Color "B" on top

Triangle Halves

Diagram 16

Line up Clearview Triangle.

ADDITIONAL CUTTING TIPS

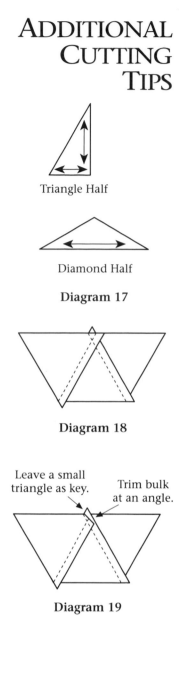

Triangle Half

Diamond Half

Diagram 17

Diagram 18

Leave a small triangle as key.

Trim bulk at an angle.

Diagram 19

1. One advantage to 60° cutting is that, for the most part, it's not necessary to worry about bias. The bias that results from these angles is less stretchy than true bias cut at a 45° angle (when cutting a square diagonally, for example). Minimal care is required to prevent distortion, and you can take advantage of the limited "give" to stretch the edges a little when necessary to line up seams. The bias of 60° shapes is easier to ease when edges are a little too long.

2. The 60°-angle fill-in pieces required to make the quilts "square" will automatically end up with the straight of grain along the outside edge when using the methods I've described in this section (Diagram 17).

3. Using these cutting and piecing methods, it is not necessary to trim corners as it is in other traditional cutting methods. After seaming, small triangles will stick out along the edges of pieced units and, like the notches in clothing patterns, are keys to help line up one unit over another accurately (Diagram 18). (If pressing has laid a little triangle key flat, you can temporarily flip it up with a finger while you line pieces up and pin.)

    After you have assembled the quilt top, check it from the front side to make sure that the dark-colored triangle points don't show through. Trim those that do.

4. Trimming is useful when seaming and pressing results in a triangle of fabrics lying across the seam edge. Trim as shown in Diagram 19 to reduce bulk. Insert the point of the scissors between layers so the small triangle key sticking out is not removed.

5. If you are making a hexagonal block from six triangle units, sew two sets of three triangles together into half hexagons first. Then sew the sets together across the center. To reduce bulk and make it easier to match the seams at the center of the hexagon, press seams in the half hexagon as shown in Diagram 20, so the center triangle is flat and the point extends above the raw edges.

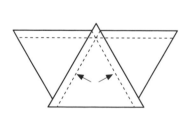

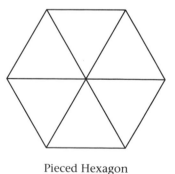

Diagram 20   Press in direction of arrows.   Pieced Hexagon

6. Seams in pieced units often have a mind of their own and want to fall a certain way. I always press from the right side and check the back afterwards. Occasionally, a seam insists on going in one direction on one end and in the other direction on the other end of the same seam. You may choose to allow the seam to twist somewhere along its length to reduce overall bulk.

Three Blocks Variation

Cubes floating in space! It's easy to achieve a three-dimensional illusion, using 60° triangles and diamonds. Just be sure to sort your fabrics by value: light, medium, dark, and an even darker background.

Dimensions: *38½" x 42¼"*

8 pieced hexagonal blocks arranged in 3 vertical rows; ¾"-wide inner border at side and top edges only and 5"-wide mitered outer border

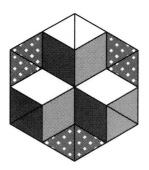

Hexagonal Block

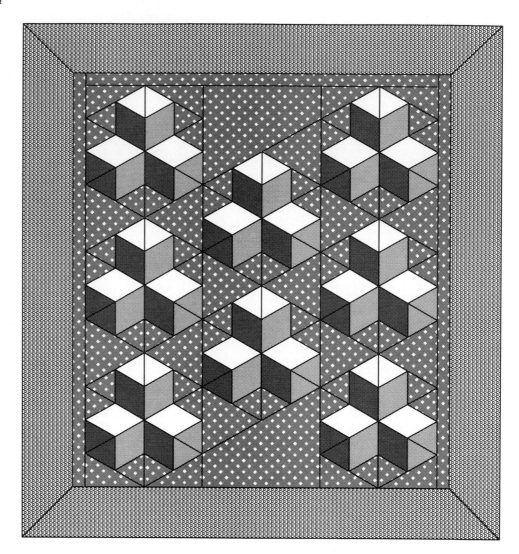

Materials: *44"-wide fabric*

Yardages listed are generous and are based on 44"-wide fabric that has been preshrunk. Strips cut across the fabric width should measure at least 42", as shown in the strip dimensions in the cutting chart.

- ½ yd. assorted dark blue prints
- ½ yd. assorted medium blue prints
- ½ yd. assorted light blue prints
- 1⅛ yds. navy blue print for background
- ⅔ yd. decorator floral fabric for border
- 1½ yds. fabric of your choice for backing
- ⅜ yd. blue for binding
- Batting and thread to finish

Cutting

All rotary-cutting dimensions include ¼"-wide seam allowances. Using a rotary cutter, the Clearview Triangle, and a rotary-cutting mat, cut the pieces listed in the chart.
Note: *Due to the scrappy nature of this project, the number of strips to cut of each color for the blocks is not given. Each 2¾"-wide strip cut across the fabric width yields twelve 2¾" 60° diamonds. Each 3"-wide strip cut across the fabric width yields nineteen 3" 60° triangles.*

FABRIC	STRIP WIDTH	NO. OF PIECES	PIECES
Assorted Light Blues	Pieced Hexagonal Blocks		
	2¾"	16	◇ 60° Diamond
	3"	16	△ 60° Triangle
Assorted Medium Blues	2¾"	16	◇ 60° Diamond
	3"	16	△ 60° Triangle
Assorted Dark Blues	2¾"	16	◇ 60° Diamond
	3"	16	△ 60° Triangle
Navy	3"	48	△ 60° Triangle
Navy	Set Triangles—Piece A		
	5¼"	12	△ 60° Triangle
	Corner Set Pieces—Piece B		
	5¾"	8	◿ Triangle Half
	Set Piece C		
	9½"	2	☐ Square*
	*See step 1 under "Quilt Top Assembly" on page 223 to cut appropriate shape.		
	Inner Border		
	1¼" x 42"	3*	
	*This quilt has an inner border only at the side and top edges.		
Decorator Floral	Outer Border		
	5¼" x 42"	4	

△ *To cut 3" (or 5¼") 60° triangles for the hexagonal blocks and set triangles, see page 213.*

◇ *To cut 60° diamonds that can be pieced to 3" 60° triangles in the hexagonal blocks, see page 214.*

◿ *To cut 5¾" triangle halves for the corner set pieces (Piece B), see page 216.*

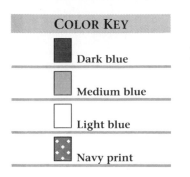

COLOR KEY

Dark blue

Medium blue

Light blue

Navy print

Directions

Blocks

1. Piece 8 blocks, following the piecing diagram (Diagram 21) and paying careful attention to the color placement of each diamond and triangle. Piece in wedges first, then sew 2 sets of 3 wedges together. Sew the sets together across the center.

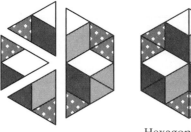

Diagram 21
Piecing Diagram

Hexagonal Block
Make 8.

2. Sew two 5¼" set triangles (Piece A) to each of 4 completed blocks to make 4 of Unit 1 (Diagram 22).

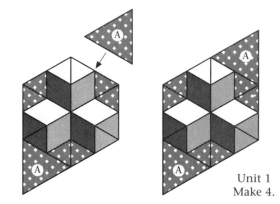

Diagram 22

Unit 1
Make 4.

3. Sew one 5¼" set triangle (Piece A) to the top right edge of 2 of the remaining blocks (Unit 2, Diagram 23) and to the bottom left edge of the final 2 blocks (Unit 3, Diagram 24). Add 2 corner set pieces (Piece B) to the bottom edge of each Unit 2 and to the top edge of each Unit 3.

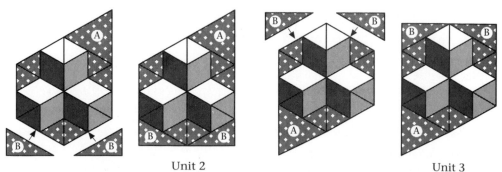

Unit 2
Make 2.

Diagram 23

Unit 3
Make 2.

Diagram 24

Quilt Top Assembly

1. Cut 2 Piece C to the correct shape, and trim to a 60° angle as shown in Diagram 25.

Diagram 25

2. Assemble quilt top in 3 vertical rows as shown in Diagram 26. Sew the rows together.

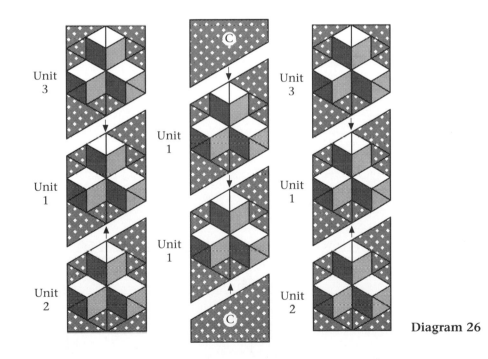

Diagram 26

Inner Border

1. Determine the required length for the top inner border by measuring across the center of the quilt top. Cut a 1¼"-wide strip of navy to that measurement and stitch to the top edge of the quilt top.

2. Measure the quilt top for the side inner borders by measuring at the center, including the top inner border. Cut 1¼"-wide navy border strips to fit, and stitch to the sides of the quilt top.

Outer Border

1. Measure the quilt top for mitered borders as shown on page 47.

2. Stitch the 5¼"-wide border strips to the quilt top, mitering the corners as shown on page 48.

Quilt Finishing

1. Layer the quilt top with batting and backing; baste.

2. Quilt in the design of your choice, or follow the Quilting Suggestion.

3. From the blue for the binding, cut and piece 170" of 2½"-wide bias for binding, following the directions on pages 52–53. Bind the quilt edges.

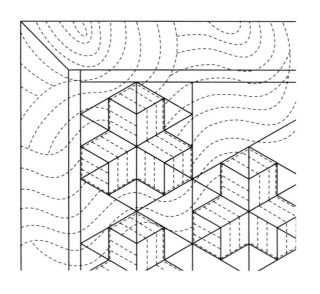

💗 Quilt a repeat wave pattern in the navy background, spacing rows 1" apart. As this wave intersects the border, it curves in different directions, introducing a more random effect.

💗 Straight-line quilt the blocks with rows spaced ¾" apart to emphasize the three-dimensional illusion.

Tumbling Blocks Wall Hanging

The Tumbling Blocks Wall Hanging is an easy remake of a favorite old pattern. Limiting the choice of fabrics to three makes it extra easy to assemble. Cutting directions include the pieces required to square up all edges of the quilt top.

Dimensions: 35½" x 42½"

9 diamond-shaped blocks arranged in 3 vertical rows with 6 fill-in units; 1¼"-wide inner border and 4¼"-wide outer border

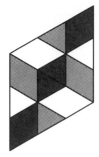

Diamond Block

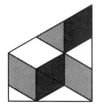

Fill-in Unit 1

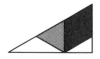

Fill-in Unit 2

Materials: *44"-wide fabric*

Yardages listed are generous and are based on 44"-wide fabric that has been preshrunk. Strips cut across the fabric width should measure at least 42".

- 1¾ yds. black print for blocks and outer border
- ¾ yd. gray print for blocks
- ¾ yd. white print for blocks
- ¼ yd. red solid for inner border
- 1½ yds. fabric of your choice for backing
- ⅜ yd. black for binding
- Batting and thread to finish

Cutting

All rotary-cutting dimensions include ¼"-wide seam allowances. Using a rotary cutter, the Clearview Triangle, and a rotary-cutting mat, cut the pieces listed in the chart.
Note: Due to the scrappy nature of this project, the number of strips to cut of each color for the blocks is not given. Each 2¾"-wide strip cut across the fabric width yields twelve 2¾" 60° diamonds. Each 3"-wide strip cut across the fabric width yields nineteen 3" 60° triangles.

FABRIC	STRIP WIDTH	NO. OF PIECES	PIECES
Black Print	Diamond Blocks		
	2¾"	22*	◇ 60° Diamond
	*Reserve 4 for Piece C on right-hand edge of quilt top.		
	3"	18	△ 60° Triangle
	Fill-In Units 1 and 2		
	2¾"	6	◇ 60° Diamond
	3"	6	△ 60° Triangle
	Piece A for Left-hand Edge		
	2¾"	4	⬭ Flat Pyramid*
	*Cut at 5¼" on the Clearview Triangle.		
	Outer Border		
	4½"	4	
Gray Print	Diamond Blocks		
	2¾"	23*	◇ 60° Diamond
	*Reserve 4 for Piece C at left-hand edge of quilt and one for Piece B at the top upper corner of the right-hand edge.		
	3"	18	△ 60° Triangle
	Fill-In Units 1 and 2		
	2¾"	6	◇ 60° Diamond
	3	6	△ 60° Triangle
	Piece A for Right-hand Edge		
	2¾"	3	⬭ Flat Pyramid*
	*Cut at 5¼" on the Clearview Triangle.		
White Print	Diamond Blocks		
	2¾"	18	◇ 60° Diamond
	3"	25*	△ 60° Triangle
	*Reserve 7 for Piece B on left- and right-hand edges of quilt top.		

(CONTINUED)

Cutting (CONTINUED)

FABRIC	STRIP WIDTH	NO. OF PIECES	PIECES
White Print	*Fill-In Units 1 and 2*		
	2¾"	3	◇ 60° Diamond
	3"	3	△ 60° Triangle
	3½"	10*	◿ Triangle Half (Piece D)
	Reserve 4 for the outer corners of the quilt top.		
	1⅞"	6	◠ Diamond Half (Piece E)
Red	*Inner Border*		
	1¾"	4	

△ *To cut 3" 60° triangles for Diamond blocks and fill-in units, see page 213.*

◇ *To cut 60° diamonds that can be pieced to a 3" 60° triangle for Diamond blocks and fill-in units, follow the directions on page 214, using the 2¾" strips.*

◿ *To cut 3½" triangle halves for Piece D, see page 216.*

◠ *To cut 1⅞" diamond halves for Piece E, see page 215.*

▱ *To cut 2¾" flat pyramids for Piece A, place the Clearview Triangle on a 2¾"-wide strip of fabric, lining up the bottom edge of the strip at the 5¼" line on the ruler. Cut as directed on page 215.*

Directions

Diamond Blocks and Fill-In Units

1. Piece 9 Diamond blocks, following the piecing diagram (Diagram 27) and paying careful attention to the color placement of each piece. Piece in half blocks first, then sew halves together.

Piecing Diagram
Diamond Block
Make 9.

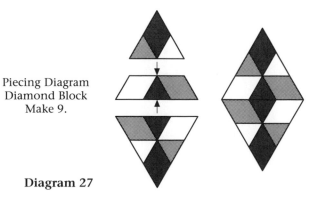

Diagram 27

2. Piece 3 of Fill-In Unit 1, following the piecing diagram (Diagram 28) and paying careful attention to the color placement of each piece. Piece half blocks first and then add remaining pieces.

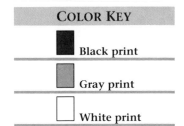

COLOR KEY

Black print

Gray print

White print

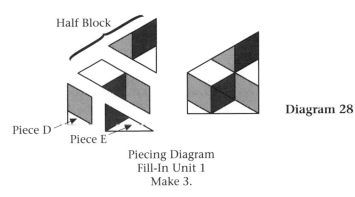

Half Block

Piece D

Piece E

Diagram 28

Piecing Diagram
Fill-In Unit 1
Make 3.

3. Piece 3 of Fill-In Unit 2, following the piecing diagram (Diagram 29).

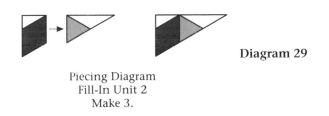

Diagram 29

Piecing Diagram
Fill-In Unit 2
Make 3.

Quilt Top Assembly

Assemble the quilt top in vertical rows as shown in Diagram 30, using the pieced Diamond blocks, the fill-in units, and the remaining cut pieces.

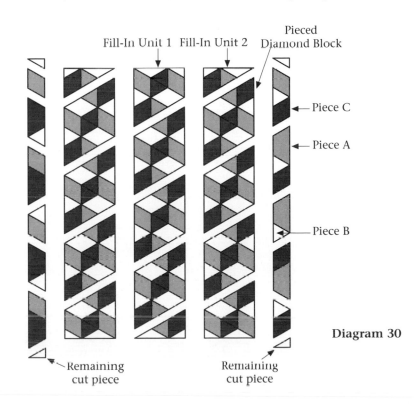

Fill-In Unit 1   Fill-In Unit 2   Pieced Diamond Block

Piece C

Piece A

Piece B

Diagram 30

Remaining cut piece

Remaining cut piece

Borders

1. Stitch each 1¾"-wide red border strip to a 4½"-wide black border strip. Press the seam toward the black border strip.

2. Measure the quilt top for mitered borders as shown on page 47. Cut to fit, and stitch the strip-pieced red/black borders to the quilt top, mitering the corners as shown on page 48.

Quilt Finishing

1. Layer the quilt top with batting and backing; baste.

2. Quilt in the design of your choice, or follow the Quilting Suggestion.

3. From the black for the binding, cut and piece 170" of 2½"-wide bias for binding, following the directions on pages 52–53. Bind the quilt edges.

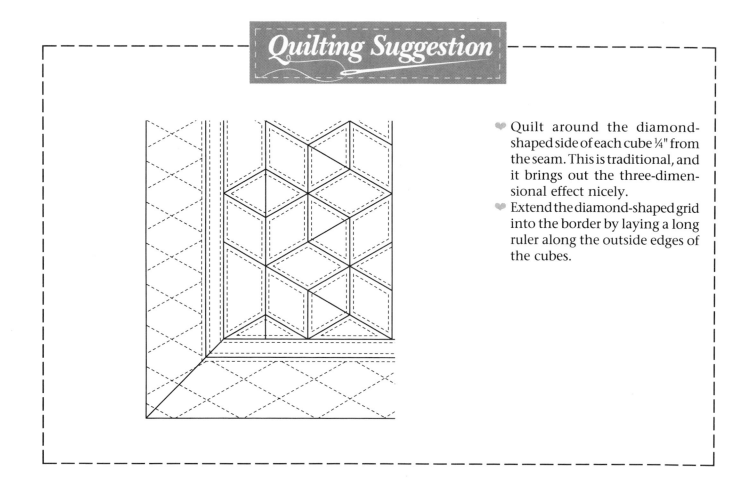

Quilting Suggestion

- Quilt around the diamond-shaped side of each cube ¼" from the seam. This is traditional, and it brings out the three-dimensional effect nicely.
- Extend the diamond-shaped grid into the border by laying a long ruler along the outside edges of the cubes.

Tumbling Blocks Quilt

The Tumbling Blocks Quilt was pieced from a damaged Tumbling Blocks and Stars quilt top, dated circa 1910. I cut it apart at the seams, evaluated each piece of fabric for usability, then cut the required shapes to make a "new" quilt from the old. Fabrics had to be carefully sorted into dark, medium, and light prints and used in the correct place in the pattern.

Reproductions of many 1800s fabrics are available to imitate the look achieved in the quilt shown. Choose an assortment of antique-looking prints in light, medium, and dark values to achieve the three-dimensional illusion.

Dimensions: *50½" x 57¼"*

30 Diamond blocks arranged in 6 vertical rows with 12 fill-in units; 5"-wide mitered border

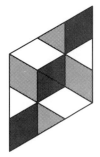

Diamond Block

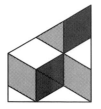

Fill-In Unit 1

Fill-In Unit 2

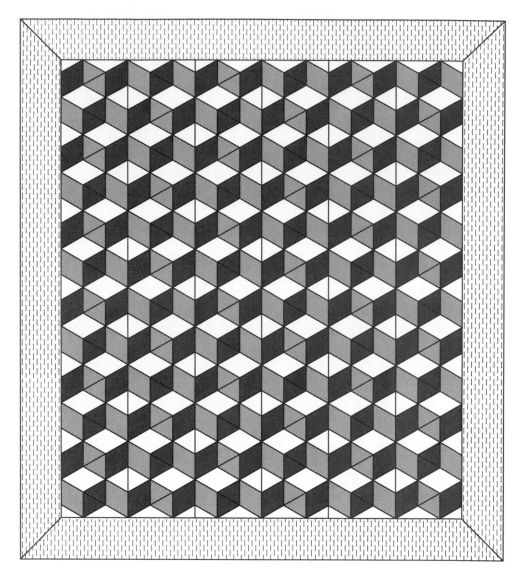

Materials: *44"-wide fabric*

Yardages listed are generous and are based on 44"-wide fabric that has been preshrunk. Strips cut across the fabric width should measure at least 42".

- ■ 1¼ yds. total of assorted dark prints for blocks
- ▨ 1¼ yds. total of medium prints for blocks
- □ 1¼ yds. total of light prints for blocks
- ▥ 1¼ yds. light print for border
- 3¾ yds. fabric of your choice for backing
- ½ yd. medium-toned print fabric for binding
- Batting and thread to finish

Cutting

All rotary-cutting dimensions include ¼"-wide seam allowances. Using a rotary cutter, the Clearview Triangle, and a rotary-cutting mat, cut the pieces listed in the chart.
Note: Due to the scrappy nature of this project, the number of strips to cut of each color (dark, medium, light) is not given. Each 2¾"-wide strip cut across the fabric width yields twelve 2¾" 60° diamonds. Each 3"-wide strip cut across the fabric width yields nineteen 3" 60° triangles.

FABRIC	STRIP WIDTH	NO. OF PIECES	PIECES
Assorted Darks	Diamond Blocks		
	2¾"	60	◇ 60° Diamond
	3"	60	△ 60° Triangle
	Fill-In Units 1 and 2		
	2¾"	12	◇ 60° Diamond
	3"	12	△ 60° Triangle
Assorted Mediums	Diamond Blocks		
	2¾"	60	◇ 60° Diamond
	3"	60	△ 60° Triangle
	Fill-In Units 1 and 2		
	2¾"	12	◇ 60° Diamond
	3"	12	△ 60° Triangle
Assorted Lights	Diamond Blocks		
	2¾"	60	◇ 60° Diamond
	3"	60	△ 60° Triangle
	Fill-In Units 1 and 2		
	2¾"	6	◇ 60° Diamond
	3"	6	△ 60° Triangle
	3½"	12	◿ Triangle Half
	1⅞"	12	◸ Diamond Half
Light Print	Border		
	5¼"	8	

△ To cut 3" 60° triangles for Diamond blocks and fill-in units, see page 213.

◇ To cut 60° diamonds that can be pieced to a 3" 60° triangle for Diamond blocks and fill-in units, follow the directions on page 214, using the 2¾" strips.

◿ To cut 3½" triangle halves for Piece D, see page 216.

◸ To cut 1⅞" diamond halves for Piece E, see page 215.

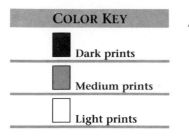

COLOR KEY

■ Dark prints

▦ Medium prints

□ Light prints

⬡ To cut 2¾" flat pyramids for Piece A, place the Clearview Triangle on a 2¾"-wide strip of fabric, lining up the bottom edge of the strip at the 5¼" line on the ruler. Cut as directed on page 216.

△ To cut 3" 60° triangles for the hexagonal blocks and set triangles, see page 213.

◇ To cut 60° diamonds that can be pieced to 3" 60° triangles in the hexagonal blocks, see page 214.

◿ To cut 5¾" triangle halves for the corner set pieces (Piece B), see page 217.

Directions

Diamond Blocks and Fill-In Units

1. Piece 30 Diamond blocks, following the piecing diagram (Diagram 31) and paying careful attention to the color placement of each piece. Piece half blocks first, then sew halves together.

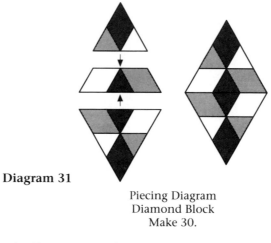

Diagram 31

Piecing Diagram
Diamond Block
Make 30.

2. Piece 6 of Fill-In Unit 1, following the piecing diagram (Diagram 32) and paying careful attention to the color placement of each piece. Piece half blocks first and then add remaining pieces.

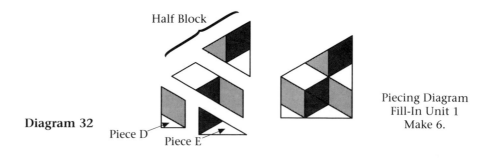

Half Block

Diagram 32

Piece D

Piece E

Piecing Diagram
Fill-In Unit 1
Make 6.

3. Piece 6 of Fill-In Unit 2, following the piecing diagram (Diagram 33).

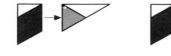

Diagram 33

Piecing Diagram
Fill-In Unit 2
Make 6.

Quilt Top Assembly

Assemble the quilt top in vertical rows as shown in Diagram 34, using the pieced Diamond blocks and the fill-in units.

Fill-In Unit 1   Fill-In Unit 2   Pieced Diamond Block

Diagram 34

Borders

1. Measure the quilt top for mitered borders as shown on page 47.

2. Piece the 4 light print borders from the 5¼"-wide border strips to equal the strip lengths required.

3. Stitch the borders to the quilt top, mitering the corners as shown on page 48.

Quilt Finishing

1. Layer the quilt top with batting and backing; baste.

2. Quilt in the design of your choice, or follow the Quilting Suggestion.

3. From the medium print for the binding, cut and piece 230" of 2½"-wide bias for binding, following the directions on pages 52–53. Bind the quilt edges.

Quilting Suggestion

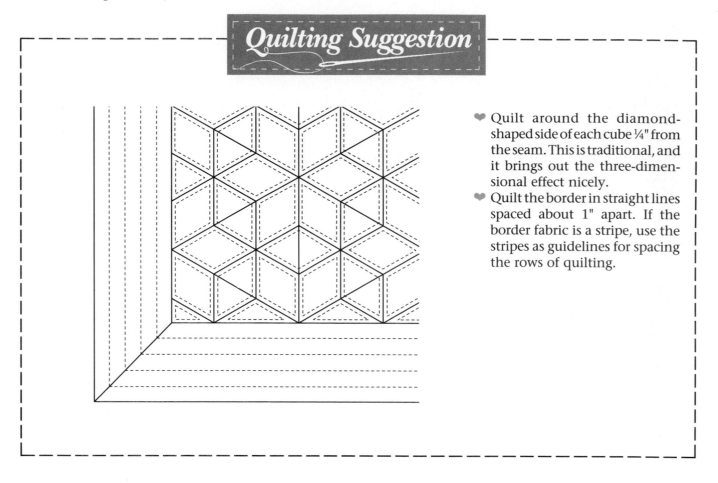

❤ Quilt around the diamond-shaped side of each cube ¼" from the seam. This is traditional, and it brings out the three-dimensional effect nicely.

❤ Quilt the border in straight lines spaced about 1" apart. If the border fabric is a stripe, use the stripes as guidelines for spacing the rows of quilting.

Sailing

Do you love lakes, oceans, and rivers? Make this quilt and keep it near you wherever you go. It's fun to choose nautical fabrics for this scrappy, pieced quilt.

Dimensions: *80¼" x 97¾"*

13 Sailboat blocks and
85 Ocean blocks set
in 7 vertical rows;
6¼"-wide border

Sailboat Block

Dark Ocean Block

Light Ocean Block

Materials: *44"-wide fabric*

Yardages listed are generous and are based on 44"-wide fabric that has been preshrunk. Strips cut across the fabric width should measure at least 42", as shown in the strip dimensions in the cutting chart.

- ½ yd. printed muslin for sails
- ½ yd. brown or black fabric for boat hulls
- 2 yds. total assorted light blue prints for water (adding lavender print accents in small quantities)
- 2 yds. total assorted medium blue print for water (adding red or brown print accents in small quantities)
- 2 yds. assorted dark blue prints for water
- ½ yd. each sky blue and medium blue-green prints for top and bottom of each vertical row
- 1½ yds. black variegated print for border
- 7½ yds. fabric of your choice for backing
- ¾ yd. black print for binding
- Batting and thread to finish

Cutting

All rotary-cutting dimensions include ¼"-wide seam allowances. Using a rotary cutter, the Clearview Triangle, and a rotary-cutting mat, cut the strips as described in the first column of the chart. Then from those strips, cut the pieces listed in the second column. Some strips do not require additional cuts at this time so no directions appear in the second column.

Fabric	FIRST CUT		ADDITIONAL CUTS	
	No. of Strips	Dimensions	No. of Pieces	Pieces
Printed Muslin	Sails for Sailboat Blocks			
	3	4½" x 42"	3	
Brown or Black	Boat Hulls and Masts for Sailboat Blocks			
	3	1" x 42"	3	
	5	3¾" x 42"	13	⬡ Flat Pyramid*
	*Cut at 7¼" line on Clearview Triangle.			
Assorted Light Blue Prints	Water for Sailboat Blocks			
	1	4" x 42"	*	△ 60° Triangle
Med. Blue Prints	1	4" x 42"	*	△ 60° Triangle
Dark Blue Prints	1	4" x 42"	*	△ 60° Triangle
	*From these 3 strips, cut a total of 13 sets of matching triangles.			
Assorted Light Blue Prints	Ocean Blocks			
	10	4" x 42"	*	
Ass't Med Blue Prt	10	4" x 42"	*	
Ass't Dark Blue Prt	10	4" x 42"	*	
	*See step 1 under "Ocean Blocks" on page 240 for piecing and cutting directions.			
Sky Blue	Fill-In Triangles for Top and Bottom Edges			
	2	6⅜" x 42"	4	6⅜" x 11"
Med. Blue-green	2	6⅜" x 42"	4	6⅜" x 11"
Black Print	Border			
	9	6½" x 42"		

△ To cut 4" 60° triangles for Sailboat blocks and Ocean blocks, see page 213.

⬡ To cut 3¾" flat pyramids for boat hulls and masts for Sailboat blocks, place the Clearview Triangle on a 3¾"-wide strip of fabric, lining up the bottom edge of the strip at the 7¼" line on the ruler. Cut as directed on page 215.

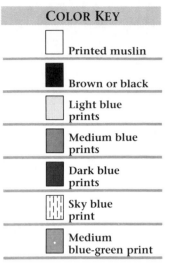

COLOR KEY

☐ Printed muslin

■ Brown or black

☐ Light blue prints

▨ Medium blue prints

■ Dark blue prints

▦ Sky blue print

▨ Medium blue-green print

Directions

Sailboat Blocks

1. Stitch each 4½"-wide muslin strip to a 1"-wide black or brown strip. Press the seam toward the dark strip in each strip-pieced sail/mast unit. Crosscut each strip-pieced unit into 7¼"-long segments (Diagram 35). Each strip should yield 5 segments.

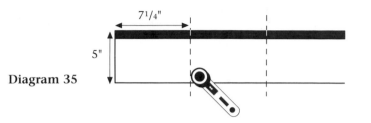

Diagram 35

2. Sew segments together into one long strip (Diagram 36).

Diagram 36

3. Cut the strip into 7¼"-tall, 60° triangles, lining up the center line of the Clearview Triangle with the center of each dark strip (Diagram 37). You will need 13 sails.

Diagram 37

4. Piece 13 Sailboat blocks, following the piecing diagram (Diagram 38) and using 1 sail, 1 hull, and 1 pair of blue print triangles in each block.

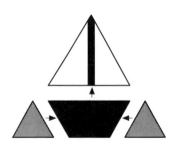

Diagram 38
Piecing Diagram

Ocean Blocks

1. With right sides together, stitch a 4"-wide strip of dark blue print to a 4"-wide strip of medium blue print along both long edges, using ¼"-wide seam allowances. Make 5 of these units. Repeat with the light blue and medium blue strips and with the remaining dark blue and light blue strips, making 5 of each of these units (Diagram 39).

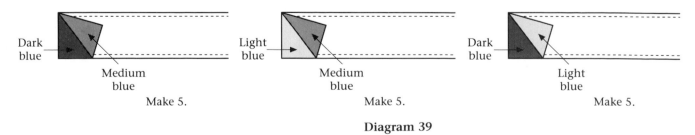

Dark blue / Medium blue — Make 5.

Light blue / Medium blue — Make 5.

Dark blue / Light blue — Make 5.

Diagram 39

2. Using the Clearview Triangle, rotary cut 4" 60° triangles from each unit (Diagram 40).

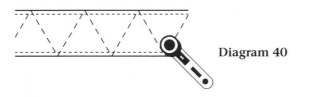

Diagram 40

3. Carefully pull the triangles apart at the tip and press the remaining seam toward the darker fabric in each resulting triangle pair (Diagram 41). You will need a total of 255 of these triangle pairs. (Cut and assemble additional 4"-wide strip units for extra triangle pairs, if needed.)

4. Piece 85 Ocean blocks, following the piecing diagram (Diagram 42). Use the triangle pairs and the remaining 4" triangles (cut earlier in assorted light, medium, and dark blues) to make dark and light blocks.

Diagram 41

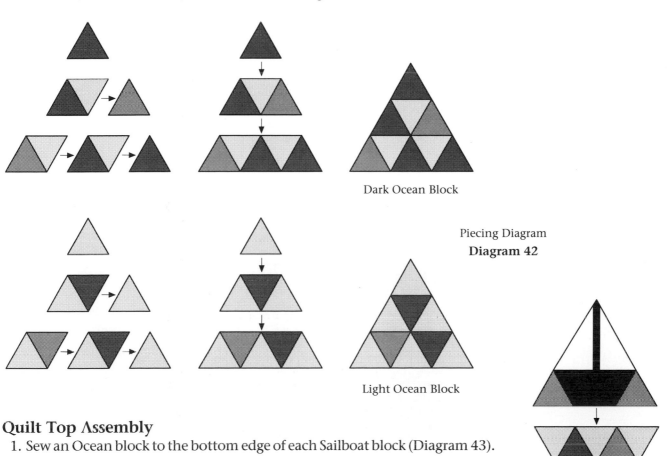

Dark Ocean Block

Light Ocean Block

Piecing Diagram
Diagram 42

Quilt Top Assembly

1. Sew an Ocean block to the bottom edge of each Sailboat block (Diagram 43).

Diagram 43

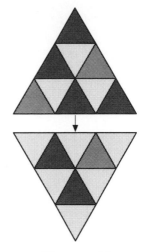

Diagram 44

2. Assemble 32 paired Ocean blocks (Diagram 44). You should have 8 single Ocean blocks remaining.

3. Layer the sky blue 6⅜" x 11" rectangles in 2 stacks of 2 rectangles each with right sides up. Repeat with the blue-green rectangles. Place a rotary ruler diagonally across one stack of sky blue rectangles, corner to corner, and cut (Diagram 45). Cut the remaining sky blue stack diagonally in the opposite direction as shown. Repeat with the blue-green stacks.

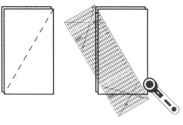

Diagram 45

4. Assemble the quilt top in 7 vertical rows as shown in Diagram 46, using the completed Sailboat blocks, single Ocean blocks, paired Ocean blocks, and the fill-in triangles (sky blue at the top edge and blue-green at the bottom edge of each row). Sew the rows together.

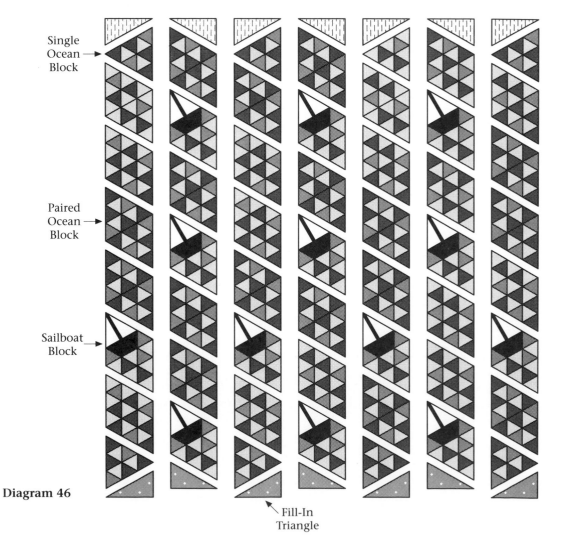

Single Ocean Block

Paired Ocean Block

Sailboat Block

Diagram 46

Fill-In Triangle

Border

1. Measure the quilt top for mitered borders as shown on page 47.
2. Cut to fit and stitch the 6½"-wide border strips to the quilt top, mitering the corners as shown on page 48.

Quilt Finishing

1. Layer the quilt top with batting and backing; baste.
2. Quilt in the design of your choice, or follow the Quilting Suggestion.
3. From the black print for the binding, cut and piece 370" of 2½"-wide bias for binding, following the directions on pages 52–53. Bind the quilt edges.

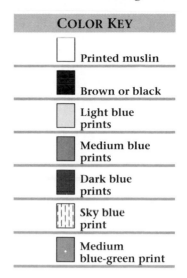

COLOR KEY

	Printed muslin
	Brown or black
	Light blue prints
	Medium blue prints
	Dark blue prints
	Sky blue print
	Medium blue-green print

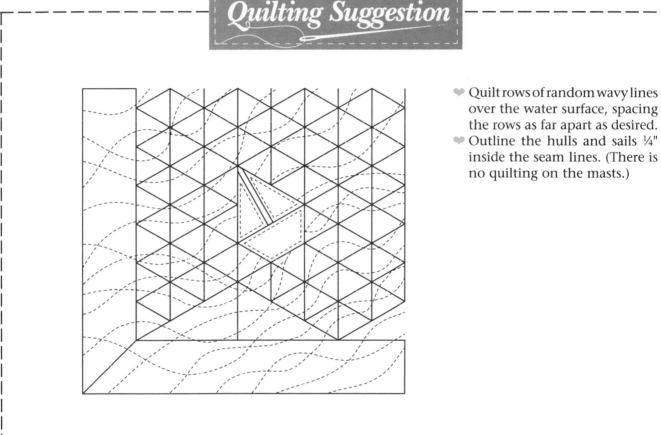

Quilting Suggestion

- Quilt rows of random wavy lines over the water surface, spacing the rows as far apart as desired.
- Outline the hulls and sails ¼" inside the seam lines. (There is no quilting on the masts.)

Tulips

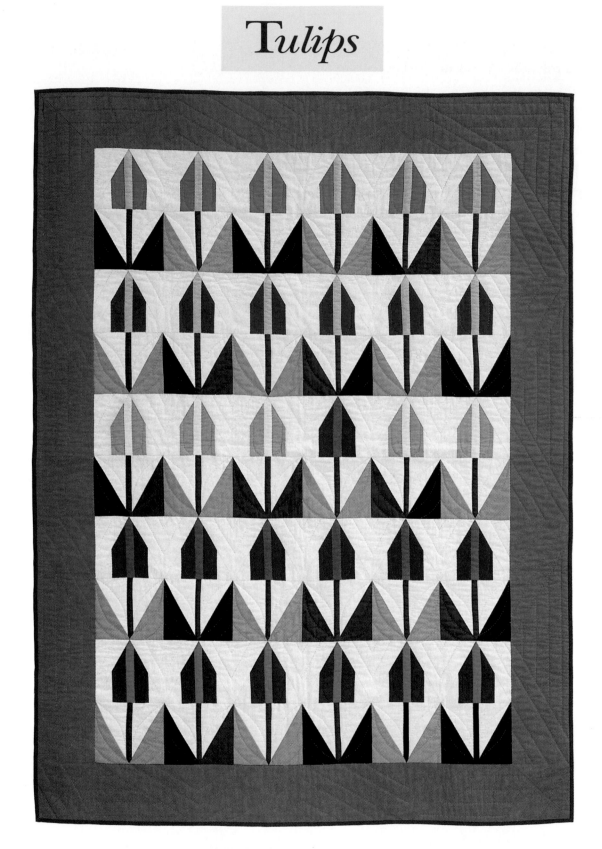

You can sleep under colorful tulips all year long if you make this cheery quilt. These bright, solid-colored flowers will bring out the sunshine in any setting. Strip piecing and sandwich piecing make this a quick project for the beginner as well as the more experienced quilter.

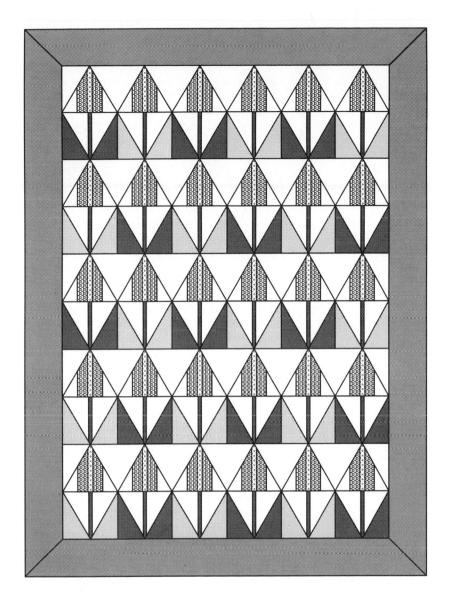

Dimensions: *47¼" x 63"*

30 tulips arranged
in 5 horizontal rows of
6 tulips each;
5¼"-wide mitered border

Petals

Leaves

Stems

Materials: *44"-wide fabric*

Yardages listed are generous and are based on 44"-wide fabric that has been preshrunk. Strips cut across the fabric width should measure at least 42", as shown in the strip dimensions in the cutting chart.

☐ 2 yds. muslin

▦ ¼ yd. each of turquoise, violet, gold, red, and dark blue for the outer tulip petals

▧ ¼ yd. each of aqua, lilac, yellow, medium pink or coral, and bright blue for center tulip petals (These should coordinate with the colors for the outer tulip petals.)

▪ ¾ yd. dark green for stems and leaves

☐ ¾ yd. light green for leaves

▪ 1¼ yds. coral pink for border

4¼ yds. fabric of your choice for backing

½ yd. red fabric for binding

Batting and thread to finish

Cutting

COLOR KEY

☐ Muslin

▨ Tulip petals

▨ Tulip centers

■ Dark green

☐ Light green

All rotary-cutting dimensions include ¼"-wide seam allowances. Using a rotary cutter, the Clearview Triangle, and a rotary-cutting mat, cut the strips as described in the first column of the chart. Then from those strips, cut the pieces listed in the second column. Some strips do not require additional cuts at this time so no directions appear in the second column.

	FIRST CUT		ADDITIONAL CUTS	
Fabric	**No. of Strips**	**Dimensions**	**No. of Pieces**	**Dimensions**
Muslin	Tulips			
	5	2" x 42"		
Outer Tulip Petals: Turquoise, Violet, Gold, Red, Dark Blue	From each of the 5 colors listed, cut the following for the outer petals:			
	2	1¾" x 42"		
Tulip Centers: Aqua, Lilac, Yellow, Medium Pink, Bright Blue	From each of the 5 colors listed, cut the following for the center petals:			
	1	1¼" x 42"		
Dark Green	Stems			
	5	1" x 42"		
Muslin	5	3⅝" x 42"		
Dark Green	Leaves			
	4	3¾" x 42"		
Light Green	4	3¾" x 42"		
Muslin	Background Triangles			
	4	6" x 42"	25	△ 60° Triangle
Dark Green	Fill-In Triangles			
	1	3¾" x 42"	4	3¾" x 6½"*
Light Green	1	3¾" x 42"	4	3¾" x 6½"*
Muslin	1	3¾" x 42"	6	3¾" x 6½"*
	*See step 1 under "Quilt Top Assembly" on page 249 for additional cutting instructions.			
Coral Pink	Border			
	6	5½" x 42"		

△ *To cut 6" 60° triangles for background triangles, see page 213.*

Directions

Tulips

1. Working with each set of tulip petal and tulip center colors separately, strip-piece the muslin, outer tulip petal, and center petal strips together as shown in Diagram 47. Press all the seams in one direction. Crosscut each of the 5 different strip-pieced units into 6" lengths. Each unit will yield 7 segments.

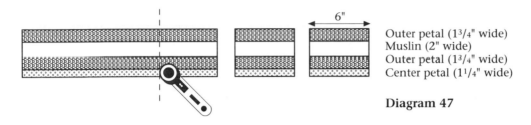

6"

Outer petal (1³/₄" wide)
Muslin (2" wide)
Outer petal (1³/₄" wide)
Center petal (1¹/₄" wide)

Diagram 47

2. Sew the segments together as shown in Diagram 48 to produce a continuous, 6"-wide strip of each tulip color.

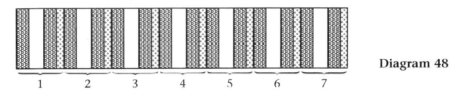

Diagram 48

1   2   3   4   5   6   7

3. Centering the perpendicular line of the Clearview Triangle in the light tulip color (tulip center) in each strip-pieced unit, cut 6" triangles from alternate sides of each strip. Gently pull off the dark tips at each side of the base of each triangle (Diagram 49). (This method reduces waste and saves time.) You will need 7 red tulips, 5 gold tulips, and 6 each of the turquoise, violet, and dark blue tulips.

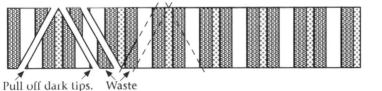

Diagram 49

Pull off dark tips.   Waste

Cut triangles from alternate sides.

Stems

1. Strip-piece 5 units, each containing 1 muslin strip, 3⅝" wide, and 1 dark green strip, 1" wide (Diagram 50). Press the seams toward the green strip in each one. Crosscut each of the strip-pieced units into 6" lengths. Each unit will yield 7 segments.

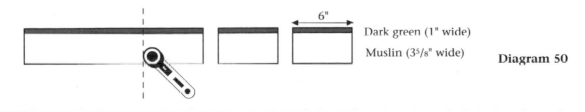

6"

Dark green (1" wide)

Muslin (3⁵/₈" wide)   **Diagram 50**

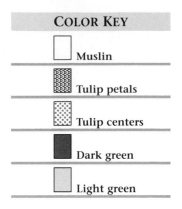

COLOR KEY

Muslin

Tulip petals

Tulip centers

Dark green

Light green

2. Sew the segments together as shown in Diagram 51 to produce a continuous, 6"-wide strip.

Diagram 51

3. Centering the perpendicular line on the Clearview Triangle in the center of each "stem," cut 30 stem triangles, 6" tall, from alternate sides of the strip (Diagram 52).

Diagram 52

Waste

Leaves

1. With right sides together and raw edges even, pair each 3¾"-wide strip of dark green with a 3¾"-wide light green strip. Stitch ¼" from both long edges. Crosscut each unit into 6½"-long segments (Diagram 53).

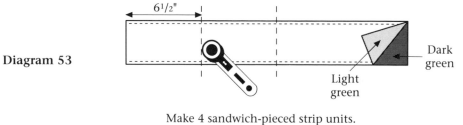

$6^1/2$"

Dark green

Light green

Diagram 53

Make 4 sandwich-pieced strip units.
Cut into $6^1/2$" segments.

Triangle tip
at upper corner

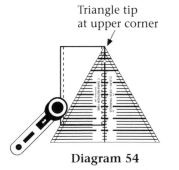

Diagram 54

2. Divide the segments into two equal piles. The same color should be facing up in each pile. Line up one long edge of a segment from one of the piles with the center line on the Clearview Triangle, placing the tip of the triangle at the upper corner. Rotary cut along the edge of the triangle (Diagram 54).

Use the triangle to check the other half for accuracy, trimming if necessary. Repeat with the remaining segments in the first pile.

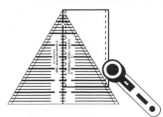

3. Cut the segments in the remaining pile, with the angled cut in the opposite direction as shown in Diagram 55.

4. Press the seam in each triangle toward the dark green triangle half and trim off the angled seam that extends at the tip of the triangle. You should have a total of 24 half-triangle units, 12 with a light green triangle on the right half and 12 with a light green triangle on the left half (Diagram 56).

 Using leftover fabrics, make one more half-triangle unit with light green on the left half.

Diagram 55

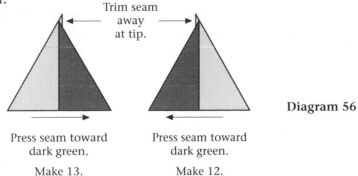

Diagram 56

Trim seam away at tip.

Press seam toward dark green.

Make 13.

Press seam toward dark green.

Make 12.

Quilt Top Assembly

1. Divide the 3¾" x 6½" muslin rectangles into 2 stacks of 3 each with all of the rectangles right side up. Cut one stack in half diagonally in one direction, using a rotary ruler and cutter. Cut the other stack in the opposite direction (Diagram 57). Use 10 of these triangles to fill in at the outer edges of the tulip rows (Diagram 59, page 250).

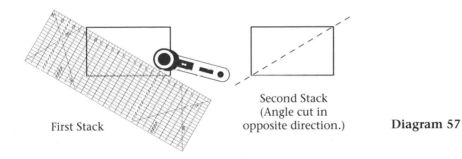

First Stack

Second Stack (Angle cut in opposite direction.)

Diagram 57

2. Divide the 3¾" x 6½" light green rectangles into 2 stacks of 2 each. Repeat with the dark green rectangles. Cut one stack in half diagonally in one direction, using a rotary ruler and cutter. Cut the other stack in the opposite direction (Diagram 58). Use 5 dark green and 5 light green triangles to fill in the outer edges of the leaf rows.

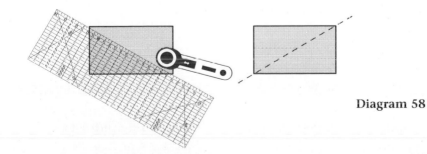

Diagram 58

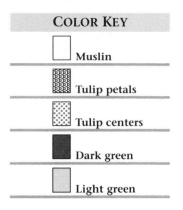

COLOR KEY

Muslin

Tulip petals

Tulip centers

Dark green

Light green

3. Arrange the tulip, stem, and leaf triangles with the fill-in and background triangles on a large, flat surface, referring to Diagram 59 and the quilt photo on page 244.

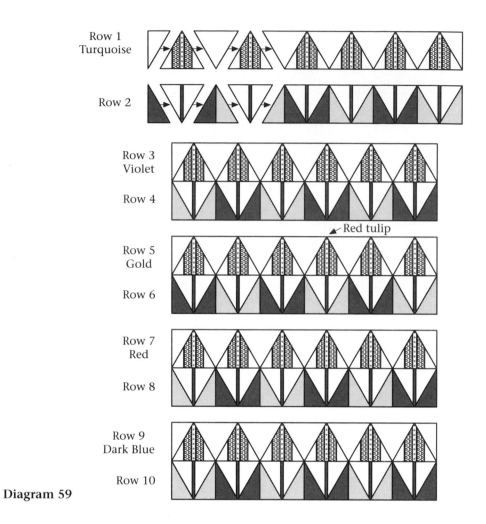

Row 1
Turquoise

Row 2

Row 3
Violet

Row 4

Red tulip

Row 5
Gold

Row 6

Row 7
Red

Row 8

Row 9
Dark Blue

Row 10

Diagram 59

4. Stitch the pieces together in horizontal rows first. Then sew the rows together, making sure that the stems are centered under each tulip. Pin, if necessary, to hold them in a matched position for stitching.

Border

1. Measure the quilt top for mitered borders as shown on page 47.

2. Cut the 5½"-wide coral pink border strips to fit the quilt top and stitch, mitering the corners as shown on page 48.

Quilt Finishing

1. Layer the quilt top with batting and backing; baste.

2. Quilt in the design of your choice, or follow the Quilting Suggestion.

3. From the red for the binding, cut and piece 240" of 2½"-wide bias for binding, following the directions on pages 52–53. Bind the quilt edges.

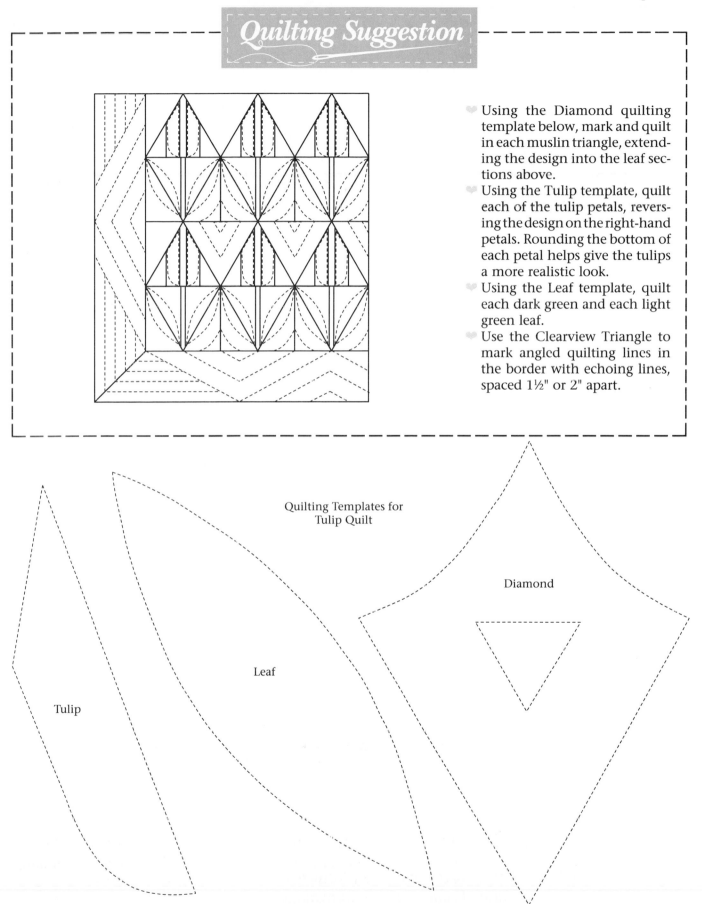

Quilting Suggestion

❤ Using the Diamond quilting template below, mark and quilt in each muslin triangle, extending the design into the leaf sections above.

❤ Using the Tulip template, quilt each of the tulip petals, reversing the design on the right-hand petals. Rounding the bottom of each petal helps give the tulips a more realistic look.

❤ Using the Leaf template, quilt each dark green and each light green leaf.

❤ Use the Clearview Triangle to mark angled quilting lines in the border with echoing lines, spaced 1½" or 2" apart.

Quilting Templates for
Tulip Quilt

Diamond

Leaf

Tulip

Tulip Field

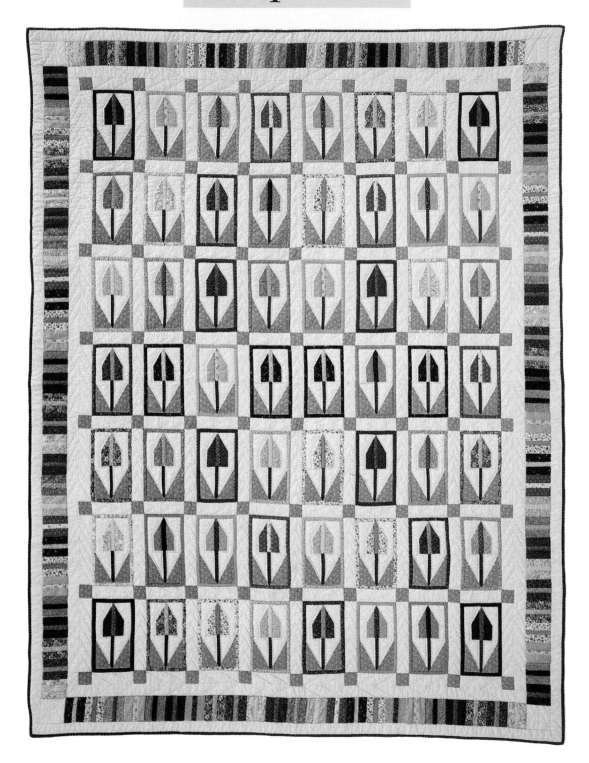

Annette Austin devised this variation of the Tulips quilt pattern (page 244) for the Busy Bee Quilters of Snohomish, Washington, my home quilting guild. It was our 1990 raffle quilt. In her design, the cameolike Tulip blocks are separated by borders and lattice strips. The multicolored strippy border makes this quilt a colorful reminder of springtime.

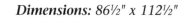

Dimensions: *86½" x 112½"*

56 bordered Tulip blocks
in 7 horizontal rows
with muslin lattice strips
and green set squares
at each block corner;
2¼"-wide inner and
outer borders of muslin
and 4"-wide strippy
middle border

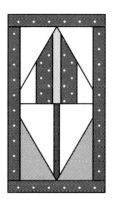

Tulip Block

Materials: *44"-wide fabric*

Yardages listed are generous and are based on 44"-wide fabric that has been preshrunk. Strips cut across the fabric width should measure at least 42", as shown in the strip dimensions in the cutting chart.

- ☐   6¾ yds. white-on-white, printed muslin for block backgrounds, lattice strips, corner squares, and inner and outer borders
- ■ ■ ▦   ¼ yd. each of 15 dark colors for tulip petals, border strips, and strippy border
- ☐ ▥ ▨   ¼ yd. each of 15 light colors for tulip centers and strippy border (These should coordinate with colors for outer tulip petals.)
- ▤   ¼ yd. dark green for stems
- ▦   1½ yds. medium green print for leaves
-   8½ yds. fabric of your choice for backing
-   ¾ yd. dark green for binding
-   Batting and thread to finish

Cutting

> *All rotary-cutting dimensions include ¼"-wide seam allowances. Using a rotary cutter, the Clearview Triangle, and a rotary-cutting mat, cut the strips as described in the first column of the chart. Then from those strips, cut the pieces listed in the second column. Some strips do not require additional cuts at this time so no directions appear in the second column.*
> ***Note:*** *Cutting directions for the strippy border appear under "Strip-Pieced Border Assembly" on page 258.*

| Fabric | FIRST CUT | | ADDITIONAL CUTS | |
	No. of Strips	Dimensions	No. of Pieces	Pieces
Muslin	Tulips			
	15	2" x 42"		
	6	6" x 42"	56	△ 60° Triangles*
	*See step 2 under "Tulip Block Assembly" on page 257 for additional cutting instructions.			
Tulip Petals	From each of the 15 dark colors, cut the following:			
	2	1¾" x 42"		
Tulip Border Strips	From each of the 15 light colors listed, cut the following for the borders around each tulip block:			
	3	1" x 42"		
Tulip Centers	From each of the 15 light colors, cut the following for the center petals:			
	1	1¼" x 42"		
Dark Green	Stems			
	15	1" x 42"		
Muslin	15	3⅝" x 42"*		
	*See step 3 under "Stems" on page 256 for additional cutting instructions.			
Medium Green	Leaves			
	6	6" x 42"	56	△ 60° Triangles*
	*See step 2 under "Tulip Block Assembly" on page 257 for additional cutting instructions.			

(CONTINUED)

Cutting (CONTINUED)

Fabric	FIRST CUT		ADDITIONAL CUTS	
	No. of Strips	Dimensions	No. of Pieces	Dimensions
Muslin	Lattice Strips			
	5	12" x 42"	72	2½" x 12"
	4	6¾" x 42"	64	2½" x 6¾"
Medium Green	Set Squares			
	5	2½" x 42"	72	2½" x 2½"
Muslin	Inner Border			
	10	2¾" x 42"		
	Outer Border and Corner Squares			
	10	2½" x 42"		
	1	4½" x 42"	4	4½" x 4½"

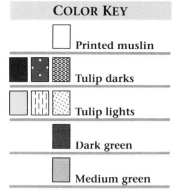

COLOR KEY

☐ Printed muslin

Tulip darks

Tulip lights

☐ Dark green

☐ Medium green

△ *To cut 60° triangles for the tulips and leaves, see page 213.*

Directions

Tulips

1. Working with each set of tulip petal and tulip center colors separately, strip-piece the muslin, outer tulip-petal strips, and center petal strips together as shown in Diagram 60. Press all seams in one direction. Crosscut each of the 15 different strip-pieced units into 6" lengths. Each unit will yield 7 segments.

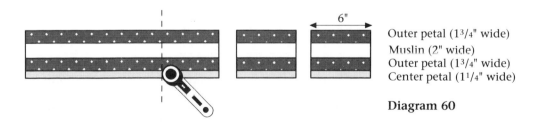

Outer petal (1³/4" wide)
Muslin (2" wide)
Outer petal (1³/4" wide)
Center petal (1¹/4" wide)

Diagram 60

2. Sew the segments together as shown in Diagram 61 to produce a continuous, 6"-wide strip of each tulip color combination.

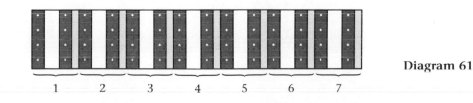

Diagram 61

1   2   3   4   5   6   7

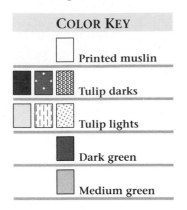

COLOR KEY

☐ Printed muslin

Tulip darks

Tulip lights

Dark green

Medium green

3. Centering the perpendicular line of the Clearview Triangle in the light tulip color (tulip center) in each strip-pieced tulip section, cut 6" triangles from alternate sides of each strip (Diagram 62). Gently pull off the dark tips at each side of the base of each triangle. (This method reduces waste and saves time.) You will need a total of 56 tulips.

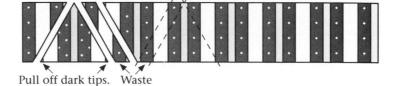

Diagram 62

Pull off dark tips.   Waste

Cut triangles from alternate sides.

Stems

1. Strip-piece 15 units, each containing 1 muslin strip, 3⅝" wide, and 1 dark green strip, 1" wide. Press the seams toward the green strip in each one. Crosscut each of the strip-pieced units into 6" lengths (Diagram 63). Each unit will yield 7 segments.

Diagram 63

6"

Dark green (1" wide)

Muslin (3⅝" wide)

2. Sew the segments together as shown in Diagram 64 to produce a continuous, 6"-wide strip. Press the seams toward the green.

Diagram 64

3. Centering the perpendicular line of the Clearview Triangle in the center of each "stem," cut 56 stem triangles, 6" tall, from alternate sides of the strip (Diagram 65).

Diagram 65

Waste

Tulip Block Assembly

1. Sew each tulip to a stem (Diagram 66).

2. Cut each muslin 60° triangle into triangle halves as shown on page 217. Repeat with the medium green print 60° triangles for the leaves.

3. Sew a muslin triangle half to each side of the tulip, lining up the triangles at the tip of the tulip (Diagram 67). Sew a medium green print triangle half to each side of the stem, lining up the triangles at the bottom of the stem. After stitching, square up the block by trimming away the excess that extends at each side of the block.

Diagram 66

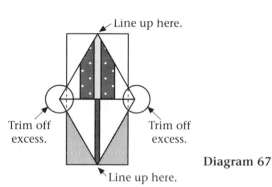

Line up here.

Trim off excess. Trim off excess.

Diagram 67

Line up here.

4. Measure each tulip block for borders as shown on page 46. Add 1" border strips to each Tulip block, matching the border strip to the outer tulip color in each one (Diagram 68). Sew the strips to the long side of each block first, then add the top and bottom borders.

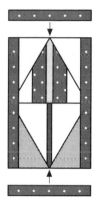

Diagram 68

Quilt Top Assembly

1. Working on a large surface, arrange the Tulip blocks to your liking in 7 horizontal rows of 8 blocks each.

2. Join the blocks in each horizontal row with the 2½" x 12" muslin lattice strips between, beginning and ending each row with a lattice strip (Diagram 69).

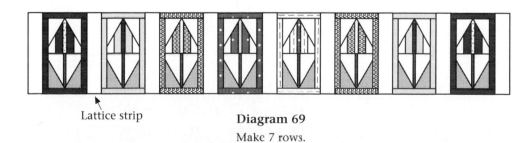

Lattice strip

Diagram 69

Make 7 rows.

3. Make 8 rows of alternating green set squares and 2½" x 6¾" muslin lattice strips, beginning and ending each row with a set square (Diagram 70).

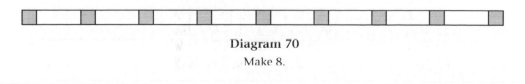

Diagram 70

Make 8.

4. Referring to the quilt plan on page 253, assemble the quilt top. Alternate the rows of blocks with the rows of lattice/set squares, beginning and ending with a lattice row.

Strip-Pieced Border Assembly

1. From the fabric remaining of each tulip color, cut and construct a total of 12 strip-pieced units that look like the one shown in Diagram 71. Cut each strip across the fabric width in the widths indicated in the diagram. Press all seams in the same direction. Use a variety of color combinations to create the strippy, scrappy look. Crosscut each strip-pieced unit into 4½"-long segments. You will need a total of 108 segments.

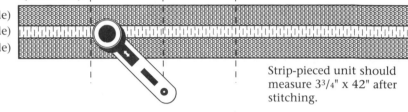

First tulip color (1¾" wide)
Second tulip color (1¼" wide)
First tulip color (1¾" wide)

4½"

Strip-pieced unit should measure 3¾" x 42" after stitching.

Diagram 71

2. Sew 23 segments, 4½" long, together for the top middle border. Repeat for the bottom middle border.

3. Sew 32 segments, 4½" long, together for each side border.

Borders

1. Measure the quilt top for borders as shown on page 46. Cut inner side borders from the 2¾"-wide muslin strips and stitch to each side of the quilt top. Press seams toward quilt top. Cut top and bottom borders to fit, and stitch to the quilt top. Press seams toward quilt top.

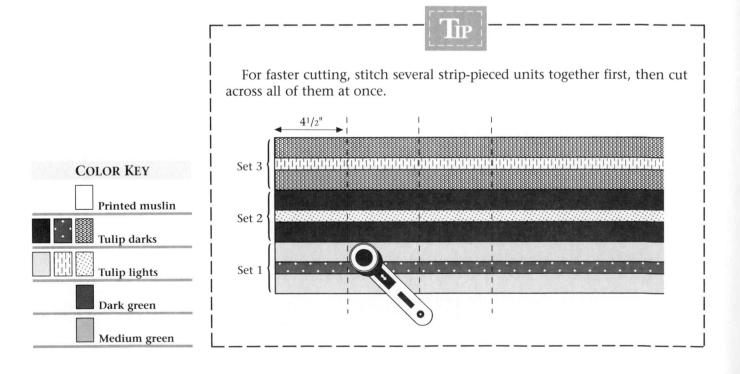

TIP

For faster cutting, stitch several strip-pieced units together first, then cut across all of them at once.

4½"

Set 3

Set 2

Set 1

COLOR KEY

Printed muslin

Tulip darks

Tulip lights

Dark green

Medium green

2. Sew the strip-pieced borders to the sides of the quilt top, adjusting the border length to fit, if necessary, by adding or removing a fabric strip.

3. Pin the top border to the quilt top to check the fit. It should end 4" shy of the outer edge of the quilt top on each side. If necessary, add or remove a strip. Unpin. Make the bottom border the same length as the adjusted top border.

4. Stitch a 4½" muslin corner square to each end of the top and bottom pieced border strips (Diagram 72).

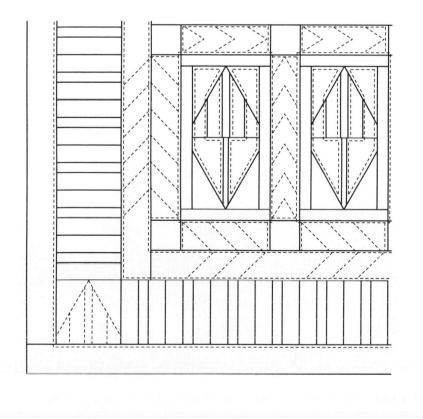

Diagram 72

5. Stitch top and bottom pieced borders to the quilt top.

6. Use the 2½"-wide muslin strips to add the outer border to the sides and then to the top and bottom edges of the quilt top, measuring and cutting the borders to fit as described on page 46.

Quilt Finishing

1. Layer the quilt top with batting and backing; baste.

2. Quilt in the design of your choice, or follow the Quilting Suggestion.

3. From the dark green fabric for binding, cut and piece 425" of 2½"-wide bias for binding, following the directions on pages 52–53. Bind the quilt edges.

Quilting Suggestion

Stitch "in the ditch" around the inside and outside edges of each frame around each block.

Stitch "in the ditch" on both edges of each tulip center.

Stitch ¼" from the seam line around the outside edges of the tulip, stem, and leaves in each block.

Quilt the vertical lattice strips in an echoing arrow pattern. Use the same pattern in the horizontal lattice strips, making the "arrows" point toward the center from both outside edges.

Stitch larger echoing arrows on the inner border.

Stitch "in the ditch" on each side of the strippy border.

Stitch "in the ditch" around each green set square.

In each muslin corner square, quilt a tulip shape that mimics the shape of the tulips in the quilt.

Gardenia Bouquet

White gardenias with bold red centers twist and twirl across the surface of this vibrant quilt. A dynamic pieced border adds drama to the overall design.

Dimensions: *81" x 102½"*

11 blocks and 20
setting units, plus corners
and fill-in pieces set
in 3 vertical rows;
3½"-wide inner border on
2 sides and bottom and
7½"-wide pieced border on
2 sides and bottom edge;
3¾"-wide top border

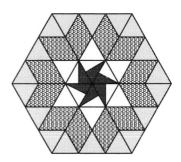

Gardenia Block

Setting Unit

Materials: *44"-wide fabric*

*Yardages listed are generous and are based on 44"-wide fabric that has
been preshrunk. Strips cut across the fabric width should measure at
least 42", as shown in the strip dimensions in the cutting chart.*

- 2¾ yds. assorted green prints and/or solids for the leaves and pieced border

- ¾ yd. red solid

- 2 yds. white-on-white muslin for the gardenias and pieced outer border

- 3½ yds. assorted tan prints for blocks, setting-unit triangles, fill-in pieces A and B, and pieced border

- 1⅛ yds. floral print for setting-unit triangles

  8 yds. fabric of your choice for backing

  ¾ yd. green print for binding

  Batting and thread to finish

Cutting

All rotary-cutting dimensions include ¼"-wide seam allowances. Using a rotary cutter, the Clearview Triangle, and a rotary-cutting mat, cut the strips as described in the first column of the chart. Then from those strips, cut the pieces listed in the second column. Some strips do not require additional cuts at this time so no directions appear in the second column.

Fabric	FIRST CUT		ADDITIONAL CUTS	
	No. of Strips	Dimensions	No. of Pieces	Pieces
Red	Gardenia Blocks			
	7	2⅝" x 42"	66	▲ Half-triangle*
Muslin	7	2⅝" x 42"	66	▲ Half-triangle*
	*Sandwich-piece as shown in steps 1–3 under "Gardenia Blocks" on pages 263–64 to create 66 half-triangles.			
	4	4" x 42"	66**	△ 60° Triangle
	**Cut 2 of these triangles from scraps, if necessary.			
Assorted Greens	17	3¾" x 42"	132	◇ 60° Diamond
Assorted Tans	12	4" x 42"	196***	△ 60° Triangle
	***Cut 192 from the strips and the 4 remaining from scraps.			
Floral Print	Setting Units			
	4	4" x 42"	60	△ 60° Triangle
	4	4" x 42"*		
Assorted Tans	4	4" x 42"*		
	*Sandwich-piece as shown in steps 1–3 under "Setting Units" on pages 264–65 to create 60 matching triangle pairs.			
Tan	Fill-In Piece A for Quilt Top and Pieced Border			
	4	7¾" x 42"	16	4½" x 7¾" rectangle*
	*See step 1 under "Fill-In Pieces A and B" on pages 265–66 for additional cutting instructions.			
	Fill-In Piece B for Quilt Top			
	1	10½" x 42"	2	10½" x 19½" rectangle*
	*See step 3 and 4 under "Fill-In Pieces A and B" on pages 265–66 for additional cutting instructions.			
	Inner Side and Bottom Borders, Top Border, and Corner Squares			
	9	4" x 42"		
	1	11¼" x 23"	2	11¼" x 11¼" square

(CONTINUED)

Cutting (CONTINUED)

Fabric	FIRST CUT		ADDITIONAL CUTS	
	No. of Strips	Dimensions	No. of Pieces	Pieces
Muslin	Pieced Border Units			
	4	6¼" x 42"	11	◺ Diamond Half
Assorted Greens	2	4" x 42"	24	△ 60° Triangle
	3	4" x 42"*		
Tan	3	4" x 42"*		
	2	2⅜" x 42"	11	◺ Diamond Half*
	*Sandwich-piece as shown in steps 1–3 under "Pieced Border" on page 267 to create 48 matching triangle pairs.			
Muslin	Pieced Border Half Units			
			2	◹ Triangle Half*
	*See step 5 under "Pieced Border" on page 267 for special cutting instructions.			
Tan	1	4½" x 4½"	2	◹ Triangle Half (1 mirror-image set)

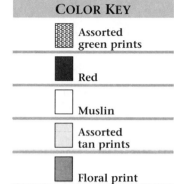

COLOR KEY

▦ Assorted green prints

■ Red

□ Muslin

▨ Assorted tan prints

▦ Floral print

△ To cut 4" 60° triangles for the Gardenia blocks, setting units, and pieced border units, see page 213.

◹ To cut 4½" triangle halves for the pieced border half units, see page 216.

◇ To cut 3¾" 60° diamonds for the Gardenia blocks, see page 214.

◺ To cut 2⅜" (or 6¼") diamond halves for the pieced border units, see page 215.

Directions

Gardenia Blocks

1. With right sides together and raw edges even, stitch each 2⅝"-wide red strip to a 2⅝"-wide muslin strip (Diagram 73). Stitch ¼" from both long edges. Make 7 of these units. Crosscut each red/muslin fabric "sandwich" into 4½" segments.

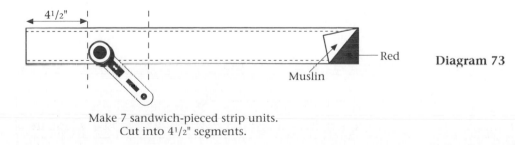

4¹/₂"

Red

Muslin

Diagram 73

Make 7 sandwich-pieced strip units.
Cut into 4¹/₂" segments.

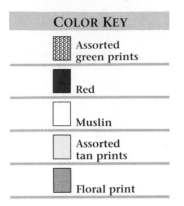

COLOR KEY

Assorted green prints

Red

Muslin

Assorted tan prints

Floral print

2. Line up one long edge of a segment with the center line on the Clearview Triangle, placing the tip of the triangle at the upper corner (Diagram 74). Rotary cut along the edge of the triangle. Check the other piece also and trim, if necessary.

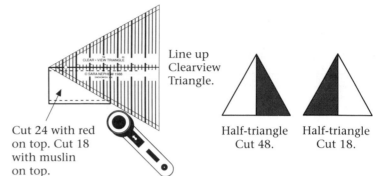

Diagram 74

Cut 24 with red on top. Cut 18 with muslin on top.

Line up Clearview Triangle.

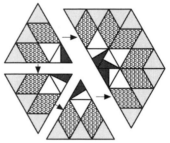

Half-triangle Cut 48.   Half-triangle Cut 18.

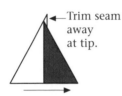

Trim seam away at tip.

Press seam toward red.

Diagram 75

3. Press the seam toward the red half-triangle and trim off the angled seam that extends at the tip of the triangle (Diagram 75).

4. Assemble 11 Gardenia blocks, following the piecing diagram (Diagram 76). Note that for 3 of the blocks the half-triangles in the center will have red on the left side.

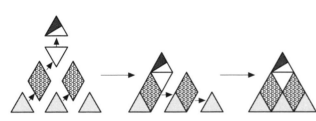

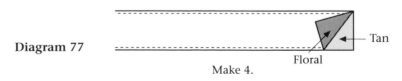

Make 6 for each block.   Piecing Diagram   Gardenia Block

Diagram 76

Setting Units

1. With right sides together and raw edges even, stitch each 4"-wide floral strip to a 4"-wide tan strip (Diagram 77). Stitch ¼" from both long edges. Make 4 of these units.

Diagram 77

Tan

Floral

Make 4.

2. Using the Clearview Triangle, rotary cut 4" triangles from each unit (Diagram 78).

Diagram 78

3. Carefully pull the triangles apart at the tip and press the remaining seam toward the darker of the two fabrics in each of the resulting triangle pairs (Diagram 79).

Pull apart here to remove stitch and open triangle.

4. Assemble 20 setting units, following the piecing diagram (Diagram 80).

Piecing Diagram

Diagram 80

Setting Unit
Make 20.

Triangle Pair

Diagram 79

5. Sew a setting unit to opposite sides of 7 Gardenia blocks to create 7 diamond-shaped units (Diagram 81).

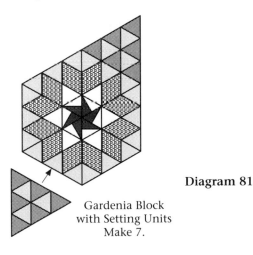

Diagram 81

Gardenia Block
with Setting Units
Make 7.

Setting Unit

Diagram 82

6. To make the 4 corner blocks, sew 1 setting unit to each of the 4 remaining Gardenia blocks (Diagram 82).

Fill-In Pieces A and B

1. To cut Fill-In Piece A, make 2 stacks of 8 rectangles each, using the 4½" x 7¾" tan rectangles. Make sure all rectangles are positioned with the right side facing up. Place a rotary ruler diagonally across each stack and cut along the edge to cut the rectangles into triangle halves. Cut half of the rectangles in one direction and the other half in the opposite direction as shown in Diagram 83.

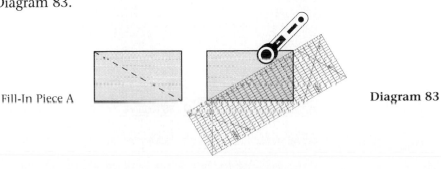

Fill-In Piece A

Diagram 83

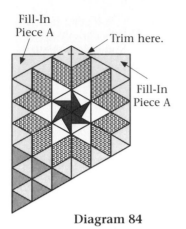

Diagram 84

2. Add 2 triangle halves (Fill-In Piece A) to each corner block and trim away the point of the hexagon that extends at the top of the block, allowing for a ¼" seam allowance as indicated by the dashed line (Diagram 84). Set aside the remaining triangle halves for the pieced border.

3. To cut the top and bottom fill-in pieces (Fill-In Piece B), fold each of the 10½" x 19½" rectangles in half crosswise as shown in Diagram 85.

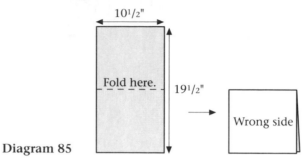

Diagram 85

4. Place the center line of the Clearview Triangle along the raw edge of each folded rectangle, with the point at the fold (Diagram 86). Cut along the edge of the triangle to cut a 30° angle. Unfold each rectangle.

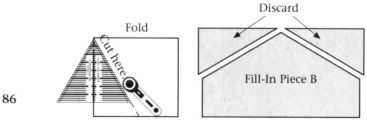

Diagram 86

5. Sew a setting unit to the top right edge of each Fill-In Piece B (Diagram 87).

Quilt Top Assembly

1. Assemble the completed Gardenia blocks, corner blocks, and Fill-In Piece B in 3 vertical rows as shown in Diagram 88.

Diagram 87

Make 2.

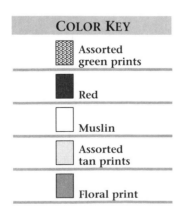

Diagram 88

Gardenia Block

Fill-In Piece B Corner Block

2. Sew the 3 rows together. The center row will extend beyond the top and bottom edge of the 2 outer rows. Trim evenly (Diagram 89).

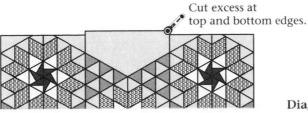

Cut excess at top and bottom edges.

Diagram 89

Pieced Border

1. With right sides together and raw edges even, stitch each 4"-wide green strip to a 4"-wide tan strip (Diagram 90). Stitch ¼" from both long edges. Make 3 of these units.

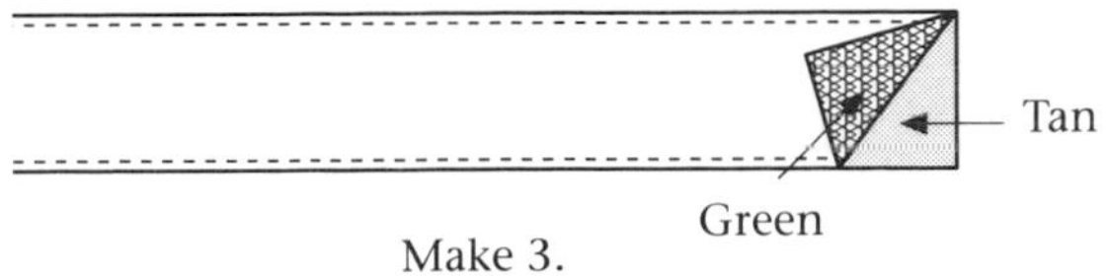

Tan

Green

Make 3.

Diagram 90

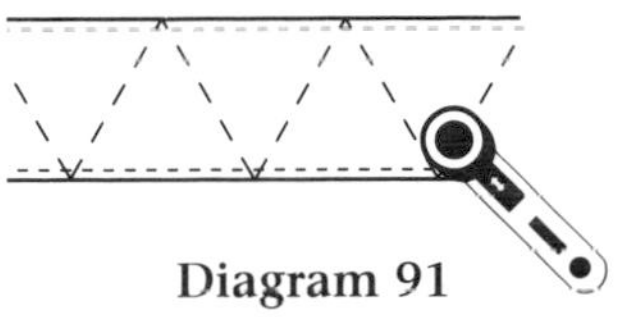

Diagram 91

2. Using Clearview Triangle, rotary cut 4" triangles from each unit (Diagram 91).

3. Carefully pull the triangles apart at the tip and press the remaining seam toward the darker of the two fabrics in each of the resulting triangle pairs (Diagram 92). You will need 44 triangle pairs for the 11 border units and 2 pairs for each of the border half-units (a total of 48 triangle pairs).

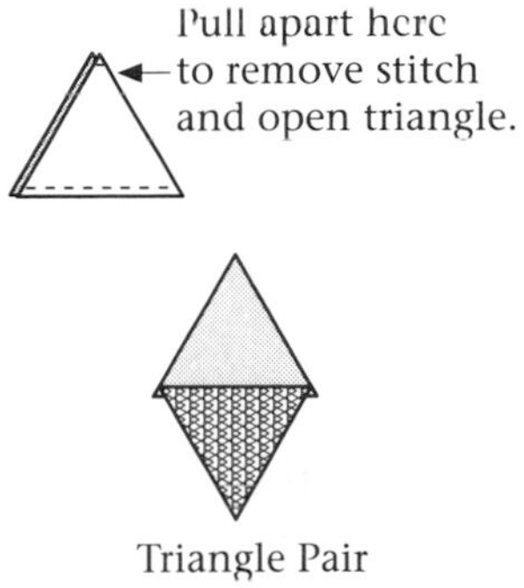

Pull apart here to remove stitch and open triangle.

Triangle Pair

Diagram 92

4. Assemble 11 border units, following the piecing diagram (Diagram 93). You should have 4 triangle pairs and 2 green triangles left for border half-units.

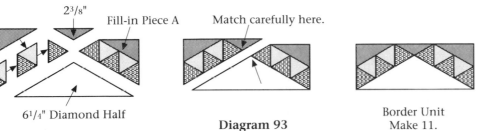

2³⁄₈" Fill-in Piece A   Match carefully here.

6¼" Diamond Half

Diagram 93

Border Unit
Make 11.

5. To cut the muslin triangle halves for the border half-units, choose 2 large scraps left over after cutting the 6¼" diamond halves. Check to be sure the 30° angle is correct and the strip is still 6¼" wide. With a chalk or light lead pencil, draw a perpendicular line from one edge of the strip to the opposite edge as shown in Diagram 94. Add a ¼" seam to this line on the side away from the angled tip and trim excess. Make 2 of these.

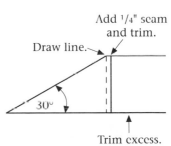

Add ¼" seam and trim.

Draw line.

30°

Trim excess.

Diagram 94

6. Assemble 2 border half-units, following the piecing diagram (Diagram 95).

Piecing Diagram

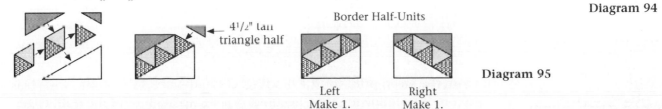

4½" tan triangle half

Border Half-Units

Diagram 95

Left
Make 1.

Right
Make 1.

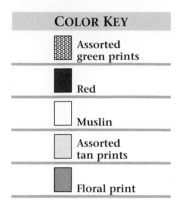

COLOR KEY

Assorted green prints

Red

Muslin

Assorted tan prints

Floral print

7. Assemble side pieced border strips, using 4 border units in each and adding a border half-unit at the top of each strip (Diagram 96). Assemble the bottom pieced border strip, using the remaining 3 border units.

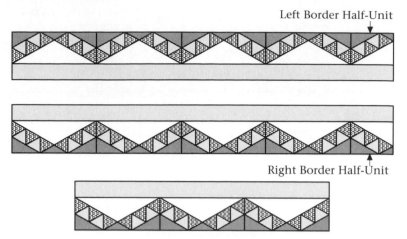

Left Border Half-Unit

Right Border Half-Unit

Diagram 96　　　　　　Bottom Border

8. Measure the quilt top for side and bottom borders as shown on page 46. Trim the 4"-wide tan border strips to correct length. Pin a pieced side border to each, matching centers and ends. Ease to fit as necessary and stitch. Repeat with the bottom pieced border. Press seams toward borders. Set aside the bottom border for step 11.

9. Sew the side borders to the quilt top.

10. Measure the width of the quilt top at the center. Cut and piece the tan top border to match this measurement. Pin to the top edge of the quilt top, matching centers and ends (Diagram 97). Stitch, easing to fit as necessary.

Top border

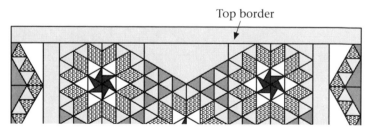

Diagram 97

11. Stitch the tan corner squares to the short ends of the bottom border strip (Diagram 98); then, stitch the border to the bottom edge of the quilt.

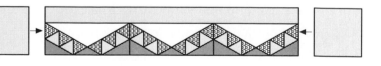

Diagram 98

Quilt Finishing

1. Layer the quilt top with batting and backing; baste.

2. Quilt in the design of your choice, or follow the Quilting Suggestion.

3. From the green print for the binding, cut and piece 380" of 2½"-wide bias for binding, following the directions on pages 52–53. Bind the quilt edges.

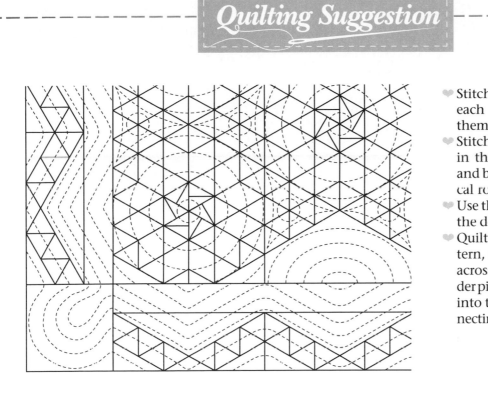

Quilting Suggestion

♥ Stitch 5 concentric circles on each Gardenia block, spacing them approximately 2" apart.

♥ Stitch 4 concentric half circles in the fill-in pieces at the top and bottom of the second vertical row of blocks.

♥ Use the template below to mark the design for the setting units.

♥ Quilt the borders in a wave pattern, spacing the waves 2" apart across the pieced and inner border pieces. Extend the wave lines into the corner blocks in a connecting curved pattern as shown.

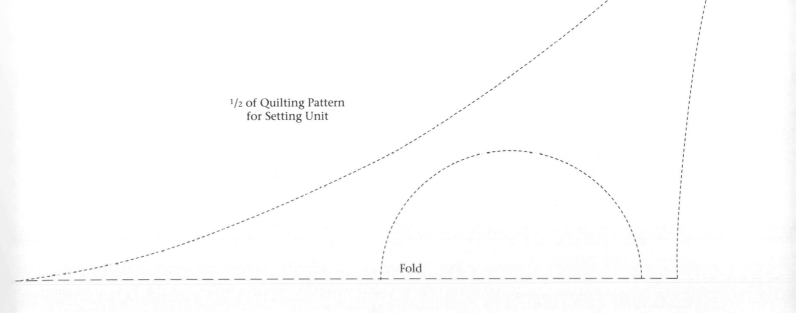

¹/₂ of Quilting Pattern
for Setting Unit

Fold

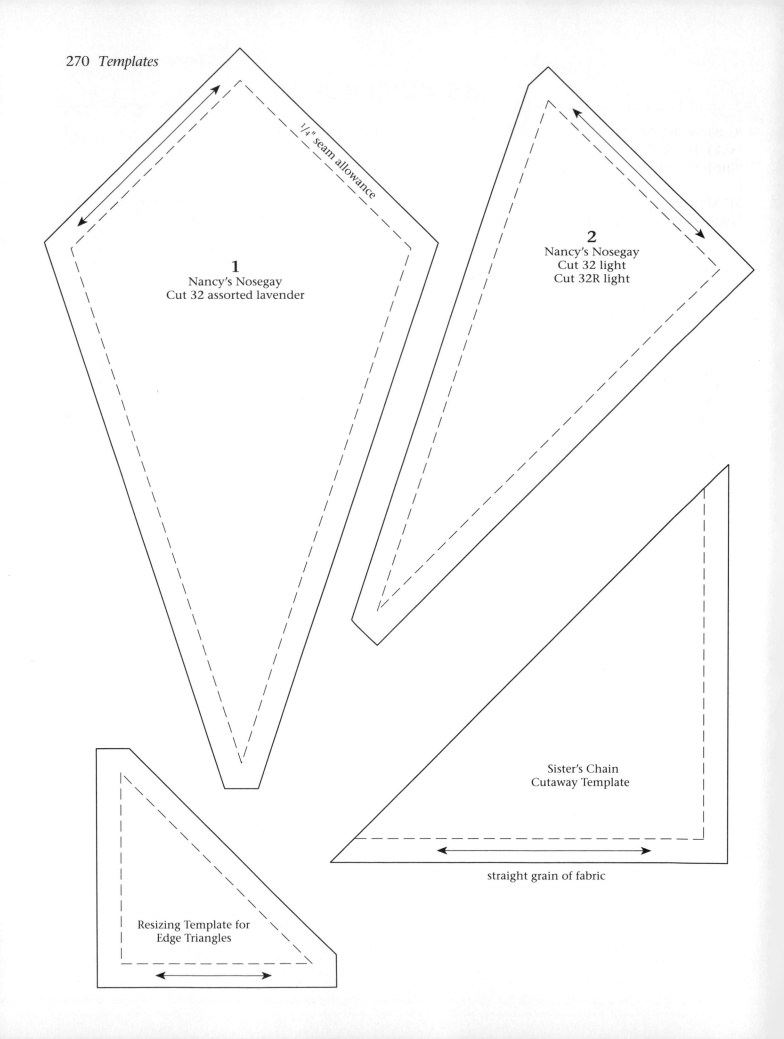

¼" seam allowance

1
Nancy's Nosegay
Cut 32 assorted lavender

2
Nancy's Nosegay
Cut 32 light
Cut 32R light

Sister's Chain
Cutaway Template

straight grain of fabric

Resizing Template for
Edge Triangles

RESOURCE LIST

Clearview Triangle
8311 180th St. S.E.
Snohomish, WA 98290

8" Mini-Pro Clearview Triangle
$9.50, plus $1.75 shipping and handling

12" Clearview Triangle
$11.50, plus $2.00 shipping and handling

Write for additional information about Sara
Nephew's books and tools.

Feathered Star Productions
2151 7th Ave. West
Seattle, WA 98119

Write to order Marsha McCloskey's *Guide to Rotary
Cutting*, $4.95 plus $1.50 shipping and handling.

Wildflower Designs
PO Box 82611
Kenmore, WA 98028-0611

Write to order Mary Hickey's Color Packet $4.00
plus $1.50 shipping and handling.

That Patchwork Place, Inc.
PO Box 118
Bothell, WA 98041-0118
USA

Write or call 1-800-426-3126 to order the Bias
Square, the BiRangle, and many other tools and
books, including those by Nancy Martin, Marsha
McCloskey, and Mary Hickey.